Cakes

250 Best Cake Recipes Of All Time

Sharon Belcher

All rights reserved. No part of this book may be reproduced in any way or form without permission in writing from the author. No part of this publication may be reproduced or transmitted in any form or by any means , mechanic, electronic, photocopying, recording, by any storage or retrieval system or transmitted by email without the permission in writing from the author & publisher.

Contents

Espresso cupcakes 14

Roasted berry cupcakes 16

Chocolate buttercream cupcakes 18

pumpkin cupcakes with maple cream 20

Vegan chocolate cupcakes 22

Chocolate cupcake with pumpkin buttercream 24

Mocha cupcakes 26

Apple pie cupcakes 28

Cinnamon roll cupcakes 29

Peppermint cupcakes 29

green cupcakes 32

Strawberry cheesecake cupcakes 33

Raspberry cheesecake cupcakes 36

Chocolate pumpkin cupcakes 38

Mango & vanilla cupcakes 40

Cupcakes with raspberry buttercream 41

Toffee cupcake 43

Kit kat cupcakes 45

Two colors 47

Ice cream cupcakes 49

Banana & chocolate cupcakes 51

Pumpkin chocolate cupcakes(2nd version) 53

Apple cider cranberry cupcakes 55

Buttered cupcakes 57

Bar cupcakes 59

Chocolate chip cookie dough cupcakes 61

Lemon meringue cupcakes 64

Nutella cheesecake cupcakes 66

Sweet potato cupcakes 68

Chocolate mocha cupcake 70

Caramel apple cupcakes 72

Dulce de leche cupcakes 74

Cheesecake cupcakes 76

Pumpkin pie cupcakes 76

Mint & chocolate cupcakes 78

Pudding cupcakes 80

Halloween cupcakes 81

Glass cupcakes(halloween) 83

Corn cupcakes 85

cupcakes with vanilla buttercream 86

Cider&caramel cupcakes 88

Pumpkin & cinnamon buttercream cupcakes 90

Black velvet cupcakes 92

Pumpkin cupcakes 94

Mint&chocolate cupcakes 96

- Chocolate blackberry cupcakes 98
- Peanut butter cupcakes 100
- Fudge cupcakes 102
- Chocolate & cookie cupcakes 103
- Pumpkin & chocolate cream cupcakes 104
- Red velvet cupcakes 106
- Classic vanilla cupcakes 108
- Simple pumpkin cupcakes 109
- The golden cupcake 110
- Berries cupcake with mascarpone 112
- Black cupcake 114
- Snickers cupcakes 116
- Chocolate & orange cupcakes 118
- Hat cupcakes 120
- Cupcakes with mint buttercream 123
- Chocolate cupcakes with strawberry buttercream 125
- Cupcakes with lemonfrosting 127
- Pumpkin & maple cream cupcakes 129
- Cheesecake cupcakes 131
- Vegan chocolate cupcake 133
- Cupcakes with caramel 135
- Dark cupcakes 137
- Coconut & lemon cupcakes 140

- Chocolate & coconut cupcakes 142
- Chocolate cream cheese cupcakes 144
- Coconut cupcakes with lemon curd 146
- Triple chocolate cupcakes 148
- Root beer cupcakes 152
- Funfetti cupcakes 154
- Flourless chocolate cupcakes 155
- Double chocolate cupcakes 157
- Egg nog cupcakes 159
- Chocolate & peanut butter cupcakes 160
- Chocolate cupcakes with caramel 163
- Apple cupcakes 165
- Mint ice cream cupcakes 168
- Classic cupcakes with chocolate buttercream 170
- Avocado cupcakes 172
- Caramel cheesecake 174
- The new 2015 brownies recipe 175
- The ultimate blueberry cake 176
- Apple cake with caramel 177
- Flourless chocolate blender cake 179
- The ultimate banana cake 180
- Coffee & chocolate cake 182
- Lemon & cheese cream cake 185

- Basic chocolate pudding cake 188
- Three colors cake 190
- Chocolate buttercream brownies cake 194
- Apple cake with caramel v2 195
- Chocolate cheesecake with cookie dough (no bake) 198
- Caramel & chocolate cupcakes 200
- Basic cream cake 202
- Chocolate bundt cake with biscuits dough (no bake) 205
- Pumpkin mousse sweet cake 207
- Easy coconut & chocolate cake with rum 209
- Easy snack cake with lots of banana chunks & chocolate 214
- Simple ducle de leche cake with banana layers 216
- Apple & coffee cake 218
- The big cake: chocolate, buttercream frosting & ganache 220
- Pumkin cake v2 224
- The simple recipe: chocolate cake newbie level 225
- Strawberry cheesecake (no bake) 227
- Blueberry cheesecake v2 229
- Dark cake 231
- Chocolate cheesecake v2 233
- Simple lava chocolate cake 236
- Oreo cake 238
- Upside-down meyer cake 241

Lemon & blueberry cheesecake 242

Chocolate brownie cake with mascarpone 245

Dark & white chocolate truffle cake 248

Peanut butter cheesecake with brownie bottom layer 253

Dark & white cake with mascarpone & caramel buttercream 255

Brownie chocolate cake with vanilla buttercream 258

French cake with blueberries 261

Strawberry cream crepe cake 264

Strawberry, champagne & rose cake 267

Chocolate & pomegranate layer cake 270

Chocolate cinnamon cake 272

Chocolate ganache cake 273

Chocolate pistachio cake 274

Flourless chocolate praline cake 276

Flourless chocolate & almond cake 277

Black forest cake 279

Velvet mocha cheesecake 281

Flourless chocolate cake 283

Cheesecake brownies 285

Mudslide cake 286

Vegan cake 288

Gluten free brownies 290

m&m's brownies 291

cinnamon cheesecake bars 292

Pumpkin & chocolate cake 294

Chocolate bundt cake 296

Angel cake 298

Red velvet cake 299

Lemon & blueberry cheesecake 301

Chocolate brownie cake with mascarpone 303

Coffee cake 307

chocolate cake with caramel & mascarpone 308

Upside-down tea cake 311

Pumpkin carrot cake 313

Crepe cheesecake 315

Meyer lemon cheesecake 318

Pumpkin spice cake 320

Strawberry upside down cake 322

Apple cider bundt cake 324

Chocolate brownie cake with mascarpone 326

Chestnut chocolate cake 329

Chocolate cake 332

Oreo cake 333

Chocolate layered cake 334

cinnamon sugar cake 336

Dark chocolate & yogurt cake 338

strawberries cake 339

Carrot cake 341

Mocha cake 343

Chocolate zucchini cake 344

Zesty citrus cheesecake 345

Herry jell-o cheesecake 346

Classic cheesecake 347

Classic new york cheesecake 347

Chocolate cheesecake 348

No-bake chocolate cheesecake 348

Gluten-free diet cheesecake 349

Layered blackberry cheesecake 350

White chocolate raspberry cheesecake 351

Walnut crust cheesecake 351

Savoiardi cheesecake 352

Layered creamy orange cheesecake 353

Moist pecan cheesecake 354

Tropical pineapple cheesecake 355

Pumpkin cheesecake 355

Pineapple cheesecake 356

Peanut butter oreo cheesecake 357

Lemon raspberry cheesecake bars 358

Zesty cheesecake brownies 359

- Caramel brownie cheesecake 360
- Cheesecake-stuffed strawberries 361
- Cheesecake tarts 362
- Cheesecake lollipops 362
- Toffee cheesecake bars 363
- Bittersweet apple cheesecake roll 364
- Cranberry cheese squares 365
- Banana cheesecake 366
- Chocolate truffle cheesecake 366
- Chocomint cheesecake 367
- Green tea mousse cheesecake 368
- Frozen blueberry & lime cheesecake 368
- Salted caramel ginger snap cheesecake 369
- Coffee cheesecake 371
- Chocolate melt cheesecake 371
- Mint cheesecake 372
- Toffee truffle cheesecake 373
- Lime cheesecake 374
- Chocolate snickers cheesecake 375
- Double layer creamy pumpkin cheesecake 375
- Caramel macchiato cheesecake 376
- Vanilla mousse cheesecake 377
- Red velvet cheesecake cups 378

Blueberry cheesecake cups 379

Honey cheese cups 379

Berry cheesecake cups 380

Mini berry cheese cups 381

Blackberry cheese cups 382

Chocolate cheesecake cups 382

Miniature cherry cheesecakes 383

Sundried tomato cheesecake 384

Roasted pepper pesto cheesecake 385

Feta cheesecake 386

Garlic mushroom cheesecake 387

Double cheese bacon cheesecake 388

Vanilla layered cheesecake 389

Raspberry cheesecake 389

Vanilla cinnamon cheesecake 390

Double berry cheesecake 391

Double-chocomalt cheesecake 392

Creamy lemon cheesecake 393

Melted marshmallow cheesecake 394

Caramel apple cheesecake 395

Butter-nutty cheesecake 395

Lemon berry cheesecake 396

Chocolate oreo cheesecake 397

Nutella cheesecake 398

Smoked salmon cheesecake 399

Ricotta asparagus cheesecake with swiss almond crust 400

Triple cheese & basil cheesecake 400

Creamy leek cheesecake 402

Pecan & olive cheesecake squares 402

Blue cheese & garlic cheesecake 403

Mexican cheesecake 404

Savory vegetable cheesecake 405

Chicken cranberry-orange cheesecake 406

Polenta pepper cheesecake 406

Blueberry cabernet cheesecake 407

Amaretto cheesecake 408

Double chocolate liqueur cheesecake 409

White chocolate frangelico cheesecake 410

Cheesecake icecream 411

Pecan liqueur cheesecake 411

Cointreau cheesecake 412

Coffee jelly cheesecake 413

Banana bourbon cheesecake 414

Rum-infused mousse cheesecake 415

White chocolate cheesecake 416

Margarita cheesecakes snacks 417

Vodka ricotta cheesecake ... 417

Rum praline cheesecake ... 418

Pina colada cheesecake ... 419

Tiramisu cheesecake ... 420

Rum & chocolate cheesecake ... 421

Vegan cheesecake ... 422

Tofu cheesecake ... 422

Cashew cheesecake ... 423

Strawberry cheesecake ... 424

Cashew lime cheesecake cups ... 425

Dulce de leche cheesecake bars ... 425

Lime cheesecake bars ... 426

Coffee cheesecake bars ... 428

One more thing ... 429

Espresso cupcakes

What you need

Cupcakes

- 1 c. Butter, softened to room temperature
- 1 3/4 c. Sugar
- 2 eggs
- 2 tsp. Vanilla extract
- 1 c. Buttermilk or 1 c. Whole milk with 1 tbs. Lemon juice
- 1/2 c. Strong coffee, cooled
- 2 c. Flour
- 3/4 c. Cocoa powder
- 1 tsp. Baking soda
- 1 1/2 tsp. Baking powder
- 1/2 tsp. Salt

Frosting

- 8 oz. Bar cream cheese, cold
- 1/2 c. Butter (1 stick), softened to room temperature
- 1 tsp vanilla extract
- 4 tbs. Kahlua coffee liqueur
- 3 1/2 c. Powdered sugar, measure next which sift

Topping

- 1/2 to 3/4 c. Kahlua coffee liqeuer*
- 1 c. Chocolate covered espresso beans

What to do

1. Heat up oven to 350 degrees f. Line 3 muffin pans with cupcake liners. Beat together butter & sugar till light & fluffy. Slowly add eggs one at a time.
2. Sift together flour, cocoa powder, baking soda, baking powder & salt. Mix the buttermilk & coffee together. Alternate adding the flour mixture & buttermilk mixture.

3. Pour right into the prepared pans. Bake for 12-15 min. Or till a toothpick inserted in the middle of the cupcake comes out clean. Let cool for at least 10 min. Next which poke holes on top of each cupcake. Drizzle about 1/2 tsp of kahlua over each cupcake.
4. With the mixer on a low speed, beat the cream cheese & butter till blended. Mix in vanilla & kahlua. Slowly add the powdered sugar, a c. At a time.
5. Once all the powdered sugar is added, increase to a higher speed to whip up the frosting till light & fluffy. Transfer frosting right into a piping bag.
6. Place the chocolate covered espresso beans inside a ziplock bag. Utilizing a rolling pin, lightly crush them right into smaller pieces. Pipe frosting on top of each cupcake.
7. Drizzle a little bit of kahlua on top of the frosting. Dash the crushed chocolate covered espresso beans on top of each cupcake.

Roasted berry cupcakes

What you need

Roasted berries

- 3 c. Assorted berries
- 1/4 c. Sugar

Cupcakes

- 1/2 c. (1 stick) unsalted butter, softened at room temperature
- 3/4 c. Granulated sugar
- 2 big eggs
- 1 tsp vanilla
- 1 1/3 c. Cake flour
- 1 1/4 tsp baking powder
- 1/4 tsp kosher salt
- 1/2 c. Buttermilk
- 1 c. Roasted berries, drained

Frosting

- 1/2 c. (1 stick) unsalted butter, softened at room temperature
- 1/2 c. Cream cheese
- 3 c. Confectioner's sugar
- 1-2 drops pink food coloring
- 1 c. Mashed roasted berries

What to do

1. Heat up the oven to 400°f. Line a small baking tray with parchment paper & scatter the berries in one layer on the tray. Dash with the sugar & roast for about 15-20 min., or till the berries are soft & have released their juices. Take away from the oven & cool completely.
2. Take the roasted berries & drain some of the excess liquid. Mash the remaining berries utilizing a fork & set this aside for the frosting.
3. Lower the oven temperature to 350°f. Prepare muffin trays by lining with cupcake liners.

4. In the bowl of a stand mixer with the whisk attachment, cream the butter till light & fluffy. Mix in the sugar till well incorporated, next which add the eggs & vanilla, scraping down the sides of the bowl periodically.
5. In a small bowl, whisk together the cake flour, baking powder & salt. Add the flour to the egg mixture, mixing till only incorporated. Add the buttermilk & mix again till the batter is smooth, but take care not to over mix.
6. Take away the mixing bowl from the stand mixer & lightly fold in the roasted berries. Spoon the batter right into the muffin trays, about 3/4 full.
7. Bake for about 20 min., or till an toothpick inserted in the middle come out with only a few moist crumbs. Put to the side to cool before icing.

Frosting

1. Whisk the butter, cream cheese & confectioner's sugar in a stand mixer with the whisk attachment on low speed. When the ingredients start to come together, increase the speed to medium & let the icing mix for about 2 min..
2. Add the food coloring & mix again. When the icing is smooth, take away the mixing bowl from the mixer.
3. Spoon the mashed berries right into the bowl, next which spoon the icing right into a piping bag outfitted with a big decorating tip.

Chocolate buttercream cupcakes

What you need

Yellow cupcakes

- 3/4 c. (1 1/2 sticks or 169g) unsalted butter, room temperature
- 1 1/2 c. (300g) granulated sugar
- 3 extra-large (3/4 cup, 56g, or 6ounces) eggs, room temperature
- 2 tsp pure vanilla extract
- 1 tsp almond extract
- 1 1/4 c. (287g) sour cream, room temperature
- 2 1/2 c. (312g) cake flour
- 2 tsp baking powder
- 1/2 tsp baking soda
- 1/2 tsp salt

Chocolate buttercream

- 1 1/2 c. (340g) butter, at room temperature
- 4 c. (500g) powdered sugar
- 3/4 c. (94g) cocoa powder
- 4 tbsp (60ml) heavy whipping cream
- 2 tsp vanilla extract
- Pinch table salt

What to do

1. Heat up the oven to 350 degrees f.
2. Cream the butter & sugar in the bowl of a stand mixer fitted with the paddle attachment for about 3 min. Or till light & fluffy.
3. With mixer on medium-low, add the eggs 1 at a time, allowing them to incorporate before adding next.
4. With mixer off, add the vanilla, almond extract, & sour cream. Turn mixer on low till incorporated next which high for about 1 minute.
5. In a separate bowl, sift together the flour, baking powder, baking soda, & salt. Sift at least 2 times.
6. With the mixer on low, add the flour mixture to the batter till only combined. Take away bowl from mixer & finish stirring with a spatula to be sure the batter is completely mixed.

7. Using a 1/4 c. Ice cream scoop or a measuring cup, divide batter right into cupcake pans.
8. Bake for 16-20 min. Or till cupcake springs back when pressed in the center.
9. Chocolate buttercream
10. In a the bowl of an stand mixer fitted with whisk attachment, whisk butter & sugar on medium-high speed till very pale & fluffy, or about five min..
11. Be sure to stop at least when & scrape the bowl.
12. With the mixer off, add in cocoa powder, vanilla, & salt.
13. Turn mixer on low & blend for about 30 sec..
14. One tbsp at a time, add in heavy cream.
15. Once all cream has been added & mixture is mostly combined, turn off the mixer & scrape down the sides of the bowl.
16. Now turn the mixer onto medium-high to high & whisk for 3-5 min. Or till mixture is light & fluffy. The frosting will be shiny & seem to have many big air bubbles throughout & this is exactly what we are going for.
17. Allow cupcakes to cool before frosting.

pumpkin cupcakes with maple cream

What you need

Cupcakes

- 1 c. All purpose flour
- 1 tsp baking powder
- ½ tsp baking soda
- 1 tsp ground cinnamon
- ¼ tsp ground ginger
- ½ tsp nutmeg
- ½ tsp salt
- 2 eggs
- 1 c. Canned pumpkin puree
- ¼ c. Granulated sugar
- ½ c. Brown sugar, lightly packed
- ⅓ c. Vegetable oil

Frosting

- 6 oz. Cream cheese, at room temperature (
- 3 tbsp unsalted butter, at room temperature
- 2 tbsp pure maple syrup
- ½ tsp pure vanilla extract
- 2 c. Powdered sugar
- For the salted maple glazed pecans:
- 4 tbsp unsalted butter
- ½ c. Brown sugar, lightly packed
- ½ tsp salt
- ¼ c. Pure maple syrup
- 1 tbsp milk
- ⅔ c. Chopped, toasted pecans

What to do

Cupcakes

1. Heat up oven to 350. Grease a muffin pan or fill with 9 paper liners.

2. In a medium bowl, whisk together the flour, baking powder, baking soda, cinnamon, ginger, nutmeg & salt.
3. In a big bowl, whisk together the eggs, pumpkin puree, sugars & vegetable oil. Add the flour mixture to the wet ingredients & mix till combined.
4. Divide the batter evenly between the 9 muffin c. & bake for 15-18 min., till a toothpick inserted in the cupcakes comes out clean.
5. Cool the cupcakes completely before spreading with frosting & topping with pecans.

Frosting

1. Beat cream cheese, butter, maple syrup & vanilla extract till combined.
2. Slowly add in powdered sugar & beat till smooth.

Pecans

1. In a saucepan over medium-high heat, melt the butter. When melted, whisk in the brown sugar & salt. Bring to a boil, reduce the heat to medium & continue to boil for 2 min., whisking frequently.
2. Add the maple syrup & boil 4 min. Longer, till the mixture has thickened, whisking frequently. Take away from the heat & straight away mix in the milk & pecans.
3. Pour onto a baking sheet that has been lined with foil. Permit to cool, next which break right into small pieces. Top the frosted cupcakes generously with the pecans.

Vegan chocolate cupcakes

What you need

Cupcakes

- 1 1/2 c. (355 milliliters) silk unsweetened original almond milk
- 1 1/2 tsp white vinegar
- 1/2 c. (113 grams) melted oil
- 2/3 c. (133 grams) brown sugar
- 1/2 c. (100 grams) granulated sugar
- 2 tsp vanilla extract
- 1 tsp espresso powder 2
- 1 1/2 c. (188 grams) flour
- 1/2 c. (58 grams) cocoa powder
- 1 1/4 tsp baking soda
- 3/4 tsp baking powder
- 1/2 tsp salt

Frosting

- 1 c. (170 grams) semi-sweet chocolate chips
- 1/4 c. (60 milliliters) silk unsweetened original almond milk
- 1/4 c. (56 grams) coconut oil
- 1 tsp vanilla extract
- 1/3 c. (40 grams) powdered sugar, sifted if lumpy4
- Pinch of salt

Decorating

- 16 chocolate peanut butter football truffles
- 1/2 c. Naturally dyed shredded coconut

What to do

Cupcakes

1. Heat up the oven to 350 °f (175 °c) & line two muffin pans with a total of 16 cupcake liners.
2. In a big mixing bowl, mix together the almond milk & vinegar. Let sit for 5 min..

3. Stir in the melted coconut oil, brown sugar, granulated sugar, vanilla extract & espresso powder.
4. In a medium mixing bowl, mix together the flour, cocoa powder, baking soda, baking powder & salt. Add this to the wet mixture & mix only till combined.
5. Fill the liners slightly more than half-way full & bake for 16-18 min. Or till a toothpick inserted in the middle comes out clean or with some moist crumbs.
6. Let cool for 5 min. & next which turn out onto a wire rack to cool completely.

Frosting

1. In a small saucepan over medium-low heat, mix together the chocolate chips, almond milk, coconut oil, & vanilla extract. Mix till melted & next which steadily whisk in the powdered sugar till completely smooth.
2. Let the pan cool for about 15 & next which put the pan in the fridge for about 10-20 min., stirring next every 5 min., or till firm enough to spread on the cupcakes.
3. Spread 1 tbsp of frosting on top of each cupcake.

Decorating

1. Dash about 1 1/2 tsp of coconut grass over the frosting. Stick a toothpick in the football truffle & put on the cupcake. Can be kept at room temperature for about 4-6 hours.
2. Place in the fridge. Let come to room temperature (about 1-2 hours) before serving.

Chocolate cupcake with pumpkin buttercream

What you need

Cupcakes

- 1/2 c. (1 stick or 115g) unsalted butter
- 2 oz. Semi-sweet baking chocolate
- 2 big eggs, at room temperature
- 3/4 c. (150g) granulated sugar
- 2 tsp vanilla extract
- 1/2 c. (115g) sour cream, room temperature
- 1/2 c. (42g) unsweetened cocoa powder
- 3/4 c. (95g) all-purpose flour
- 1/2 tsp baking soda
- 1 tsp baking powder
- 1/4 tsp salt

Pumpkin buttercream

- 1/2 c. Butter (113g), room temperature
- 1/2 c. (110g) pumpkin puree
- 1 tsp vanilla
- 3 c. (380g) confectioners sugar
- 1 tbsp pumpkin spice

What to do

Cupcakes

1. Heat up the oven to 350f degrees. This recipe makes 12-14 cupcakes, so prepare one with cupcake liners.
2. Melt the butter & chocolate together in the microwave. Microwave in 30-second increments, stirring in between each time. Put to the side.
3. In the bowl of a stand mixer with the whisk attachment; add the eggs, sugar, vanilla, & sour cream & whisk on medium speed till smooth.
4. In a medium sized bowl, sift the cocoa powder, flour, baking soda, baking powder, & salt together till thoroughly combined.
5. Add the cooled butter/chocolate to the stand mixer & whisk till smooth, about 30 sec..
6. Slowly add in the flour mixture, about 1/4 c. At a time with the stand mixer on low.

7. Fill the cupcake liners 2/3 of the way full with batter. Bake for 15-18 min..

Pumpkin buttercream

Place all ingredients in bowl of stand mixer with paddle attachment & turn on to low speed.

Once all ingredients are combined, turn mixer speed to medium-high & mix for 2-3 min..

Mocha cupcakes

What you need

- 1/2 c (118 ml) strong brewed coffee, room temp
- 1 1/2 tsp espresso powder
- 1/2 c (118 ml) whole milk
- 1 tsp vanilla extract
- 1 1/3 c (189 g) flour
- 1/3 c (30 g) cocoa powder
- 1 tsp baking powder
- 1/2 tsp baking soda
- 1/4 tsp salt
- 1/2 c (118 g) butter, room temp
- 1/2 c (99 g) granulated sugar
- 1/2 c (71 g) brown sugar
- 1 egg, room temp

Swiss meringue buttercream

- 1 1/2 c (300 g) sugar
- 7 egg whites
- 27 tbsp (381 g) unsalted butter, room temp
- 2 tbsp instant coffee
- 2 tbsp warm water

What to do

1. Heat up the oven to 350f. Line a cupcake pan with 12 liners & put to the side.
2. Mix the espresso powder/instant coffee granules right into the brewed coffee. Add the milk & vanilla put to the side to cool.
3. In a small bowl, mix the flour, cocoa powder, baking powder, baking soda & salt. Put to the side.
4. In a separate medium-sized bowl, beat the butter till creamy. Add the sugars & beat till light & fluffy, about five min..
5. Add the egg & beat till fully incorporated, scarping down the sides & the bottom of the bowl.

6. Add about 1/3 of the flour mixture to the batter, & mix slowly to combine. Scrape down the sides & add half of the coffee mixture. Scrape down the sides of the bowl again & continue alternating wet & dry, ending with dry. Mix only till combined.
7. Scoop batter right into the prepared liners. Bake 17-20 min. Or till the cupcakes spring back when pressed. Cool on a rack in pans for 3 min., next which take away the cupcakes from the pans & permit to cool thoroughly before frosting.

Swiss meringue buttercream

1. In a double boiler, cook the egg whites & sugar over medium heat, whisking continously , till the sugar is completely dissolved.
2. Pour right into an additional bowl & whip on high speed till room temp.
3. On a medium-low speed, add the butter, waiting till each piece is completely incorporated before adding the next.
4. Whereas it's beating, mix the water & instant coffee. Pour right into whipped buttercream as you would an extract, & beat to combine.

Apple pie cupcakes

What you need

- 4 tbsp unsalted butter
- 2 big granny smith apples, peeled, cored & chopped in to 1/4-inch cubes
- 1/2 tsp ground cinnamon
- 1/8 tsp salt
- Juice of half lemon (about 1 1/2 tbsp)
- 1/4 c. All purpose flour
- 1/4 c. + 2 tbsp packed brown sugar
- 1/4 c. Chopped walnuts
- 1 can (12.4 oz) pillsbury refrigerated cinnamon rolls
- Whipped cream
- Caramel-flavored syrup

What to do

1. Heat oven to 400°f. Lightly spray 8 regular-size muffin c. With cooking spray.
2. In 10-inch skillet, melt 2 tbsp butter over medium-high heat. Add apples; cook about 5 min., stirring often, till softened.
3. Dash with 2 tbsp brown sugar, the cinnamon & salt. Cook 5 min. Longer or till tender. Mix in lemon juice.
4. In the meantime , in small bowl, mix butter, flour, 1/4 c. Of brown sugar & walnuts with fork or hands till crumbly. Put to the side.
5. Separate dough right into 8 rolls. Flatten each right into 4-inch round; put in muffin cup. Divide apple filling evenly onto rolls in muffin cups. Divide flour mixture evenly over apples.
6. Bake 10 to 12 min. Or till bubbly & tops are lightly browned. Cool slightly before removing from muffin cups.
7. Cool completely, about 30 min..serve cupcakes topped with whipped cream & a drizzle of syrup.

Cinnamon roll cupcakes

What you need

- 2 1/4 tsp or 1 packet (1/4 oz./7 g) dry active yeast
- 1/2 c. Sugar, divided
- 1 c. Warm milk (approximately 110 degrees fahrenheit)
- 2 eggs, room temperature
- 1/3 c. Butter, melted
- 1 tsp salt
- 4 1/2 c. Bread flour
- 1 c. Brown sugar, packed
- 2 1/2 tbsp ground cinnamon
- 1/3 c. Butter, softened

What to do

1. Dissolve the yeast & 1/4 c. Of the granulated sugar in the warm milk in a big bowl & let stand for about 10 min. Till foamy.
2. Mix in the eggs, butter, salt, & other 1/4 c. Of granulated sugar. Add flour & mix till well blended & the dough forms a ball. Put in a bowl, cover & let rise in a warm put till doubled in size.
3. After the dough has doubled in size, turn it out onto a lightly floured surface, cover & let rest for 10 min.. In a small bowl, mix brown sugar & cinnamon. Line cupcake pan with cupcake liners, & lightly spray over the top of them with cooking spray.
4. Roll dough right into a 12x22 in. Rectangle. Spread dough with 1/3 c. Butter & dash evenly with sugar/cinnamon mixture. Roll up dough & cut right into 24 rolls.
5. Place each roll in a cupcake liner. Cover & let rise till nearly doubled, about 30 min.. In the meantime , heat up oven to 400 degrees fahrenheit.
6. Bake rolls in heat uped oven till golden brown, about 10-12 min.. Let rolls cool completely before frosting.

Peppermint cupcakes

What you need
Cupcakes

- 2 2/3 c. All-purpose flour
- 2/3 c. Unsweetened cocoa powder
- 2-3 tsp. Espresso powder
- 2 tsp. Baking powder
- 1 tsp. Baking soda
- ½ tsp. Salt
- 1 c. Whole milk
- 1 c. Strong brewed coffee
- 1 tsp. Peppermint extract
- 1 c. (2 sticks) unsalted butter, at room temperature
- 1 c. Granulated sugar
- 1 c. Light brown sugar
- 2 big eggs

Frosting

- 6 big egg whites
- 1¾ plus 2 tbsp. Granulated sugar
- 1½ c. (3 sticks) unsalted butter, at room temperature
- 4 tsp. Peppermint extract
- 1-2 tsp. Vanilla extract

What to do

1. To make the cupcakes, heat up the oven to 350° f. Line two cupcake pans with paper liners.
2. In a medium bowl, mix the flour, cocoa powder, espresso powder, baking powder, baking soda & salt; mix together. Mix the milk, coffee & peppermint extract in a liquid measuring cup.
3. In the bowl of a stand mixer fitted with the paddle attachment, mix the butter & sugars. Beat on medium-high speed till light & fluffy, 2-3 min., scraping down the sides of the bowl as needed. Blend in the eggs one at a time.
4. Alternately mix in the dry & liquid ingredients, beginning & ending with the dry ingredients & mixing only till incorporated.

5. Divide the batter evenly between the prepared cupcake liners. Bake 18-20 min., or till a toothpick inserted in the middle comes out clean. Let cool in the pan 5-10 min., next which transfer to a wire rack to cool completely.

Frosting

1. Combine the egg whites & sugar in a heatproof bowl set over a pot of simmering water. Heat, whisking frequently, till the mixture reaches 160° f & the sugar has dissolved.
2. Transfer the mixture to the bowl of a stand mixer fitted with the whisk attachment. Beat on medium-high speed till stiff peaks form & the mixture has cooled to room temperature, about 8 min..
3. Reduce the speed to medium & add the butter, 2 tbsp at a time, adding more when each addition has been incorporated.
4. Stir in the peppermint & vanilla extracts & mix only till incorporated, next which pipe or spread the frosting onto the cupcakes.
5. Take away about half of the frosting to a bowl.take the remaining frosting in the mixing bowl, add red gel coloring & mix till you have achieved the desired shade. Fit a pastry bag with a big tip. Fill one side of the pastry bag with the white frosting, & next which fill in the other side with the red frosting pipe a test streak till you see both colors coming out of the tip.

green cupcakes

What you need

- 1 pkg. (2-layer size) white cake mix
- 2 oz. Baker's semi-sweet chocolate, melted
- 1 tbsp. Green food coloring
- 4 oz. (1/2 of 8-oz. Pkg.) Cream cheese, softened
- 1 jar (7 oz.) Marshmallow creme
- 1 tsp. Vanilla
- 1 tub (8 oz.) Whipped topping, thawed

What to do

1. Heat oven to 350°f.
2. Prepare & bake cake batter as directed on package for 24 cupcakes, blending melted chocolate & food coloring right into batter before spooning right into prepared muffin cups. Cool completely.
3. Beat cream cheese, marshmallow creme & vanilla in big bowl with mixer till blended. Add the whipped topping; beat only till blended.
4. Spoon whip mixture right into resealable plastic bag. Cut corner off one bottom corner of bag; use to pipe whip mixture onto tops of cupcakes.

Strawberry cheesecake cupcakes

What you need

Graham cracker crust

- 1 ¼ c. Graham cracker crumbs
- 1/3 c. Sugar
- 5 tbsp unsalted butter, melted

Cupcakes

- 2 1/2 c. Sifted cake flour
- 1 tbsp baking powder
- 1/2 tsp salt
- 1 c. Milk, at room temperature
- 2 big egg whites, at room temperature
- 1 whole egg, at room temperature
- 1 tsp vanilla extract
- 1/4 tsp almond extract
- 1 1/2 c. Sugar
- 8 tbsp (1 stick) unsalted butter, at room temperature
- 1/2 c. Heavy cream, cold

Cheesecake filling

- 1 (8 ounce) package cream cheese, at room temperature
- ¼ c. (4 tbsp) unsalted butter, at room temperature
- ½ tsp vanilla extract
- 1 ¼ c. Confectioners' sugar, sifted

Strawberry buttercream frosting

- ¾ c. (1.5 sticks) unsalted butter, at room temperature
- 3 c. Confectioner's sugar, sifted
- 1/2 c. Fresh strawberries
- 1/2 tsp vanilla extract
- For the strawberry topping:
- 1 c. Chopped strawberries

- ¼ c. Graham cracker crumbs

What to do

Cupcakes

1. Heat up the oven to 350 degrees f. Line 2 muffin pans with cupcake liners.
2. In a medium bowl mix the flour, baking powder & salt. In a glass measuring cup, whisk the milk, eggs, vanilla & almond extract.
3. In an electric mixer fitted with the paddle attachment, cream the butter & sugar on medium speed till pale & creamy, about 5 min.. Alternate additions of the flour mixture & liquid mixture, beginning & ending with the flour mixture (3 dry additions, 2 wet), beating next each addition till incorporated. Continue mixing on medium speed for 2 min..
4. Chill a clean stainless mixer bowl in the freezer for 5 min.. Return bowl to mixer fitted with the whisk attachment & next which whisk the heavy cream on medium-high speed till soft peaks form.
5. Fold whipped cream right into the cake batter.
6. Divide the batter evenly among cupcake liners (about 2/3 full) & bake till a toothpick comes out with only a few crumbs, about 16-18 min.. Take away from pan & let cool on wire racks. Repeat with second muffin pan.

Graham cracker crust

1. In a small mixing bowl, mix the graham cracker crumbs, sugar & melted butter; mix well with a fork. Drop about 1 tbsp of the graham cracker mixture in the bottom of each cupcake liner & press down to line the bottom.
2. Bake for 5 min.. Take away from the oven, & maintain the oven temperature.

Filling

1. In the bowl of a stand mixer fitted with the paddle attachment beat the cream cheese & butter till creamy.
2. Add the vanilla next which steadily add the confectioners' sugar.
3. Beat till well combined.

Strawberry frosting

1. Puree the strawberries in a food processor. Strain the puree through a fine mesh sieve placed over a bowl to take away the seeds. In an electric mixer fitted with the paddle attachment, mix butter & half of the sugar.

2. Beat on low speed till well blended. Add the other half of the sugar & two tbsp of strawberry puree, mixing till combined.
3. Increase speed to medium & add additional puree, a tbsp at a time, till desired color & flavor is reached. Add vanilla & beat on high for about 30 sec. To lighten the frosting.

Assemble

1. Take away a small amount of the middle part of the cupcake utilizing a cupcake corer or pairing knife.
2. Divide the cheesecake filling evenly among the cupcakes, filling the hole in the middle of the cupcake. Pipe frosting around the edge of each cupcake, leaving a well for the strawberry topping.
3. Divide strawberry topping among cupcakes & dash with graham cracker crumbs.

Raspberry cheesecake cupcakes

What you need

Crust

- 3/4 c. + 2 tbsp graham cracker crumbs
- 1 1/2 tsp granulated sugar
- 3 1/2 tbsp salted butter, melted

Raspberry swirl

- 4 oz fresh raspberries
- 2 tbsp granulated sugar

Cheesecake filling

- 3/4 c. Granulated sugar
- 1 tbsp all-purpose flour
- 2 (8 oz) pkg cream cheese, softened well but not melted
- 1 tsp lemon zest
- 2 big eggs
- 1 tsp vanilla extract
- 1/4 c. Sour cream

What to do

Crust

1. Heat up oven to 325 degrees. In a mixing bowl, utilizing a fork, mix together graham cracker crumbs & sugar, next which pour in melted butter & mix till evenly moistened.
2. Add 1 slightly heaping tbspful to 12 paper lined muffin cups. Press crust firmly right into an even layer.
3. Bake in heat uped oven 5 min. Next which take away from oven & permit to cool.

Raspberry swirl

1. Add raspberries & 2 tbsp granulated sugar to a food processor & pulse till well pureed, about 30 sec. - 1 minute.
2. Press mixture through a fine mesh strainer right into a bowl.
3. Put to the side.

Cheesecake filling

1. In a mixing bowl, whisk together granulated sugar & flour. Add cream cheese & lemon zest utilizing an electric hand mixer, blend mixture only till smooth.
2. Mix in eggs one at a time. Mix in vanilla & sour cream only till combined.
3. Tap bowl forcefully against countertop, about 10 times, to release big air bubbles. Divide mixture evenly among c. Over crust layer, adding about 1/3 c. To each & filling nearly full. Jiggle pan to level cheesecake filling next which dollop about 5 small circle of raspberry sauce over each cupcake, about 3/4 tsp total over each one.
4. Using a toothpick, swirl raspberry filling with cheesecake mixture to create a marbled design. Bake in heat uped oven 22 - 25 min. Till cupcakes are puffed & nearly set.
5. Take away from oven & permit to cool completely, next which chill in fridge 3 hours, till set. Store in fridge in an airtight container.

Chocolate pumpkin cupcakes

What you need

Cupcakes

- 1½ c. Flour
- 1 tsp baking powder
- ¼ tsp baking soda
- ¾ tsp pumpkin spice
- ½ tsp salt
- ½ c. Brown sugar
- ½ c. Granulated sugar
- ½ c. Canola oil
- 2 eggs
- ¾ c. Pumpkin puree
- 1 tsp vanilla

Ganache

- 3 oz. (1/2 cup) semi sweet chocolate
- 6 tbsp whipping cream

Frosting

- 4 oz. Cream cheese, room temperature
- ¼ c. Butter (1/2 stick), room temperature
- ½ tsp vanilla
- ¼ tsp cinnamon
- Pinch of nutmeg
- Pinch of salt
- 2 c. Powdered sugar

What to do

Cupcakes

1. Heat up oven to 350 degrees & line a muffin tin with 12 paper cupcake liners.
2. In a mixing bowl, mix flour, baking powder, baking soda, pumpkin spice, & salt together. Put to the side.

3. In the bowl of a standing mixer fitted with the paddle attachment, mix sugars together till there are no lumps. Mix in the oil & next which the eggs one at a time. Add the pumpkin & vanilla & mix well. Steadily mix in the dry ingredients till combined.
   Spoon batter right into the cupcake liners filling ¾ full (about ¼ cup).
4. Bake for 20-25 min. Till toothpick comes out clean.
5. Let cupcakes cool in muffin tin for 5 min. & next which permit to cool completely on a wire rack.

Ganache

1. Microwave heavy whipping cream for 45 sec. & next which add the chocolate chips & let it sit for 2 min. & next which whisk together till smooth.
2. Allow to sit & cool for 5 min. & next which spoon about 1 tsp onto the top of each cupcake. Let the ganache cool & set for about 10 min. Before piping on frosting.

Frosting

1. Beat cream cheese & butter together till smooth. Mix in the vanilla & next which add the cinnamon, nutmeg, salt, & the powdered sugar a little at a time mixing on low.
2. Cream till fluffy & smooth. Put frosting in a piping bag fitted with a star tip & pipe on top of the ganache covered cupcakes.

Mango & vanilla cupcakes

What you need

- 1 & ⅓ c. All-purpose flour
- ½ tsp baking powder
- ¼ tsp baking soda
- ¼ tsp salt
- ½ c. Unsalted butter, melted & cooled
- 1 c. Sugar
- 1 big egg
- ¼ c. Coconut flavored yogurt (or vanilla)
- ¾ c. Milk
- 1 tsp vanilla

Buttercream

- ¾ c. Unsalted butter, room temperature
- ½ c. Mango puree ¼ tsp salt
- ½ tsp vanilla extract
- 4 c. Icing sugar

What to do

1. Heat up oven to 350°f & line a muffin pan with 12 paper liners.
2. In a big bowl, toss together flour, baking powder, baking soda & salt.
3. In a medium bowl, whisk the melted butter with the sugar. Add the egg, yogurt, milk & vanilla. Mix together, next which lightly pour right into the dry ingredients. Mix till smooth & try not to over mix.
4. Fill the paper liners ¾ full with batter & bake for about 18-20 min. Or till a toothpick inserted right into the centre comes out clean. Let cupcakes cool completely before frosting.

Buttercream

1. Whip the butter till light & fluffy. Add the mango puree, salt & vanilla, mix till somewhat incorporated. Add the icing sugar, one c. At a time, blend till smooth.

Cupcakes with raspberry buttercream

What you need

Cupcakes

- ½ c. Unsalted butter, softened
- ¾ c. Sugar
- 2 eggs plus one egg yolk, room temperature
- ½ tsp vanilla extract
- 1½ c. All purpose flour
- ¼ tsp salt
- 1½ tsp baking powder
- 4 oz. Milk, room temperature

Raspberry buttercream

- 1 c. Fresh raspberries
- ½ c. Unsalted butter, softened
- 2 c. Powdered sugar

What to do

Cupcakes

2. Heat up oven to 350 degrees. In a stand mixer with the paddle attachment cream butter & sugar till fluffy.
3. Add in eggs & vanilla extract. Mix to combine.
4. In a separate bowl mix together the dry ingredients. Mix the flour, salt, & baking powder.
5. Alternatively add the dry ingredients & milk in two parts to the egg mixture.
6. Fill a cupcake lined pan with batter ⅔ of the way up.
7. Place in the oven & bake for 12-15 min..
8. Allow the cupcakes to cool completely before frosting.

Raspberry buttercream

1. Add raspberries to a food processor. Pulse till they become a thick sauce.
2. Push the raspberry puree through a sieve to extract the juice & get rid of the seeds. Set raspberry sauce aside.
3. In a stand mixer with the paddle attachment cream butter on high for about 2-3 min. To get a creamy fluffy texture.

4. Add in the powdered sugar & raspberry sauce on low speed till combined.
5. Pipe the icing onto cool cupcakes & decorate as desired. Cupcakes can be stored on the counter at room temperature for a day or two & in the fridge for up to 5 days.
6. Top with a raspberry.

Toffee cupcake

What you need
Cupcake

- 1 c. (4.5 ounces) all purpose flour
- 1 c. Plus 2 tbsp (7.3 ounces) sugar
- 1/3 c. Plus 2 tbsp (1.5 ounces) unsweetened natural cocoa powder
- 1/2 tsp baking soda
- 1/4 tsp salt
- 1/2 c. (1 stick) unsalted butter, melted & warm
- 2 big eggs
- 1 tsp pure vanilla extract
- 2 tbsp instant coffee granules
- 1/2 c. Hot coffee
- 1/2 c. Chocolate covered toffee bits

Caramel frosting

- 5 big egg whites
- 11/2 c. Granulated sugar
- 4 sticks unsalted butter, chopped & softened
- 1/4 tsp salt
- 1 tbsp vanilla
- 1/3 c. Caramel sauce

Chocolate dipping sauce

- 2/3 c. Dark chocolate
- 2 tbsp heavy cream
- 4 tbsp powdered sugar, sifted
- 5-8 tbsp water, warm

What to do
Cupcake

1. Position a rack in the lower third of the oven. Heat the oven to 350 degrees.

2. In a big bowl, mix & mix together flour, cocoa powder, sugar, baking soda & salt. Add in butter, eggs, & vanilla & beat for one minute. Scrape down the sides of the bowl & add the instant coffee granules & hot coffee, beat till batter is smooth, about 20-30 sec..
3. Divide it evenly among the lined cups. Bake 18-22 min. Only till a toothpick inserted right into a few of the cupcakes comes out clean. Set the pan on a rack to cool.
4. Frost the cupcakes when they are completely cool. Store & serve at room temperature.

Caramel frosting

1. Combine egg whites & sugar in a bowl placed over simmering water. Bring mixture to 150 degrees f whereas whisking continously .
2. Transfer mixture to stand mixer bowl, fitted with a whisk attachment & beat on medium speed till mixture cools & doubles in volume.
3. Add butter in one piece at a time, mixing to incorporate next each addition. The mixture may appear clumpy & just about curdled looking-this is normal.
4. Keep mixing & it will become even & smooth again. Add salt & vanilla & mix to combine. Add caramel sauce & mix to combine.

Chocolate dipping sauce

1. Place chocolate & heavy cream in a bowl over simmering water. Let chocolate & cream sit for 2-3 min. To melt without stirring.
2. Slowly mix mixture to combine. Add powdered sugar & mix to combine. Add water one tbsp at a time, mixing next each addition till pouring consistency is reached. Put to the side & let sauce cool to warm.

Assemble

1. To frost the cupcakes: fill a pastry bag fitted with a big round tip & start piping from the outside working in to the middle to create one even layer.
2. Freeze cupcakes for 20 min. Before dipping in warm chocolate sauce, so that the frosting does not melt. Take away cupcakes & dip in warm chocolate sauce, & next which rim with chocolate covered toffee bits.
3. Return cupcakes to freezer for five min. For chocolate to set. Take away from freezer & finish piping frosting on top.

Kit kat cupcakes

What you need

Cupcakes

- 1 c. All-purpose flour
- 1 c. Sugar
- ⅓ c. Unprocessed cocoa powder
- 1 tsp baking soda
- ½ tsp baking powder
- ½ tsp salt
- 1 egg, at room temperature
- ½ c. Buttermilk, at room temperature
- ½ c. Hot coffee or hot water
- ¼ c. Vegetable oil
- 1½ tsp vanilla extract

Frosting

- 1 c. (2 sticks) unsalted butter, at room temperature
- 3-4 c. Powdered sugar
- 2 tsp pure vanilla extract
- Pinch of salt
- 2-3 tbsp heavy cream
- 6-7 snack size kit kats, chopped finely

What to do

Cupcakes

1. Heat up oven to 350 degrees f. Line muffin tins with cupcake liners. Sift together all the dry ingredients right into a big bowl. In a medium bowl, mix all the wet ingredients, including egg, utilizing a whisk. Be sure to whisk the last right into the wet ingredients to avoid scrambling with the hot coffee.
2. Using a mixer, mix the dry ingredients on low speed for 1 minute. Stop the mixer & add the wet ingredients. Mix for 2 min. On medium speed & scrape down the sides & bottom of bowl. Mix for additional minute on medium speed.
3. The batter will be thin. Divide evenly among the cupcake liners.
4. Bake for 12-15 min. Or till a toothpick inserted in the middle comes out just about clean.

5. Cool cupcakes on wire racks completely. In the meantime you could start on the frosting.

Frosting

1. Whip butter on medium speed for about 2-3 min. In the bowl of a stand mixer fitted with the paddle attachment till light & creamy.
2. Add the powdered sugar, vanilla extract, salt & heavy cream & mix on low for 1 minute till combined. Increase speed to medium-high & whip for 6 min.. Add in the chopped kit kats & mix till combined.
3. Use frosting straight away to frost cooled cupcakes.

Two colors

What you need

Chocolate cake

- 1 box devil's food cake mix
- 3 eggs
- ½ c. Oil
- 1 c. Milk
- 1/3 c. Sour cream
- 2 tsp. Vanilla extract

Vanilla cake

- 1 box white cake mix
- 3 eggs
- 1/3 c. Oil
- 1 c. Milk
- 1/3 c. Sour cream
- 1 tbsp. Vanilla extract

Strawberry buttercream

- 2 c. Butter, softened
- ¼ c. Strawberry puree
- 2 tsp. Vanilla extract
- 6-8 c. Powdered sugar

What to do

1. Heat up your oven to 350 degrees & line pans with cupcake liners.
2. Sift both cake mixes right into two separate bowl & put to the side.
3. Chocolate cake: in a big bowl, mix eggs, oil, milk, sour cream & vanilla extract. Add cake mix & mix till smooth.
4. Vanilla cake: in an additional big bowl, mix eggs, oil, milk, sour cream & vanilla extract. Add cake mix & mix till smooth.
5. Place a small scoop of chocolate batter in the side of each cupcake liner. Then, put a small scoop of vanilla batter next to the chocolate.
6. Bake for 16-20 min., or till an inserted knife comes out clean.

7. Strawberry buttercream: beat butter for 2 min., scrape down bowl & beat again. Add strawberry puree & vanilla extract. Slowly add powdered sugar till you reach your desired consistency.

8. Pipe buttercream onto cooled cupcakes & top with a fresh strawberry.

Ice cream cupcakes

What you need
Cupcakes

- 1⅔ c. All-purpose flour
- 2 tsp baking powder
- 1 c. White sugar
- 1 c. Butter, softened
- 3 eggs
- ⅔ c. Buttermilk
- 2 tsp vanilla extract
- ½ c. Rainbow dashs
- Pinch of salt, to taste

Vanilla buttercream

- 1⅔ c. Powdered sugar
- 2 tsp vanilla extract
- ½ c. Butter, softened
- 1 tbsp whole milk
- Pinch of salt, to taste

Decor

- 1 c. Milk chocolate chips
- 1 tbsp vegetable oil
- Rainbow dashs

What to do
Cupcakes

1. Heat up oven to 350 degrees f. Line a cupcake tin with paper wrappers.
2. In a big bowl, cream butter & sugar together. Mix in eggs, milk, & vanilla.
3. Add in salt & baking powder. Steadily mix in flour a little at a time till only combined.
4. Fill each wrapper 2/3 of the way full & bake for 20-25 min. .
5. Cool completely.

Vanilla buttercream

1. Cream butter. Mix in vanilla & salt.
2. Steadily add powdered sugar a little at a time, adding milk as needed.

Assemble

1. In a microwave safe bowl, melt chocolate chips for 30-60 sec. Or till smooth.
2. Take away from heat & mix in vegetable oil.
3. Use an ice cream scoop to put icing onto the top of each cupcake. Shape with a knife as needed.
4. Spoon chocolate on top of the frosting. Top with rainbow dashs.

Banana & chocolate cupcakes

What you need
Cupcakes

- 1 1/2 c. (212g) all-purpose flour
- 1/2 tsp baking soda
- 1/4 tsp salt
- 6 tbsp (3 oz) unsalted butter, softened
- 3/4 c. (165g) granulated sugar
- 1 big egg
- 1 big egg yolk
- 1/2 tsp vanilla extract
- 3/4 c. Mashed overripe chiquita bananas
- 1/2 c. (120ml) buttermilk
- 1/2 c. (86g) mini semi-sweet chocolate chips, plus more for garnish
- 1 1/2 chiquita bananas sliced, for garnish

Frosting

- 8 oz cream cheese, nearly at room temperature
- 1/2 c. (4 oz) unsalted butter, nearly at room temperature
- 2 1/2 c. (310g) powdered sugar
- 1 tsp vanilla extract

What to do
Cupcakes

1. Heat up oven to 350 degrees. In a mixing bowl whisk together flour, baking soda & salt for 20 sec.. In the bowl of an electric stand mixer fitted with the paddle attachment, whip together butter & granulated sugar till pale & fluffy.
2. Mix in egg next which mix in egg yolk & vanilla. Blend in mashed bananas. Add 1/3 of the flour mixture next which mix only till combined, pour in 1/2 of the buttermilk & mix only till combined, repeat process with flour & buttermilk when more.
3. Finish by adding in remaining 1/3 of the flour mixture & the chocolate chips & mix only till combined. Scrape down sides & bottom of bowl & fold batter.

4. Divide batter among 12 paper lined muffin cups, filling each about 3/4 full. Bake in heat uped oven till toothpick inserted right into middle of cupcake comes out clean, about 20 - 25 min..

Frosting

1. In the bowl of an electric stand mixer cream together cream cheese & butter till smooth.
2. Mix in powdered sugar & blend till light & fluffy.

Assemble

3. Cool in pan several min. Next which transfer to a wire rack & cool completely. Frost with cream cheese frosting, top with 2 banana slices & dash with chocolate chips.
4. Store in fridge in an air tight container & permit to rest at room temperature about 5 - 10 min. Before serving.

Pumpkin chocolate cupcakes (2nd version)

What you need
Chocolate batter

- ⅓ c. Flour
- 2 tbsp cocoa powder
- ¼ tsp baking soda
- ¼ tsp instant espresso powder
- 4 tsp neutral-flavored oil
- ½ tsp vanilla extract
- ¼ packed c. Light brown sugar
- ⅓ c. Buttermilk
- 1 big egg yolk

Pumpkin batter

- 7 tbsp flour
- ½ tsp baking powder
- ⅛ tsp baking soda
- ¼ tsp salt
- ½ tsp cinnamon
- ¼ tsp freshly grated nutmeg
- ¼ tsp ground ginger
- 1 big egg white
- ½ c. Canned pumpkin puree
- ¼ packed c. Light brown sugar
- 3 tbsp neutral-flavored oil
- 3 tbsp granulated sugar

Vanilla buttercream

- 4 tbsp unsalted butter, softened
- 1½ c. Powdered sugar
- ½ vanilla bean, scraped
- ¼ tsp vanilla extract
- Pinch of salt

- 1-2 tbsp heavy cream

What to do

Heat up the oven to 350, & line 6 c. In a muffin pan with liners.

Chocolate batter

1. Whisk together the flour, cocoa powder, baking soda & espresso powder. Put to the side.
2. Whisk together the oil, vanilla, brown sugar, buttermilk, & egg yolk. Put to the side.

Pumpkin batter

1. Whisk together the flour, baking powder, baking soda, salt, & spices. Put to the side.
2. Whisk together the egg white, pumpkin, brown sugar, oil, & granulated sugar. Put to the side.
3. When ready to fill the pan, mix the dry ingredients for the chocolate cupcakes right into its wet ingredients.
4. Mix the dry ingredients for the pumpkin cupcakes right into its wet ingredients.
5. Layer the batters in the cupcake liners.
6. Bake the cupcakes for 17-20 min., or till a toothpick inserted comes out with only moist crumbs.
7. Let the cupcakes cool in the pan for 1 minute, & next which move to a cooling rack to cool completely.

Frosting

1. Beat the butter till light & fluffy, about 1-2 min.. Slowly add the powdered sugar, vanilla bean, vanilla extract, & salt whereas continuously beating.
2. Add the heavy cream, starting with only 1 tbsp of the cream, & add more if needed.
3. Frost the cupcakes with the vanilla bean frosting, & serve.

Apple cider cranberry cupcakes

What you need
Cupcakes

- 2 c. All-purpose flour
- 1 tsp baking powder
- 1 tsp saigon cinnamon
- ½ tsp kosher salt
- ½ c. Unsalted butter, melted & cooled
- 1 c. Light brown sugar, packed
- 4 big eggs
- 1 tsp vanilla extract
- 1 c. Apple cider, natural & fresh

Frosting

- 8 oz. Cold cream cheese
- ½ c. Unsalted butter, cold but still firm
- 1/8 tsp kosher salt
- ½ tsp saigon cinnamon
- 3 ½ c. Powdered sugar, sifted
- ½ tsp vanilla
- Heavy cream if needed
- Spiced apple cider cranberry sauce

Cinnamon sugar pie crusts

- Your favorite pie crust
- ¼ tsp saigon cinnamon
- ¼ c. Sugar + more for rolling

What to do
Cupcakes

1. Heat up the oven 350°. Line standard muffin tins with cupcake liners.
2. Whisk flour, baking powder, cinnamon & salt together in a medium bowl & put to the side.

3. Using a hand mixer beat together the butter & sugar on medium-high speed till thick & lighter in color, 2-3 min..
4. Add the eggs one at a time, beating well next each addition. Add the vanilla with the last egg. Scrape down the sides of the bowl between each addition.
5. Alternately add flour & apple cider in three additions on low speed beginning & ending with flour, scraping down the sides of the bowl as needed.
6. Scoop or pour the batter right into the liners ¾ full. Bake in heat uped oven for 15-20 min..
7. Take away from tins straight away & let cool on a wire rack. They must be completely cool before frosting.

Frosting

1. Using the paddle attachment of your stand mixer, beat cream cheese, butter, salt & cinnamon on medium-high speed till smooth & creamy, approximately 2-3 min..
2. Reduce speed to low & steadily add the powdered sugar, mixing till incorporated. Add the vanilla next the last addition & mix till incorporated.

3. Pie crusts
4. Dash a generous amount of sugar over a solid surface. Roll out your pie crusts in granulated sugar.
5. Cut out little leaves or shapes & put 1 in. Apart on a baking tray.
6. Dash generously with the cinnamon sugar mixture. Bake in heat uped oven for 15-20 min. Or till they puff up & are brown around the edges.

Buttered cupcakes

What you need

- 3 1/4 c. Sifted cake flour
- 4 1/2 tsp baking powder
- 1/2 tsp salt
- 1 tsp vanilla extract
- 1 c. + 2 tbsp whole milk
- 1/2 c. + 6 tbsp softened butter
- 1 3/4 c. Sugar
- 5 egg whites (room temperature)
- 24+ buttered pop corn jelly belly beans

Frosting

- 5 egg whites (room temperature)
- 1 c. + 2 tbsp sugar
- Small pinch of salt
- 2 c. Softened butter
- 1/2 tsp vanilla extract
- Yellow food color

What to do

1. Sift together the cake flour, baking powder & salt. Put to the side.
2. With an electric mixer, or stand mixer, beat the egg whites till stiff peaks start to form. Put to the side.
3. With an electric mixer, or stand mixer cream the softened butter till smooth. Scrape down the sides of the bowl, add the sugar & beat again till the mixture starts to looked whipped.
4. Begin adding the flour mixture & milk in intervals, mixing in between. Add in the vanilla extract as well.
5. Fold the whipped egg whites right into the batter utilizing a rubber spatula. Cut through the batter down the center, next which swiftly mix to one side. Keep mixing in this manner till nearly no lumps remain & the batter looks cohesive in texture.
6. Spoon batter right into prepared baking cups. Add a jelly bean the middle of each cupcake.

7. Bake at 350° for 20-22 min. For standard size, & 17-18 min. For mini size cupcakes.

Frosting

1. Combine the egg whites & sugar in a metal or glass mixing bowl. Set this over a pot of simmering water. Whisk till the egg whites are slightly warmed & the sugar & completely dissolved.
2. Using an electric mixer or stand mixer, beat the egg whites till stiff, glossy peaks form.
3. With the mixer running on low, add the softened butter a few tbsp at a time.
4. Turn the mixer up a few notches to whip the batter for a few sec..

Bar cupcakes

What you need

Cupcakes

- 1½ c. All purpose flour
- 1½ tsp baking powder
- ½ tsp salt
- 1 c. Sugar
- ½ c. Butter, at room temperature
- 2 eggs
- 1 tsp vanilla extract
- 1 c. Buttermilk

Milky way frosting

- 12 oz (about 12 fun-sized) milky way candy bars
- ⅓ c. Butter
- 1½ tbsp milk
- 1 tsp vanilla
- 2 c. Powdered sugar
- Additional chopped or cut milky way candy bars, for garnish

What to do

Heat up the oven to 325f. Line 18 cupcake tins with paper liners.

In a bowl, whisk together the flour, baking powder & salt.

In the bowl of a stand mixer, beat together the sugar & the butter till light & fluffy, about 2 min.. Add in the eggs, one at a time, beating well next each addition. Scrape the sides of the bowl as needed. Beat in the vanilla.

Add one-third of the flour mixture, beat to combine, next which half of the buttermilk. Repeat with an additional third of the flour & the remaining buttermilk, followed by the remaining flour, beating only till combined between each addition.

Divide the mixture between the 18 cups, filling each about ⅔ full. Bake till a tester comes out clean, about 18 min.. Take away from the pans & cool completely.

Frosting

1. Bring a small saucepan with about 1 in. Of water to a simmer. Mix the candy bars, butter & milk in a big heat-proof bowl & set over the simmering water. Cook for 10-12 min., stirring frequently, till the candy bars have melted & the mixture is smooth.
2. Take away the bowl from the heat & mix in the vanilla. Add the powdered sugar & beat with a hand mixer till the mixture is smooth.
3. Let the mixture sit for 10 to 15 min. Till only warm to the touch. Transfer the frosting to a piping bag fitted with a big round tip. Pipe the frosting onto the cooled cupcakes.
4. Top with a candy bar piece.

Chocolate chip cookie dough cupcakes

What you need

Cookie dough

- 1 1/2 c. Flour
- 1/4 tsp. Baking soda
- 1/4 tsp. Salt
- 1/2 c. Softened, unsalted butter
- 1/4 c. White sugar
- 1/4 c. Brown sugar
- 2 tsp. Vanilla
- 1 egg, at room temperature
- 1 c. Semi-sweet chocolate chips

Chocolate cupcakes

- 1/2 c. Plus 1 tbsp. Cocoa powder
- 1/2 c. Plus 1 tbsp. Hot water
- 2 1/4 c. All-purpose flour
- 3/4 tsp. Baking soda
- 3/4 tsp. Baking powder
- 1/2 tsp. Salt
- 2 sticks plus 1 tbsp. (17 tbsp. Total) butter, at room temperature
- 1 2/3 c. Granulated sugar
- 3 big eggs, at room temperature
- 1 tbsp. Vanilla extract
- 3/4 c. Sour cream

Frosting

- 3 sticks unsalted butter, room temperature
- 3/4 c. Light brown sugar
- 1 tsp. Kosher salt
- 2 1/2 c. Powdered sugar
- 2 1/2 tsp. Vanilla
- 1 c. Flour

- 3-4 tbsp. Milk

What to do

Cookie dough

1. Mix the flour, baking soda, & salt in a bowl & put to the side. In an additional bowl, beat the butter & sugars till they are light & fluffy, about 2 to 3 min..
2. Add the egg & vanilla & mix till mixed, about 1 minute. Steadily add flour & mix till a dough forms. Fold in the chocolate chips. Form dough right into no larger than tbsp.-sized balls & freeze.

Cupcakes

1. Heat up the oven to 350 f. Line 2 standard cupcake pans with paper liners. In a glass liquid measuring cup, mix the cocoa powder & hot water & whisk till smooth.
2. In a medium bowl whisk together the flour, baking soda, baking powder, & salt; put to the side.
3. In a medium saucepan over medium heat, mix the butter & sugar.
4. Cook, whisking often, till the mixture is smooth & the butter is completely melted. Transfer the mixture to the bowl of an electric mixer & beat on medium-low speed till the mixture is cool, about 4-5 min..
5. Add the eggs one at a time, mixing well next each addition & scraping down the sides of the bowl as needed. Blend in the vanilla & next which the cocoa mixture till smooth. With the mixer on low speed, add the flour mixture in three additions alternating with the sour cream, beginning & ending with the dry ingredients & mixing each addition only till incorporated.
6. Place one frozen cookie dough ball in each paper liner of one tray.
7. Divide the batter evenly between the prepared liners, filling no more than 2/3 full. If you live at a high altitude or have had overflowing cupcakes in the past, err on the side of filling the liner of one cupcake 1/2 full & baking it alone first to judge how the cupcake will rise in the oven.
8. Bake the cupcakes for about 18-20 min.. Take away the cupcakes to a wire rack to cool completely.
9. Repeat process with remaining cake batter & cookie dough. Cool cupcakes to room temperature before frosting, about 1 hour.

Frosting

1. Beat butter, brown sugar, & salt together with mixer till light & fluffy, 3-4 min.. Add powdered sugar & vanilla till combined.
2. Add flour & mix till only combined. If necessary, add 1 tbsp. Milk at a time till desired consistency is reached.

Lemon meringue cupcakes

What you need

Cupcakes

- 240ml / 1 c. Almond milk
- Juice & zest from 1 medium lemon
- 150g / 1¼ c. Self-raising flour
- 2 tbsp corn starch
- 80ml / ⅓ c. Mild olive oil
- 150g / ¾ c. Caster sugar
- 1 tsp vanilla extract

Lemon curd

- Juice from 2 big lemons (to make about 120ml / ½ cup)
- 120ml / ½ c. Almond milk
- 150g / ¾ c. Caster sugar
- 2 tbsp corn starch
- 1 tbsp dairy-free butter

Frosting

- Liquid from a 400g tin of chickpeas
- 50g / ½ c. Icing sugar
- ½ tsp cream of tartar
- 1 tsp vanilla extract

What to do

Lemon cupcakes

1. Heat up the oven to 170c & line a cupcake tray with liners.
2. Mix the almond milk & lemon juice & zest together in a big bowl & leave to for a few min..
3. In the meantime , mix the flour & corn starch together in a separate bowl.
4. Add the oil, sugar & vanilla extract to the almond milk & next which the flour mixture. Mix everything till only combined.

5. Divide equally between 12 cupcake cases & bake for 20-25 min. Till golden brown & spongey to the touch.
6. Leave to cool completely before coring the centre of the cupcakes.

Lemon curd

Whilst the cupcakes are baking, make the curd by mixing the lemon juice, half of the almond milk, sugar, & corn starch together in a small saucepan.

Continually whisk over medium heat till it starts to boil. The mixture should start thickening.

Take away from heat & whisk in the remaining of the almond milk & dairy-free butter.

It should be a smooth, thick, runny consistency. Leave it to cool in the fridge where it will thicken some more.

Once cooled, pour right into the centre of the cupcakes till it reaches the brim.

Frosting

1. In a stand mixer, whisk the chickpea water on high for a few min., till it starts to turn frothy
2. Slowly add in the icing sugar, a little at a time.
3. Add the cream of tartar.
4. Keep whisking on high speed for approximately 10 min. Till the mixture forms stiff peaks.
5. Add the vanilla & whisk again for an additional minute.
6. Add the mixture to a piping bag fitted with a big star nozzle. Pipe swirls on top of the cupcakes.

Nutella cheesecake cupcakes

What you need

- 12 oreos, finely crushed
- 1 1/2 tbsp salted butter, melted
- 6 tbsp granulated sugar
- 1 1/2 tbsp all-purpose flour
- 12 oz cream cheese, well softened
- 2 big eggs
- 1/4 c. Milk
- 1/4 c. Sour cream
- 1/2 tsp vanilla extract
- 1/2 c. Nutella

Topping

- 1 c. Heavy cream
- 3 tbsp powdered sugar
- 1/4 c chopped, toasted hazelnuts
- Chopped chocolate, for garnish

What to do

1. Heat up oven to 325 degrees. In a mixing utilizing a fork, blend together crushed oreos & butter. Divide mixture evenly among 12 paper lined muffin cups, adding a heaping 1 tbsp to each. Press crumbs right into an even layer. Bake in heat uped oven 5 min.. Take away from oven & permit to cool whereas preparing filling.
2. In a mixing bowl whisk together granulated sugar & flour. Add in cream cheese & utilizing an electric hand mixer, whip only till smooth. Blend in eggs. Add in milk, sour cream & vanilla & mix only till combined, next which add in nutella & mix only till combined.
3. Tap bowl forcefully against countertop about 30 times to release some of the air bubbles. Divide mixture among muffin cups, pouring over crusts & filling each c. Nearly full, about 1/4 c. Batter in each. Bake in 325 degree oven 20 - 24 min. Till centers only jiggle slightly.
4. Take away from oven & permit to cool at room temperature 30 min., next which cover loosely with plastic wrap or foil & transfer to fridge & chill 3 hours. Serve with sweetened whipped cream, hazelnuts, chopped chocolate or chocolate. Store in fridge in an airtight container.

5. In a mixing bowl, utilizing an electric hand mixer, whip heavy cream on high speed till soft peaks form. Add in powdered sugar & whip till stiff peaks form. Store in fridge.

Sweet potato cupcakes

What you need

- 1 1/2 c. Firmly packed brown sugar
- 1/3 c. Butter, room temperature
- 2 eggs
- 1 tsp vanilla
- 2 3/4 c. All purpose flour
- 1 tbsp baking powder
- 1 tsp pumpkin pie spice
- 3/4 tsp salt
- 3/4 c. Whole milk
- 1 c. Cooked sweet potatoes
- 1/3 c. Bourbon

Candied pecans

- 1 c. Sugar
- 1 c. Water
- Pecan halves

Vanilla glaze

- 2 c. Sifted confectioner's sugar
- 1 tbsp butter, room temperature
- 1 tsp vanilla
- 3-4 tbsps milk

Syrup

- 1 1/2 c. Sugar
- 1/2 c. Water
- 1 tsp butter
- 2 tsp vanilla
- 2 tbsp bourbon

What to do

1. Heat up oven to 350 degrees.
2. Line cupcake trays with 24 baking cups.
3. Whisk together flour, baking powder, pumpkin pie spice & salt in a big bowl.
4. In an additional big mixing bowl, mix brown sugar, butter & eggs till fluffy.
5. Add sweet potatoes & vanilla. Mix well.
6. Add 1/3 of flour mixture to sugar mixture till combined. Add bourbon. Add second 1/3 of flour mixture. Add milk. Add final 1/3 flour mixture.
7. Mix well with each addition.
8. Fill baking cups.
9. Bake for 12-15 min. Or till done.
10. Cool completely.

Candied pecans

1. Add equal parts sugar & water to a pot. Add pecans. Simmer for about six min.. Drain syrup off.
2. In a deep fryer at about 375 degrees add pecans to oil. Heat for about 30 sec. To a minute or till frying noise.
3. Lay on parchment paper lined tray & cool slightly.
4. Dash some extra sugar on top to make them prettier.
5. Allow to dry completely.

Vanilla glaze

1. In a medium bowl, mix sugar & butter. Add vanilla.
2. Add milk 1 tbsp at a time till you get the desired consistency.
3. Mix till smooth.

Syrup

1. In a small saucepan, bring sugar & water to a boil.
2. Boil for five min. & add remaining ingredients. Cook till a syrupy consistency.
3. Add one candied pecan to each cupcake if you don't eat them all first.

Chocolate mocha cupcake

What you need

Cupcake

- 1 c. (4.5 ounces) all purpose flour
- 1 c. Plus 2 tbsp (7.3 ounces) sugar
- 1/3 c. Plus 2 tbsp (1.5 ounces) cocoa powder
- 1/2 tsp baking soda
- 1/4 tsp salt
- 1/2 c. (1 stick) unsalted butter, melted & warm
- 2 big eggs
- 1 tsp pure vanilla extract
- 2 tbsp instant coffee
- 1/2 c. Hot coffee
- 1/2 c. Crushed whoppers

Chocolate swiss meringue

- 5 big egg whites
- 1 1/2 c. Sugar
- 4 sticks unsalted butter, chopped & softened
- 1/4 tsp salt
- 1 tbsp vanilla
- 2 tbsp unsweetened cocoa powder
- 10 oz. Bittersweet chocolate, melted & cooled

Chocolate sauce

- 2/3 c. Dark chocolate
- 2 tbsp heavy cream
- 4 tbsp powdered sugar, sifted
- 4-5 tbsp water, warm

What to do

Cupcake

1. Add flour, cocoa powder, sugar, baking soda, & salt in a bowl & mix thoroughly to combine. Add in the butter, eggs, & vanilla & beat on medium speed for one minute.
2. Add instant coffee & half of the hot coffee right into the mixture & beat for 20 sec.. Scrape the sides of the bowl & add remaining coffee. Beat for 20-30 sec. Till the batter is smooth. The batter will be thin enough to pour.
3. Divide it evenly among the lined cups. Bake 18-22 min. Only till a toothpick inserted right into a few of the cupcakes comes out clean. Set the pan on a rack to cool. Frost the cupcakes when they are completely cool.

Chocolate swiss meringue

1. Combine egg whites & sugar in a bowl placed over simmering water. Bring mixture to 160 degrees f whereas whisking continously .
2. Transfer mixture to stand mixer bowl, fitted with a whisk attachment & beat on medium high speed till mixture cools & doubles in volume & forms stiff peaks; about 10-12 min..
3. Add butter in one piece at a time, mixing to incorporate next each addition. The mixture may appear clumpy & just about curdled looking-this is normal. Keep mixing & it will become even & smooth again. Add salt & vanilla & mix to combine. Add cooled chocolate & mix to combine.

Chocolate sauce

1. Place chocolate & heavy cream in a bowl over simmering water. Let chocolate & cream sit for 2-3 min. To melt without stirring.
2. Stir slowly mixture to combine. Add powdered sugar & mix to combine. Add water 1 tbsp at a time, mixing next each addition till pouring consistency is reached. Put to the side & let sauce cool to warm.

Assembly

1. Frost cooled cupcakes. Freeze frosted cupcakes for ten min.. Drizzle chocolate pour over chocolate frosting.
2. Dash crushed whoppers on chocolate sauce. Finish with a small swirl of frosting & a whopper.

Caramel apple cupcakes

What you need

Cupcakes

- 1 2/3 c. All purpose flour
- 1/2 c. Brown sugar
- 1/2 c. Sugar
- 1/4 tsp baking soda
- 1 1/4 tsp baking powder
- 1 tsp cinnamon
- 1/8 tsp nutmeg
- 3 egg whites
- 2 tsp vanilla extract
- 1/2 c. Sour cream
- 1/2 c. Milk
- 3/4 c. Salted butter, slightly melted
- 1 big apple, chopped

Buttercream

- 1 c. Butter
- 1 c. Shortening
- 8 c. Powdered sugar
- 3/4 c. + 2 tbsp caramel sauce

What to do

1. Heat up oven to 350 degrees.
2. Whisk together flour, sugars, baking soda, baking powder, cinnamon & nutmeg in a big mixing bowl.
3. Add egg whites, vanilla extract, sour cream, milk & butter & mix on medium speed only till smooth. Do not over mix.
4. Stir in chopped apples
5. Fill cupcake liners about 3/4 full.
6. Bake 17-19 min..
7. Allow to cool for 1-2 min., next which take away to cooling rack to finish cooling.

8. To make the buttercream, mix butter & shortening & mix till smooth. Add 4 c. Of powdered sugar & mix till smooth.
9. Add caramel sauce & mix till smooth. Add remaining powdered sugar & mix till smooth.
10. Top cupcakes with icing & a drizzle of caramel.

Dulce de leche cupcakes

What you need

- 2 tbsp canola oil
- 1 stick unsalted butter, melted & slightly cooled
- 1/2 c. Semi-sweet chocolate chips
- 1/2 c. Granulated sugar
- 1/2 c. Light brown sugar
- 2 big eggs + 1 big egg yolk, at room temperature
- 1/2 tsp vanilla
- 3/4 c. + 3 tbsp all-purpose flour, not packed
- 1/2 tsp baking soda
- 1 tsp baking powder
- 1/2 c. Unsweetened cocoa powder
- 3/4 tsp salt
- 1/2 c. Full fat sour cream
- 1/2 c. Boiling water
- 1/2 c. Dulce de leche

Buttercream

- 1 stick unsalted butter, very soft
- 3 c. Confectioners sugar, sifted
- 3/4 c. Unsweetened cocoa powder, sifted
- 3 tbsp half & half, more if needed
- 1 heaping tbsp dulce de leche
- 1/2 tsp salt

Topping

- Dulce de leche, for drizzling
- Flaky sea salt

What to do

Cupcakes

1. Heat up the oven to 350 degrees (f). Line a 12-cup cupcake/muffin tin with cupcake liners & lightly spray the liners with non-stick spray.
2. Melt the oil, butter, and chocolate together in the microwave, heating in 30 second increments, & stirring between increments each time. Whisk mixture till completely smooth. Put to the side to cool.
3. In a medium sized bowl mix the flour, baking soda, baking powder, cocoa powder, & salt; mix together till thoroughly combined; put to the side.
4. In a big bowl, whisk together the eggs, yolk, sugars, & vanilla; beat till smooth. Add the cooled oil/butter/chocolate mixture & whisk till smooth.
5. Add half of the flour mixture, next which half of the sour cream. Repeat the process till everything is added, & be sure to mix till only combined.
6. Quickly mix in the hot water till evenly combined.
7. Divide the batter among the 12 liners in your prepared pan. Bake for 16-18 min..
8. Once cooled, use a small sharp knife to carve out a small hole on the top of each not carving too wide or deep. Fill each hole with 1-2 tsp of dulce de leche.

Buttercream

1. Sift together the confectioners sugar & cocoa powder, whisking well.
2. Using a mixer beat the butter on medium-high speed till creamy; about 2 min.. Reduce speed to low & slowly add the sifted sugar/cocoa powder, alternating with the half & half; add in the dulce de leche & salt.
3. Once all of the ingredients have been added, beat on medium-high speed till light & creamy & combined; at least 2 min.. Add more cream to the frosting if it seems too thick; add a touch more sugar to the frosting if it seems too thin.
4. Frost cooled, filled cupcakes & top with more dulce de leche & flaky sea salt.

Cheesecake cupcakes

What you need

- 2 pkg. (8 oz. Each) cream cheese, softened
- 1 c. Granulated sugar
- 1 tsp. Butter extract
- 2 eggs
- 12 vanilla wafers
- 1 c. Seedless raspberry jam
- 1 pt. Fresh raspberries
- 2 tbsp. Powdered sugar for dusting

what to do

1. Heat oven to 350°f.
2. Place a paper cupcake liner in each of 12 muffin cups.
3. Beat cream cheese with a hand-held electric mixer till fluffy. Add granulated sugar & butter extract, beating well. Add eggs, one at a time, beating well next each addition.
4. Place a vanilla wafer, flat-side down, in each muffin cup. Spoon cream cheese mixture over wafers. Bake for 20 min..
5. Allow tarts to cool completely. When cool, top each cheesecake cupcake with 1/2 tbsp. Of raspberry jam & fresh raspberries. Dust with powdered sugar.

Pumpkin pie cupcakes

What you need

- 3 tbsp coconut flour
- 1 tsp pumpkin pie spice
- 1/4 tsp baking powder
- 1/4 tsp baking soda
- Pinch salt
- 1 c. Pumpkin puree
- 1/3 c. Swerve sweetener

- 1/4 c. Heavy cream
- 1 big egg
- 1/2 tsp vanilla

What to do

1. Heat up oven to 350f & line 6 muffin c. With paper liners.
2. In a small bowl, whisk together the coconut flour, pumpkin pie spice, baking powder, baking soda, & salt.
3. In a big bowl, whisk pumpkin puree, sweetener, cream, egg, & vanilla till well combined. Whisk in dry ingredients.
4. Divide among prepared muffin c. & bake 25 to 30 min., till only puffed & barely set. Take away from oven & let cool in pan.
5. Refrigerate for at least one hour before serving. Dollop whipped cream generously on top.

Mint & chocolate cupcakes

What you need

Chocolate cupcakes

- 105 grams (3/4 cup) plain flour
- 20 grams (1/4 cup) cocoa powder
- 20 grams (1/4 cup) dutch processed cocoa powder
- 1/2 tsp baking soda
- 1/2 tsp baking powder
- 100 grams (1/2 cup) caster sugar
- 45 grams (1/4 cup) brown sugar
- 115 grams (1/2 c. Or 1 stick) unsalted butter
- 2 big eggs
- 1 tsp vanilla extract
- 120 ml (1/2 cup) buttermilk

Mint frosting

- 115 grams (1/2 c. Or 1 stick) unsalted butter, softened
- 435 grams (3 & 1/2 cups) icing or powdered sugar
- 3 tbsp milk
- 1 tsp peppermint or mint extract
- A few drops of green food colouring
- 6 whole mint chocolate cookie or biscuit, cut in half

What to do

1. Heat up the oven to 180c (360 f). Line a 12 hole muffin tin with patty cases. In a big mixing bowl, sift the flour, cocoa powders, baking soda, baking powder & next which add the sugars & give it a stir. Pop the butter right into the microwave for a short burst, 10 sec. Or so at a time, till it is melted.
2. Give it a mix with a fork to eliminate any lumps. In a separate mixing bowl, add the eggs, vanilla & butter & whisk together till smooth.
3. Then add the wet mixture right into the dry mixture, along with the buttermilk & lightly fold till only combined.

4. Spoon the mixture right into the prepared patty cases & pop right into the oven. Bake for 18-20 min. Or till only cooked through. Set cakes out onto a wire rack & leave to cool completely.

Mint frosting

1. Add the butter to a big mixing bowl & beat with an electric mixer till pale & creamy. Lightly sift in the icing sugar, one c. At a time. Add a tbsp or two of milk to help loosen up the mixture. Add the mint extract & continue to beat.
2. Add a tbsp of milk if needed. The icing should be nice & creamy but thick enough to hold its shape. Add in green food colouring till it reaches your desired colour. Pipe the icing onto the cupcakes utilizing a piping bag & a big star tip. Top each cupcake with half a chocolate mint cookie.

Pudding cupcakes

What you need

- 1 3.4-ounce box instant chocolate pudding mix
- 1 3/4 c. Whole milk
- 12 ounce container whipped topping, thawed, divided use
- 24 chocolate cupcakes, baked & cooled
- 15 chocolate sandwich cookies, crushed right into crumbs
- 24 campfire ghoster roasters

What to do

1. In a big bowl, beat pudding mix & milk on medium speed till thoroughly combined & thickened. Fold 1 c. Whipped topping right into the pudding till no streaks remain. Cover & refrigerate for one hour.
2. Using a sharp paring knife, or an apple corer, core the middle of each cupcake. Reserve the cake pieces that were take awayd.
3. Fill a piping bag or big zip-top bag with the chilled pudding.
4. Pipe pudding right into the middle of each cupcake. Cover the pudding with reserved cake pieces that you cored from the cupcake.
5. Fill a big piping bar or big zip-top bag with remaining whipped topping.
6. Pipe whipped topping onto cupcakes. Dash each cupcake with crushed cookies & top with a campfire® ghoster roaster.
7. Refrigerate cupcakes till ready to serve.

Halloween cupcakes

What you need
Chocolate cupcakes

- ½ c. Boiling water
- ¼ c. Unsalted butter, softened
- 1 c. Sugar
- ⅓ c. Good quality cocoa powder
- 1½ c. All purpose flour
- ½ tsp salt
- ½ tsp baking powder
- ½ tsp baking soda
- 1 big egg, beaten
- ½ c. Sour cream
- 1 tsp vanilla extract

Buttercream frosting

- 1⅓ c. Unsalted butter, softened
- 8oz marshmallow fluff (about 2 cups)
- 1 tbsp vanilla extract
- 1 tsp heavy cream
- 2⅔ c. Confectioners sugar
- 24 mini chocolate chips (for eyes)

What to do
Chocolate cupcakes

1. Heat up over to 350 degrees.
2. Line a 12-count muffin tin with cupcake cups. Reserve.
3. In the bowl of a stand mixer, mix the butter, the sugar, the cocoa powder & the boiling water. Beat on low till smooth & the sugar is dissolved.
4. In a separate bowl, mix the flour, the salt, the baking powder & the baking soda. Reserve.
5. In a third bowl, beat the egg & add the sour cream & the vanilla extract. Whisk till smooth. Reserve.

6. With the mixer on low, add ½ the dry ingredients to the butter/sugar/boiling water mixture. Then, add the egg/sour cream & finish with the remaining of the flour. Mix only till the flour is incorporated.
7. Pour the batter right into the cupcake cups, about ⅔ full.
8. Bake the cupcakes for 20 to 25 min. Or till a toothpick inserted in the middle of a cupcake comes out clean.
9. Cool in the pan for 5 min.. Take away from the pan & cool completely before frosting.

Frosting

1. In the bowl of a stand mixer, mix the butter & the marshmallow fluff. Beat till creamy & smooth.
2. Add the vanilla extract & the heavy cream & beat till incorporated.
3. With the mixer on low, slowly add the confectioners sugar. When incorporated, turn the speed up & beat for 1 minute, till light & fluffy. Add a pinch of salt if the frosting is too sweet.
4. Frost cooled cupcakes & decorate with the eyes.

Glass cupcakes (halloween)

What you need

Cupcakes

- 2 c. All-purpose flour
- 2 c. Sugar
- 2 tbsp sugar
- 1 c. Unsweetened dark cocoa powder
- 2 tsp baking soda
- 1 tsp baking powder
- 1/2 tsp salt
- 2 eggs
- 1 c. Cold coffee
- 1 c. Buttermilk
- 1/2 c. Vegetable oil

Frosting

- 1 c. Unsalted butter, slightly softened
- 1 package cream cheese
- 2 tsp pure vanilla extract
- 4 to 4½ c. Confectioners' sugar

Glass

- ½ c. Sugar
- ¼ c. Light corn syrup
- Parchment paper

Blood

- ½ c. Corn syrup
- 1 tbsp water
- 1 tbsp of red food coloring
- 1 tbsp of chocolate syrup
- 1 tbsp of cornstarch

What to do

Cupcakes

1. Heat up oven to 350 degrees. Put 24 liners in cupcake tin. In a big bowl, mix flour, sugar, cocoa, baking soda, baking powder & salt.
2. Make a well in the middle & pour in the eggs, coffee, milk & oil. Mix till smooth; batter will be thin. Spoon right into prepared cupcake pan.
3. Bake in the heat uped oven 14-17 min., or till a toothpick inserted right into the middle of the cupcake comes out clean. Permit to cool completely.

Frosting

1. Using an electric mixer & big bowl, beat butter till creamy. Add cream cheese & vanilla; beat till fully incorporated.
2. Steadily increase mixer speed to high & continue beating till light & fluffy, scraping down the sides of bowl as necessary with rubber spatula.
3. Steadily add 4 c. Confectioners' sugar, beating on low speed (stir), till well combined. Add additional confectioners' sugar till desired consistency for piping. Beat on high speed till well combined & smooth whereas scraping down sides of bowl as necessary, about 1 to 2 min..
4. Glass

    mix sugar & corn syrup in a microwave-safe glass. Cover glass with plastic wrap & microwave 2 min. Take away plastic wrap prudently to avoid steam. Mix & cover with a new piece of plastic wrap. Microwave 1 minute.
5. Prudently pour onto parchment lined baking sheet, spread as thinly as possible, permit to cook completely, & break by smacking baking sheet on counter. Store shards in airtight container till ready to use.

Blood

1. Mix all of the ingredients in the blender for a few sec..

Assembly

2. Pipe icing on cupcake utilizing an open star cupcake tip in a swirl working from the outside to the center. Add glass shards drizzle with blood.

Corn cupcakes

What you need

- 1 white cake mix
- 2 eggs
- 1 c. Sour cream
- ½ c. Milk
- ⅓ c. Vegetable oil

Garnish

- Candy corns
- Orange dashs

Frosting

- 1 c. Butter
- 4 c. Powdered sugar
- ¼ tsp salt
- 1 tsp vanilla extract
- ⅓ c. Heavy whipping cream

What to do

3. Heat up oven to 350 degrees & line cupcake pan with paper liners.
4. Combine all ingredients in a big bowl till incorporated. Scrape sides of bowl & next which beat on medium-high speed for 3 min..
5. Divide batter in half & color one half orange & the other half yellow.
6. Fill paper liners with about 1-2 tbsp of yellow batter. Next which top with 1-2 tbsp of orange batter. Bake according to cake mix package directions - about 15-18 min.. Cool cupcakes.

Frosting

7. In a mixing bowl, cream butter till fluffy. Add sugar & continue creaming till well blended. Add salt, vanilla, & whipping cream.
8. Blend on low speed till moistened. Beat at high speed till frosting is fluffy.

cupcakes with vanilla buttercream

What you need

Cupcakes

- 2¼ c. All-purpose flour
- ¾ c. Unsweetened dutch-process cocoa powder
- ½ c. Granulated sugar
- ¾ c. Brown sugar
- 1½ tsp baking soda
- ½ tsp salt
- 1 c. Milk
- 1¼ c. Original malted milk powder
- 1 c. Vegetable oil
- 3 big eggs, at room temperature
- 1 c. Sour cream, at room temperature
- 1 tsp vanilla extract

Buttercream

- 1½ c. Unsalted butter, at room temperature
- ¾ c. Original malted milk powder
- 2½ c. Powdered sugar
- ½ tsp vanilla extract

What to do

Cupcakes

1. Heat up the oven to 350ºf. Line 30 muffin tins with cupcake liners.
2. In a big bowl, mix the flour, cocoa powder, granulated sugar, brown sugar, baking soda & salt. Whisk to combine.
3. Combine the milk & the malted milk powder in the bowl of a stand mixer & mix till the malted milk powder has dissolved. Add in the oil, next which add in the eggs, one at a time, beating till combined.
4. Scrape down the sides of the bowl, next which add in the dry ingredients. Mix only till combined. Add the sour cream & vanilla, & mix only till combined.
5. Divide the batter between the prepared cups. Bake 20 min.. Let cool completely before frosting.

Buttercream

1. Place the butter in the bowl of a stand mixer & beat till very light, about 2 min..
2. Add in the malted milk powder & mix an additional minute. Start adding in the powdered sugar, ½ c. At a time, till combined, next which add in the vanilla.
3. Continue to beat for a couple more min., till light & fluffy.
4. Frost the cupcakes as desired.

Cider & caramel cupcakes

What you need

Cupcakes

- 1/3 c. Butter
- 1 egg, room temperature
- 1 c. Buttermilk, room temp
- 1 c. Dark brown sugar
- 1/3 c. Sugar
- 1/2 tbsp vanilla extract
- 2 1/2 c. Unbleached all-purpose flour
- 1/2 tbsp cinnamon
- 1/2 tsp nutmeg
- 1 tsp salt
- 1 tbsp baking soda
- 1 c. Hard apple cider, room temperature

Apple filling

- 3 tbsp butter
- 2 big (or 3 small) honey crisp apples peeled, cored, & chopped
- 1/4 c. Dark brown sugar
- 1/4 tsp cinnamon
- 1/4 tsp kosher salt
- 1 1/2 tsp vanilla extract
- 1 tsp cornstarch
- 2 tbsp whiskey

Buttercream

- 1 c. Butter, at room temperature
- 3½ c. Powdered sugar
- 1/4 tsp cinnamon
- 1 tsp vanilla extract
- 1-2 tbsp whiskey

What to do

Cupcakes

1. Heat up oven to 350.
2. In a small saucepan, heat the butter over low-medium heat, whisking continously . When you see brown specks appear on the bottom, take away from the heat & continue whisking for 30 sec.. Pour right into an additional bowl so that the butter doesn't continue to cook.
3. Once the butter is cool, add the buttermilk, egg, sugars & vanilla, & mix till well combined.
4. In a separate bowl, sift together the flour, cinnamon, nutmeg, salt, & baking soda.
5. Steadily add the flour to the wet ingredients, scraping down the sides of the bowl next each addition.
6. Once the flour is fully incorporated, mix in the hard cider.
7. Line a muffin pan with liners, & spray them with non-stick spray. Fill each muffin tin slightly more than midway with the batter.
8. Bake for 15-18 min., till a knife inserted in the middle of a cupcake comes out clean.

Filling

1. Melt the butter in a medium-sized saucepan over medium heat.
2. Add the apples, sugar, cinnamon, salt, & vanilla. Cook for about 10 min., till the apples are soft & have released their juices.
3. In a separate bowl, whisk together the whiskey with cornstarch, & next which add to the pan with the apples & cook for about 3 min., till the liquid thickens. Put to the side to cool.

Frosting

1. Cream the butter for about 30 sec.. Add the powdered sugar, cinnamon, & vanilla extract. Beat on medium speed till creamy.
2. Add the whiskey & beat on high for 2-3 min., till fluffy & whipped.

Assembly

1. Core each cupcake with a cupcake corer, or with a knife angled at 45-degrees.
2. Fill the cupcake with apples, next which top with buttercream, top the frosting with more apples.

Pumpkin & cinnamon buttercream cupcakes

What you need

- 1½ c. Spelt flour
- ¾ c. Organic cane sugar
- 1 tsp baking soda
- ½ tsp salt
- 1 tsp cinnamon
- ½ tsp ginger
- ⅛ tsp nutmeg
- Pinch cloves
- 1 c. Of pumpkin puree
- ⅓ c. Organic canola oil
- 1 tsp vanilla extract
- 1 tsp apple cider vinegar
- ½ c. Water

Frosting

- 3 tbsp vegan buttery spread
- 2½ c. Powdered sugar
- 1-2 tbsp unsweetened coconut milk
- ½ tsp cinnamon
- ½ tsp ginger
- Pinch of cloves

What to do

1. Heat up the oven to 350 degrees. Line a cupcake tin with paper liners.
2. In a medium bowl, whisk together the flour, sugar, baking soda, salt, cinnamon, ginger, nutmeg, & cloves. Put to the side.
3. In a big bowl, mix the pumpkin puree, organic canola oil, vanilla, apple cider vinegar, & water. Mix well.
4. Add the dry ingredients to the wet ingredients & mix well to combine.
5. Spoon the batter right into the cupcake liners, filling them about ⅔ full.
6. Bake at 350 degrees for about 16-18 min., or till a toothpick inserted in the middle comes out clean.

Frosting

1. Beat the buttery spread till fluffy. Sift the powdered sugar right into the bowl & drizzle in a little coconut milk.
2. Alternate adding more sugar & milk till the frosting is thick & creamy.
3. Add the spices & mix again.
4. Spread or pipe frosting onto cooled cupcakes. Store leftover cupcakes in the fridge.

Black velvet cupcakes

What you need

Cupcakes

- 1 c. Granulated sugar
- 1/4 c. Butter, room temperature
- 2 tbsp vegetable oil
- 1 egg
- 1 tsp black food coloring or soft gel paste
- 3 tbsp dark dutch-process cocoa powder
- 1 tsp pure vanilla extract
- 1/2 tsp salt
- 1/2 c. Buttermilk, room temperature
- 1/2 tsp white vinegar
- 1 1/4 c. Flour
- 1/4 tsp baking soda

Frosting

- 1 8 oz. Package of cream cheese, room temperature
- 1/4 c. Butter, room temperature
- 3 1/2 c. Powdered sugar
- 1 tsp pure vanilla extract
- 1 tsp black food coloring or gel paste

What to do

Cupcakes

1. Sift together the cocoa powder, flour, salt & baking powder in one bowl & put to the side. Fitted with the whisk attachment, use your mixer to mix together the sugar, butter, oil & vanilla till fluffy.
2. Add the food coloring & beat to combine. Mix in the egg. Add 1/3 of the dry ingredients & alternate with the buttermilk till all ingredients are combined. Lastly, mix in the vinegar.
3. Distribute the batter among 12-14 cupcake liners & bake on 350 degrees for about 20 min. Till an inserted toothpick comes out clean. Take away from oven to cool on a wire rack.

Frosting

1. To make this spooky black frosting, beat together the cream cheese & butter with a paddle attachment. Slowly mix in the powdered sugar till you reach your desired sweetness .
2. Then mix in the vanilla extract & black coloring till the frosting reaches its proper color.
3. Once the cupcakes have cooled, pipe the frosting onto the . Let in cool in the fridge.

Pumpkin cupcakes

What you need

Cupcakes

- 2 c. All-purpose flour
- 1½ tsp ground cinnamon
- ½ tsp ground nutmeg
- ½ tsp ground ginger
- ¼ tsp ground cloves
- ½ tsp salt
- 2 tsp baking powder
- 1 tsp baking soda
- ½ c. Butter, softened
- 1 c. Light brown sugar, packed
- ⅓ c. Granulated sugar
- 2 eggs
- 1 c. Buttermilk
- 1 c. Pumpkin puree
- 1 tsp vanilla extract

Frosting

- 1 - ¼ oz packet of unflavored gelatin
- ¼ (scant) c. Cool water
- 3 c. Heavy whipping cream
- 2 tsp vanilla extract
- ⅔ c. Confectioners sugar

What to do

Cupcakes

1. Heat up the oven to 350 degrees.
2. Sift together the flour, spices, salt, baking powder, & baking soda; put to the side.
3. Cream butter & both sugars with an electric mixer till light & fluffy.
4. Add the eggs one at a time.
5. Add the buttermilk & pumpkin puree, blending well & scraping down sides as needed.

6. Stir in the flour mixture, next which the vanilla, mixing till only incorporated.
7. Divide the batter right into cupcake wrapper lined c. Of a muffin tray.
8. Bake about 15-18 min. Or till a toothpick comes out clean.
9. Cool in the pans for 5 min. Before removing to cool completely on a wire rack.

Frosting

1. Combine gelatin & water in a small saucepan & let stand till thick.
2. Warm over low heat & mix till gelatin is softened & take away & cool, but do not permit to set.
3. Whip the heavy cream till thickened. Add confectioners sugar & vanilla, beating till it holds soft peaks.
4. Steadily add the gelatin to the whipped cream, beating continously .
5. Continue to beat on med/high speed till it holds stiff peaks.
6. Frost cooled cupcakes straight away & serve, or refrigerate frosting till ready to use.

Mint&chocolate cupcakes

What you need

Chocolate cupcakes

- 75 g (2.7 oz.) Butter
- ½ tsp. Vanilla essence
- 100 ml (3.4 fl. Oz.) Hot water
- 150 ml (5.1 fl. Oz.) Whole milk
- 1 big egg, lightly beaten
- 300 g (10. 6 oz.) Plain flour
- 100 g (3.5 oz.) Dutch processed cocoa powder
- 1 tsp. Bicarbonate of soda
- 1 tsp. Baking powder
- 250 g (8.8 oz.) Caster sugar
- Pinch of salt

Mint frosting

- 1 ½ (3 sticks) c. Unsalted butter, softened
- 3 tbsp. Heavy cream
- 1 tsp. Vanilla extract
- 1 tbsp. Peppermint essence
- ¼ tsp salt
- 3 c. (12 oz.) Icing sugar
- 1 c. (6.2 oz.) Dark chocolate chips
- 3 tbsp. Fresh mint leaves, chopped

What to do

Chocolate cupcakes

1. Heat up an oven to 175 c (350 f). Line a 12 hole cupcake pan with cupcake liners.
2. Over a low heat, melt the butter. When melted, take away from the heat & mix in the vanilla essence, water, milk & beaten egg. Put to the side.
3. In a separate big bowl sift together the flour, cocoa powder, bicarbonate of soda, baking powder, sugar & salt.

4. In two batches, pour the liquid ingredients right into the bowl with the dry ingredients & whisk till uniform, combined & smooth.
5. Divide the mixture evenly among the cupcake liners, filling them no more than ⅔rds full. Bake for 15 to 18 min. Or till a skewer inserted comes out clean. Leave to cool completely on a wire rack before frosting.

Mint frosting

1. Beat the butter, cream, vanilla, peppermint & salt together on medium speed till smooth, 2-3 min..
2. Reduce speed to low & slowly, in batches, add in the icing sugar. Beat till incorporated & smooth, 4 – 6 min..
3. Increase the mixer speed to medium-high & beat till the frosting is light & fluffy, 5 – 8 min.. Add the chocolate chips & chopped mint leaves, & mix till only combined.

Chocolate blackberry cupcakes

What you need

- 10 oz. (285 grams) fresh blackberries
- 1 1/2 c. (190 grams) all-purpose flour
- 3/4 c. (150 grams) granulated sugar, divided
- 1/3 c. (60 grams) cocoa powder
- 2 tsp espresso powder
- 1 tsp baking soda
- 1/2 tsp salt
- 1 tsp vanilla extract
- 1/3 c. (78 ml) vegetable oil
- 1 c. (237 ml) milk of choice
- 6 oz. (170 grams) semi-sweet or bittersweet chocolate, chopped finely
- Fresh blackberries, for garnish

What to do

In a big saucepan, mix the blackberries with 1/4 c. Granulated sugar. Bring to a boil over medium heat & cook for about 10 min., stirring often, till the berries burst & are swimming in their juices. Take away from heat.

Using a fine mesh strainer, strain out the liquid & save it for later use. Put the solid fruit back right into the saucepan & put to the side.

Heat up oven to 350 degrees f (180 degrees c). Line a cupcake pan with baking cups.

In a mixing bowl, whisk together the flour, sugar, cocoa, espresso powder, baking soda, & salt. Add the vanilla extract, oil, & milk. Utilizing a spatula, mix the batter till smooth. Fold in the blackberry solids.

Divide batter evenly between 12 baking c. (about 3/4 full). Bake for 18-22 min., or till a toothpick inserted right into the middle comes out clean. Take away from baking pan & permit to cool to room temperature.

Frosting

1. Place chopped chocolate right into a mixing bowl. Warm the blackberry juice back up to boiling & pour over the chocolate, allowing it to set for 5 min. Before stirring till smooth.
2. Allow frosting to rest on the counter, stirring often, till it cools down & thickens.

3. Beat the chocolate ganache for several min. Till it incorporates air & feels lighter.
4. Place frosting in a pastry bag & pipe frosting onto the cooled cupcakes. Garnish with fresh blackberries.

Peanut butter cupcakes

What you need

Cupcakes

- 1 c. All-purpose flour
- 1 tsp baking powder
- 1/4 tsp salt
- 6 tbsp unsalted butter, at room temperature
- 3/4 c. Chunky or smooth peanut butter
- 1 c. Packed brown sugar
- 1 egg
- 1 1/2 tsp vanilla
- 1/2 c. Milk

Ganache

- 2 oz. Bittersweet chocolate, chopped
- 1/2 tsp instant coffee granules
- 2 oz. Heavy cream

Peanut butter buttercream

- 1 c. Unsalted butter, at room temperature (2 sticks)
- 1 c. Powdered sugar, or more, to taste
- 1/8 tsp salt
- 1/2 tsp vanilla extract
- 3/4 c. Peanut butter, at room temperature

What to do

1. Heat the oven to 350 degrees. Line 12 muffin tin c. With paper cupcake liners.
2. Sift the flour, baking powder & salt in a medium bowl & put to the side.
3. Using a stand mixer, beat the butter, peanut butter & brown sugar, on medium speed, till smooth & light in color, about 1 minute.
4. Mix in the egg. Add the vanilla & beat for 1 minute, or till the batter is smooth. On low speed, add the flour mixture in 3 additions & the milk in 2 additions, beginning & ending

with the flour mixture & mixing only till the flour is incorporated & the batter looks smooth.
5. Fill each paper liner with batter, about 1/3 in. Below the top of the liner. Bake only till the tops feel firm & are lightly browned, about 20 min.. There will be a few cracks on top. Cool the cupcakes for 10 min. In the pan on a wire rack. Prudently take away cupcakes from pan to finish cooling.

Ganache

1. Place the chocolate & coffee granules in a heatproof bowl. Heat the cream in a small sauce pan over medium heat, till it comes to a boil.
2. Pour the hot cream right into the bowl with the chocolate & mix till completely mixed & glossy.

Peanut butter buttercream

1. Beat everything in a bowl till smooth & blended.
2. Add in more powdered sugar, if needed, according to your preference.

Assembly

1. Spread a layer of chocolate ganache on top of the cupcake & next which frost with the peanut butter buttercream.
2. Dash with chopped nuts & chocolate dashs.

Fudge cupcakes

What you need

- 250 g butter (150 g for the cakes & 100 g for the frosting)
- 150 g sugar
- 3 big eggs
- 225 g self-raising flour
- 100 g mini fudge pieces (75 g for the cakes & 25 g for decorating the frosting)
- 200 g icing sugar
- 2 tbsp of clear honey
- 2 tabs honeycomb pieces (for decor)

What to do

Fudge cupcakes

1. Pre-heat the oven 180 c.
2. Beat together the butter & sugar till light & fluffy.
3. Beat the eggs & steadily beat right into the butter & sugar with a spoon or two of the flour to prevent curdling.
4. Fold in the remaining of the flour to form a smooth thick batter. It needs to be thicker than a normal sponge mix otherwise the fudge pieces will sink.
5. Fold in 75 g of the fudge pieces & spoon the mixture evenly right into 12 big muffin cases.
6. Bake for 20 min. Or till risen & golden brown.

Frosting

1. Combine 100 g of butter with 200 g of icing sugar & 1 tbsp of clear honey. If the mix is too dry next which add the second spoon of honey.
2. Pipe or spread onto the cakes & dash with the remaining 25 g of fudge pieces & the honeycomb pieces.

Chocolate & cookie cupcakes

What you need
Cookie dough

- 1 c. Unsalted butter at room temperature
- 3/4 c. Sugar
- 3/4 c. Brown sugar
- 4 tbsp whole milk
- 1 tbsp vanilla
- 2 1/2 c. All-purpose flour
- 1/4 tsp. Salt
- 1 c. Mini chocolate chips

Cupcakes

- 1 1/2 c unsalted butter, room temperature
- 1 1/2 c. Light brown sugar, packed
- 4 big eggs, room temperature
- 2 2/3 c. All-purpose flour
- 1 tsp. Baking powder
- 1 tsp. Baking soda
- 1/4 tsp. Kosher salt
- 1 c. Whole milk, room temperature
- 2 tsp. Vanilla extract

What to do
Cookie dough

1. Combine the butter & sugars in a mixing bowl & cream on medium-high speed till light & fluffy. Beat in milk & vanilla till incorporated & smooth.
2. Mix in the flour & salt till only combined. Mix in the chocolate chips.
3. Using a small scoop, shape the dough right into balls or tubes. Freeze on a parchment lined baking sheet overnight.

Pumpkin & chocolate cream cupcakes

What you need

- ¾ c. Unsweetened cocoa powder
- 1½ c. All-purpose flour
- 1½ c. Sugar
- 1½ tsp baking soda
- ¾ tsp baking powder
- 1 tsp salt
- 2 big eggs
- ½ c. Warm water
- ¾ c. Buttermilk
- 5 tbsp safflower oil
- 1 tsp pure vanilla extract

Frosting

- 7 tbsp butter, softened
- 5 oz. Cream cheese, softened
- ¾ c. Pumpkin puree
- 2 ½ c. Powdered sugar, sifted

What to do

1. Heat up oven to 350 degrees. Line standard muffin tins with paper liners; put to the side. In the bottom of a stand mixer, whisk together cocoa powder, flour, sugar, baking soda, baking powder, & salt.
2. Switch to the paddle attachment, turn the mixer on low & add eggs, warm water, buttermilk, oil, & vanilla, & mix till smooth.. Scrape down the sides & bottom of bowl to ensure everything is incorporated.
3. Divide batter evenly among muffin cups, filling each ⅔ full. Bake till tops spring back when touched, about 20 min., rotating when midway through baking. Transfer to a wire rack; let cool completely.
4. In the bottom of a stand mixer, utilizing the paddle attachment cream the butter & cream cheese till light & fluffy on a medium-high speed, about two to three min..

5. Add in pumpkin puree, mix an additional minute. Slowly add in powdered sugar, about a ½ c. At a time till fully incorporated. If the icing is not thick enough, add more powdered sugar. Transfer to a ziplock bag or pastry bag. Chill for at least an hour or even overnight.
6. When cupcakes have cooled completely, pipe frosting. Store in the fridge. When ready to use, let sit at room temperature for 20 min..

Red velvet cupcakes

What you need
Cupcakes

- 2½ c. All-purpose flour
- 1½ c. Granulated sugar
- 1 tsp baking soda
- ½ tsp salt
- 1 tbsp cocoa powder
- 1 c. Vegetable oil
- ½ c. (1 stick) unsalted butter, room
- 1 c. Buttermilk
- 2 eggs, room temperature
- 1 tsp distilled white vinegar
- Red food coloring

Cream cheese frosting

- 16 oz. Cream cheese, room temperature
- ½ c. (1 stick) unsalted butter, room temperature
- 3 heaping c. Confectioners sugar
- 1 tsp vanilla

What to do

1. Heat up oven to 350 degrees & line a cupcake pan with liners.
2. In a mixer fitted with a paddle attachment, mix together butter, oil, buttermilk, eggs, vanilla & vinegar. Mixture may be lumpy.
3. In a separate bowl, sift together flour, cocoa powder, salt & baking soda. With mixer on low-speed, steadily add dry

ingredients to the wet ingredients. Mix till smooth & no longer lumpy, but careful to not over mix.
4. Add food coloring to your liking & mix to combine. Because of the cocoa powder, the cupcakes will be a dusty red color. If you want light or bright red cupcakes, omit the cocoa powder.
5. Fill cupcake liners about ⅔ full. For mini muffins, bake for 11 min., turning cupcakes half way through baking process. For regular size muffins, bake for about 20 min., turning half way through. Check doneness by inserting a tooth pick right into cupcakes - if the toothpick comes out clean, they're done.
6. To make cream cheese frosting, add butter & cream cheese to a mixer & whip till creamy & completely combined. With mixer on low-speed, steadily add confectioners sugar till frosting is smooth & fluffy. Lastly, add vanilla & mix for a few sec. Till combined. Frost cupcakes.

Classic vanilla cupcakes

What you need

- 1 1/2 c. All-purpose flour
- 1 1/2 tsp baking powder
- 1/4 tsp fine salt
- 2 big eggs, at room temperature
- 2/3 c. Sugar
- 1 1/2 sticks (6 ounces) unsalted butter, melted
- 2 tsp pure vanilla extract
- 1/2 c. Milk

What to do

1. Heat up the oven to 350 f & position a rack in the middle of the oven. Line one 12-cup standard muffin tin or two 24-cup mini-muffin tins with cupcake liners.
2. Whisk the flour, baking powder & salt together in a medium bowl.
3. In an additional medium bowl, beat the eggs & sugar with an electric mixer till light & foamy, about 2 min.. Whereas beating, steadily pour in the butter & next which the vanilla.
4. Whereas mixing slowly, add half the dry ingredients. Next which add all the milk & follow with the remaining of the dry ingredients. Take care not to overmix the batter. Divide the batter evenly in the prepared tin.
5. Bake till a tester inserted in the middle of the cakes comes out clean, rotating the tin about midway through, 18 to 20 min. (10 to 12 min. For minis). Cool the cupcakes on a rack in the tin for 10 min., & next which take away from the tin. Cool on the rack completely.

Simple pumpkin cupcakes

What you need
For the cupcakes

- 1 can pumpkin or 1 1/2 c. Pumpkin puree
- 2 very ripe bananas
- 1/2 c. Coconut sugar
- 1 1/2 tsp cinnamon
- 1/4 tsp ginger
- 1/4 tsp nutmeg
- 1/4 tsp sea salt

For the whip topping

- 1 can full fat coconut milk
- 2 t maple syrup
- 1 tsp vanilla beans

What to do

1. Heat up oven to 350.
2. In a food processor, mix all the cupcake ingredients & blend till smooth.
3. Spoon the mixture right into lined muffin pans.
4. Bake for 20-25 min..
5. Let these cool completely before removing from the muffin liners. Since they are soft like pumpkin pie.
6. To make the whip topping, open up your can of coconut milk that has been in the fridge overnight. Scoop the fatty white part off & put in a mixing bowl with the vanilla & maple syrup. Use the whipping attachment & whip the coconut right into a cream. Scoop a little on top of each muffin.

The golden cupcake

What you need
Yellow cake

- 20-24 golden oreos
- 1 box yellow cake mix
- 3 eggs
- 1/3 c. Oil
- 3/4 c. Sour cream
- 1/2 c. Milk or butter milk
- 2 tsp. Vanilla extract

Cream cheese frosting

- 8 oz. Cream cheese
- 1/2 c. Butter, softened
- 2 tsp. Vanilla extract
- 1 tbsp. Milk
- 3-4 c. Powdered sugar
- Extra golden oreos for decoration

What to do

1. Heat up oven to 350 degrees & line pans with cupcake liners.
2. Place an oreo on the bottom of each liner.
3. Sift cake mix right into a big bowl to take away any lumps.
4. Add eggs, oil, sour cream, milk & vanilla extract & mix till smooth.
5. Fill cupcake liners (over oreos) till about 3/4 full.
6. Bake for 15-20 min. Or till an inserted knife comes out clean. (depending on your oven you may want to bake on a higher rack to not burn the oreos on the bottom, some ovens get extra hot from below, so be careful!)
7. Let cool.
8. Cream cheese frosting: beat cream cheese & butter till smooth. Add vanilla extract, milk & 2 cups. Powdered sugar an beat again.

Continue to add more powdered sugar till you reach your desired consistency.
9. Pipe onto cooled cupcakes & top with an extra golden oreo.

Berries cupcake with mascarpone

What you need

Mini cornmeal cakes

- 3/4 c. + 2 tbsp (100 grams) unbleached all-purpose flour
- 1/4 c. (30 grams) stone ground yellow cornmeal
- 1/2 c. + 3 tbsp (140 grams) granulated sugar
- 1 & 1/2 tsp baking powder
- 1/4 tsp kosher salt
- 3 big whole eggs
- 10 tbsp (145 grams or 5 ounces) unsalted butter, very soft

Whipped mascarpone frosting

- 1/2 c. (113 grams) mascarpone cheese
- 1/2 c. (120 ml) chilled heavy cream
- 3 tbsp (24 grams) powdered sugar
- 1/2 tsp pure vanilla extract

Assembly

- Powdered sugar, for dusting
- Fresh raspberries & blackberries (roughly 2 oz. Of each)
- Fresh lemon zest, for garnish

What to do

1. Prepare the mini cornmeal cakes: heat up the oven to 375 degrees fahrenheit. Line a standard muffin tin with 11 liners. Put to the side. In a medium bowl, whisk together the all-purpose flour, cornmeal, granulated sugar, baking powder, & salt. Put to the side.
2. In a stand mixer, fitted with a paddle attachment, mix the whole eggs & softened butter. Add all of the dry ingredients to the bowl. Turn on the mixer to medium speed (4) & beat the batter for 2 min., or till all of the ingredients are evenly incorporated & batter is smooth.

3. Divide the batter evenly among the lined muffin cups. The batter should be reach about half-way up each cup. Bake at 375 degrees for 14 to 16 min., or till the cornmeal cakes are golden brown & springy to touch. Take away from the oven & permit to cool in the baking tin, on a rack, for 5 min.. Take away the cornmeal cakes from the tin & permit to cool to room temperature on a cooling rack.
4. Prepare the whipped mascarpone: in a clean mixer bowl, fitted with a paddle attachment, mix the mascarpone cheese, heavy cream, powdered sugar, & vanilla extract. Beat at low speed, slowly increasing to medium speed, till mixture thickens & forms soft peaks.
5. Using a spoon, add a dollop of whipped mascarpone in the middle of each cooled cornmeal cake. Utilizing a fine-meshed sieve, dust the cakes lightly with powdered sugar.
6. Top each cake with a mixture of fresh blackberries & fresh raspberries, & freshly grated lemon zest. Serve straight away.

Black cupcake

What you need
For the brownie layer

- 4 big eggs
- 2 c. Sugar, sifted
- 8 oz. / 2 sticks melted butter
- ½ c. Cocoa, sifted
- 2 vanilla beans, seeds only
- ¾ c. Flour, sifted
- ½ tsp kosher salt
- ½ tsp pumpkin spice

Pumpkin buttercream

- 2½ sticks unsalted butter, room temperature
- 3 c. Confectioners sugar
- 3 tbsp pumpkin puree
- ½ tsp pumpkin spice
- 5 drops orange gel color

What to do

1. Adjust oven rack to middle position & heat oven to 300 degrees f. Line a standard muffin/cupcake tin with paper or foil liners.
2. In a mixer fitted with the whisk attachment, beat the eggs at medium speed till fluffy & light yellow, add the sugar & beat till combined. Add remaining ingredients, & mix to combine.
3. Pour the batter evenly right into the cupcake tins & bake for 40 min.. Check for doneness by inserting a toothpick right into the middle of the cupcake, it should come out with only a few crumbs attached.
4. When done, take away from oven & transfer cupcakes to a cooling rack. Cool cupcakes to room temperature before frosting.

5. Using the wire whisk attachment of a stand mixer, whip the butter on medium-high speed for 5 min., stopping to scrape the bowl when or twice.
6. Reduce the speed to low & steadily add the confectioner sugar & pumpkin spice. When incorporated, increase the speed to medium-high & add the pumpkin puree & gel color, mixing till combined. Whip at medium-high speed till light & fluffy, about 2 min., scraping the bowl as needed.
7. Unused buttercream can be stored in the fridge in an airtight container. Let it come to room temperature & next which give it a quick whip in the mixer before utilizing it.
8. If the frosting is too soft, add more sugar - ½ c. At a time, if the frosting is too tough add some milk, 1 tbsp as a time.
9. Transfer frosting to a piping bag & decorate the cupcakes, garnish with dashs.

Snickers cupcakes

What you need
Chocolate cupcakes

- 1 1/2 c. All-purpose flour
- 1 c. Unsweetened cocoa powder
- 1 tsp. Baking soda
- 1 1/2 tsp. Baking powder
- 1/2 tsp. Salt
- 4 eggs, at room temp
- 1 c. Sugar
- 1 c. Brown sugar, packed
- 2/3 c. Oil
- 1 c. Buttermilk or milk
- 1 tbsp. Vanilla extract

Chocolate peanut butter frosting

- 3/4 c. Butter softened
- 1/2 c. Peanut butter, creamy
- 1/2 c. Unsweetened cocoa powder
- 2 tsp. vanilla extract
- 2-3 tbsp. Milk
- 3-4 c. Powdered sugar
- Snickers bars & caramel sauce

What to do

1. Heat up oven to 350 degrees & line pans with cupcake liners.
2. In a medium bowl, mix cocoa flour, cocoa powder, baking soda, baking powder & salt. Put to the side.
3. In a big bowl, mix eggs, sugar, brown sugar, oil, buttermilk & vanilla extract.
4. Pour half the dry ingredients right into the wet & stir. Next which add the remaining of the dry ingredients & mix again. Don't over mix.

5. Fill cupcake liners 2/3 full & bake for 18-22 min. Or till an inserted knife comes out clean. Let cool.
6. Frosting: beat butter & peanut butter till smooth. Add cocoa powder, vanilla extract & 2 tbsp milk. Slowly add in powdered sugar till thick. If it becomes thick like cookie dough, stream in more milk!
7. Pipe onto cooled cupcakes & top with snickers & caramel sauce.

Chocolate & orange cupcakes

What you need
Cupcakes

- 1 1/2 c. All-purpose flour
- 2/3 c. Dark cocoa powder
- 1 1/3 c. Granulated sugar
- 1 tsp baking soda
- 1/2 tsp baking powder
- 1/2 tsp salt
- 2 big eggs
- 1/3 c. Vegetable oil
- 1 tsp vanilla extract
- 2/3 c. Milk
- 2/3 c. Hot water

Frosting

- 1 c. Unsalted butter (2 sticks)
- 7 c. Confectioners sugar, sifted
- 1/2 c. Milk
- 1 tsp vanilla extract
- 2 tsp orange extract
- Orange food coloring

What to do

1. Heat up oven to 350°f & line muffin tins with cupcake liners.
2. In a big bowl, whisk the flour, cocoa powder, sugar, baking soda, baking powder, & salt together.
3. Add the eggs, vegetable oil, vanilla extract, & milk to the bowl with the dry ingredients & mix till only combined.
4. Pour in the hot water & mix on medium speed with the hand mixer for about 1-2 min.. Batter will be very liquidy.
5. Fill cupcake liners about 2/3 full & bake in the oven for 15-17 min. Or till a toothpick inserted in the middles comes out clean.

6. Take away cupcakes from oven, let cool for about 5 min.. Next which put cupcakes on a cooling rack to cool completely.
7. Make frosting.
8. Cut butter right into cubes & put right into a stand mixer bowl fitted with the paddle attachment. Mix on medium speed for 30 sec..
9. Add 4 c. Of the sifted confectioners sugar, the milk, vanilla & orange extracts. Mix on low for 10 sec. So the sugar doesn't fly everywhere, next which turn mixer up to medium speed for 5 min..
10. Scrape the sides & bottom of the bowl in case any butter stuck to bottom or sides of bowl & didn't get mixed in. Next which add the remaining of the confectioners sugar & mix again on low speed for 10 sec.. Add 2 drops of orange food coloring, next which up the speed to high for 2-3 min..
11. Prepare your piping bag with a big round tip, fill piping bag with frosting, next which pipe big dollops onto each cupcake.
12. Top each cupcake with a chocolate orange slice and/or some orange peel.

Hat cupcakes

What you need
Chocolate cupcakes

- 105 grams (3/4 cup) plain flour
- 40 grams (1/2 cup) cocoa powder
- 1/2 tsp baking soda
- 1/2 tsp baking powder
- 100 grams (1/2 cup) caster sugar
- 45 grams (1/4 cup) brown sugar
- 115 grams (1/2 c. Or 1 stick) unsalted butter
- 2 big eggs
- 1 tsp vanilla extract
- 120 ml (1/2 cup) buttermilk

Marshmallow frosting

- 4 egg whites, room temperature
- 200 grams (1 cup) caster sugar
- 1/4 tsp cream of tartar
- 1 tsp vanilla extract

Chocolate coating

- 300 grams (2 cups) good quality dark chocolate, pieces
- 2 tbsp vegetable oil

What to do

1. Heat up the oven to 180c (360 f). Line a 12 hole muffin tin with patty cases. In a big mixing bowl, sift the flour, cocoa powder, baking soda, baking powder & next which add the sugars - give it a little stir. Pop the butter right into the microwave for a short burst, 10 sec. Or so at a time, till it is only melted. Give it a mix with a fork to eliminate any lumps.
2. In a separate mixing bowl, add the eggs, vanilla & butter & whisk together till smooth. Next which add the wet mixture right into

the dry mixture, along with the buttermilk & lightly fold till only combined.

3. Spoon the mixture right into the prepared patty cases & pop right into the oven. Bake for 18-20 min. Or till only cooked through. Set cakes out onto a wire rack & leave to cool completely.
4. To make the marshmallow frosting, fill a medium saucepan with a few in. Of water & pop on a medium heat.
5. In a small heatproof bowl, add your eggs whites, caster sugar & cream of tartar. Whisk together. Next which pop the bowl over the saucepan, ensuring the bottom of the bowl does not touch the water. As the egg whites heat, whisk lightly by hand the entire time. You'll want to heat the egg whites to 50 c / 120 f which you can test by sticking a candy thermometer right into the mixture or go by feel (the mixture should be hot to the touch) - should be around 5-6 min. Or so.
6. Then take away the bowl from the saucepan & put the mixture in the base of a stand mixer (or simply use a hand beater) & beat on medium speed for approximately 5 min. Or till the mixture is fluffy, white & voluminous. Add the vanilla & beat for 30 sec. Or so.
7. Then grab your piping bag fitted with a big round or star shaped tip. Fill with the marshmallow fluff & pipe tall swirls onto each cupcake. Pop the cupcakes right into the freezer for at least 20 min. For the frosting to firm up slightly. Next which its time for the chocolate.
8. Melt your dark chocolate & oil over the stove utilizing the boiler method. Put a few in. Of water in a medium saucepan & next which put a medium bowl over the top, with the chocolate & oil inside. Ensure that the bottom of the bowl does not touch the water, next which put on a medium heat. Lightly mix as the steam melts the chocolate till silky & smooth. Put the chocolate in a deep & high sided container.
9. Gently dip each cupcake upside down right into the chocolate, let the chocolate drip off lightly & next which put the right side

up onto a wire rack. Continue with all the cupcakes & leave them to harden slightly at room temperature for about 20 min. Before placing in the fridge to firm completely. These cupcakes keep quite well for 2-3 days, simply store in the fridge.

Cupcakes with mint buttercream

What you need

For the chocolate cupcakes

- ⅔ c. Cocoa powder
- 1 tsp baking soda
- 1 c. Water, boiling
- ½ c. Butter, melted
- 5 tbsp vegetable oil
- 1½ c. White sugar
- 2 tsp vanilla extract
- ½ tsp salt
- 4 eggs
- ½ c. Heavy creamy
- 1½ c. All purpose flour

For the mint chocolate chip buttercream

- 1½ c. Butter, softened
- 2 tsp mint extract
- 2 tsp vanilla
- 5 c. Powdered sugar
- 1 tbsp whole milk
- 1 c. Mini chocolate chips
- Green food coloring
- Pinch of salt, to taste

What to do

1. Heat up oven to 350 degrees f. In a big mixing bowl mix cocoa powder & baking soda. Pour boiling water over the mixture & mix till combined.
2. In a separate big mixing bowl mix melted butter, oil, sugar, vanilla, salt, & eggs till combined. Blend in cocoa mixture & heavy cream.
3. Steadily mix in flour a little at a time & mix till only combined.

4. Divide batter evenly between lined cupcake bakers. Bake for 20-22 min. Or till a tooth pick inserted in the middle comes out clean. Cool completely.
5. For the mint chocolate chip buttercream:
6. Stir butter till light & fluffy. Mix in mint & vanilla extracts.
7. Steadily mix in powdered sugar a little at time, adding milk as needed.
8. Stir in food coloring if desired. Fold in mini chocolate chips.
9. Scoop a generous amount of frosting onto the cupcakes with an ice cream scoop.

Chocolate cupcakes with strawberry buttercream

What you need

Strawberry buttercream

- 1 c. Butter
- 1 two-pound bag powder sugar (about 7-8 cups)
- 2 tsp strawberry extract
- 4 tbsp milk
- Dash salt
- 1-2 drops pink food coloring

Vanilla buttercream

- 1 c. (2 sticks) unsalted butter, softened
- 6-8 c. Confectioner's sugar
- 1/2 c. Milk
- 2 tsp vanilla extract

Chocolate buttercream

- 1 c. Unsalted butter (2 sticks) at room temp.
- 4 c. Powdered sugar
- 1/2 c. Good quality cocoa powder
- 1/2 tsp table salt
- 2 tsp vanilla extract
- 1/2 c. Whole milk or heavy cream

What to do

1. Put room temperature butter, strawberry extract, & salt right into mixer. Add in powder sugar one c. At a time, alternating with the milk till you have used it all.
2. Add in food coloring a drop at a time to determine desired color.
3. If your frosting is too thick you can certainly add more milk.
4. In a big mixing bowl, mix 4 c. Of confectioner's sugar with butter.

5. Stir in milk & vanilla.
6. On medium speed, beat till smooth & creamy 3-5 min.. Steadily add remaining sugar 1 c. At a time till desired consistency. You may not use all the sugar.
7. Place room temperature butter & vanilla right into a stand mixer & beat at medium-high for about three min.. You want it to appear lighter & fluffier.
8. Whereas butter is in mixer add powdered sugar, cocoa, & salt to a bowl & mix with a whisk. (sift)
9. With mixer off, add in one c. Of the powdered sugar & cocoa mixture. Turn mixer on to low & next which slowly add in remaining powdered sugar mixture, one c. At a time.
10. With mixer still on low, add in milk. Turn mixer to medium high & blend for at least two min..
11. Frosting will appear very light, but it will darken as it sets.

Cupcakes with lemonfrosting

What you need
Lemon cupcakes

- 1 1/3 c. (185g/6.5 oz.) All-purpose flour
- 1 tsp baking powder
- 1/4 tsp salt
- 1 c. (200g/7 oz.) Granulated sugar
- 1 tbsp lemon zest
- 1/2 c. (1 stick/113g) unsalted butter, softened
- 2 big eggs
- 1 tsp pure vanilla extract
- 1/4 c. Plus 2 tbsp (90 ml) whole milk
- 2 tbsp (30ml) freshly squeezed lemon juice

Lemon buttercream frosting

- 1/2 c. (1 stick/113g) unsalted butter, softened
- 1 1/2 – 2 1/2 c. (180g-280g) powdered sugar, sifted
- 1 tbsp heavy cream or whole milk
- 1 tbsp freshly squeezed lemon juice
- 2 tsp lemon zest

What to do

1. For the cupcakes: heat up oven to 350f/180c. Line a muffin tin with cupcake liners. Put to the side.
2. In a medium bowl, sift together flour, baking powder, & salt. In an additional small bowl, toss together sugar & lemon zest till combined.
3. Using a mixer fitted with the paddle attachment, beat together butter & lemon-sugar mixture on medium speed till light & fluffy, about 2-3 min.. Scrape down the sides & bottom of the bowl as necessary. On medium speed, beat in eggs, one at a time, beating well next each addition. Add vanilla extract & beat till combined. With the mixer on low speed, add half of the dry ingredients & beat only till combined. Add milk & lemon juice &

beat till combined. Add the other half of the dry ingredients & beat slowly till only combined.
4. Divide batter evenly between the cups, filling them about 3/4 full. Bake for 15-20 min. (or 8-10 min. For mini cupcakes), till a toothpick inserted right into the middle comes out clean or with only a few moist crumbs. Permit cupcakes to sit for 10 min., next which take away from pan & permit to cool completely on a wire rack.
5. Unfrosted cupcakes can be kept tightly covered at room temperature for up to 3 days, or in the freezer for up to 2 months. Thaw, still covered, on the counter or overnight in the fridge.
6. For the frosting: in the bowl of an electric mixer fitted with the paddle attachment, beat butter on medium speed till smooth, creamy, & the consistency is much like mayonnaise, about 2 min.. Add 3/4 c. (90g) sugar & beat well till smooth. Add cream, lemon juice, & lemon zest & beat till combined & smooth. Add an additional 3/4 c. Sugar & beat till completely smooth & fluffy. Beat in more sugar as needed, till desired consistency (thick enough to pipe). Frost cupcakes when they've cooled.
7. If you wish to add lemon curd filling: when the cupcakes have cooled, cut a 1/2-inch (1.5cm) hole in the middle of each cupcake utilizing a spoon or melon baller. Spoon about a tsp of lemon curd right into the hole, next which frost the cupcakes.

Pumpkin & maple cream cupcakes

What you need
Cake

- 1 c. Vegetable oil
- 4 eggs
- 1 c. Sugar
- 1 c. Brown sugar
- 1 (15-16oz) can pure pumpkin
- 2 tsp. Baking soda
- 2 tsp. Baking powder
- 1 tsp. Salt
- 2 c. Flour
- 1 tsp. Cinnamon
- 1 tsp. Ginger
- 1 tsp nutmeg
- 24 cupcake liners

Frosting

- 8 oz cream cheese, softened
- 1/4 c. Butter, softened
- 1 tsp. Vanilla extract
- 1 1/2 tsp. Maple extract
- 3 c. Powdered sugar

What to do

1. In a mixer mix oil, eggs, both sugars, & pumpkin.
2. In a separate bowl whisk together baking soda, baking powder, salt, flour, cinnamon, ginger, & nutmeg. Slowly add the flour mixture to the liquid mixture till combined.
3. Add cupcake liners to tins & fill 2/3 of the way full with batter. Bake for 18-20 min. At 350°. Cool completely before frosting.
4. To make the frosting, mix cream cheese & butter with an electric hand mixer till smooth; add vanilla extract & maple extract.

5. Add powdered sugar one c. At a time till combined. Frost cupcakes when cooled.

Cheesecake cupcakes

What you need
Mini cheesecake cupcakes

- 1 c. Graham cracker crumbs
- 4 tbsp unsalted butter, melted
- 2 tbsp sugar
- 16 oz. Cream cheese, softened
- ½ c. Sour cream
- ¼ c. Sugar
- 2 eggs
- 1 tsp vanilla extract
- Caramel sauce or strawberry sauce for topping, optional
- 3 ingredient strawberry sauce
- 1 c. Strawberries, halved
- ½ tsp lemon juice
- 2 tsp sugar

Easy caramel sauce

- 2 c. Light brown sugar
- 1 stick plus 4 tbsp unsalted butter
- 1 c. Heavy cream
- 2 tsp vanilla extract
- Sea salt for serving, if desired

1. What to do

2. Mini cheesecake cupcakes
3. Heat up oven to 325 degrees.
4. Line a muffin pan with paper liners.

5. Combine graham cracker, butter & sugar in a small bowl. Texture should be much like wet sand. Divide crust evenly right into the bottom of the lined muffin tin.
6. Bake for 5-6 min. Or till golden brown.
7. Take out of the oven & cool completely.
8. In the meantime assemble the cheesecake filling. Beat cream cheese in a stand mixer with the paddle attachment.
9. Add in sour cream, sugar, eggs & vanilla. Mix till combined. Ensure to scrap the sides of the bowl.
10. Pour cheesecake mixture right into cooled muffin tin. It will be about 2 tbsp of filling each. Fill just about all the way to the top.
11. Place in the oven & bake for 20 min. Or till the cheesecakes are set. They will still giggle a bit. Do not over cook them. If they start to crack they are getting over cooked.
12. Allow them to cool in the muffin tin completely. Put in the fridge to chill & serve cold with your favorite toppings.

Ingredient strawberry sauce

1. Add strawberries, lemon juice & sugar to a small saucepan. Simmer on low for 15 min., mashing up strawberries with the back of a wooden spoon. Take off heat & permit to cool.
2. Place in a food processor & pulse till creamy & thick. Put back in the fridge & serve cold.

Easy caramel sauce

1. Add all of the ingredients excluding for the vanilla to a saucepan. Cook over low-medium heat till thickened stirring often. About 8 min.. If the sauce isn't getting a lot thicker turn up the heat a bit & keep & eye on it making sure to whisk continously . (the sauce will thicken as it cools in the fridge).
2. Stir in vanilla.
3. Take off of the heat & permit to cool in the saucepan. Transfer to a container & put in the fridge to firm up & cool.

Vegan chocolate cupcake

What you need

- 1 c. Of almond milk or any non-dairy/dairy milk
- 1/2 c. Pumpkin puree
- 3/4 c. Packed light brown sugar
- 1 tsp vanilla extract
- 1 c. Whole wheat flour
- 1/3 c. Unsweetened cocoa powder
- 1/2 tsp baking powder
- 3/4 tsp baking soda
- 1/4 tsp salt

Chocolate ganache

- 4 oz bitter/semi sweet chocolate squares, chopped
- 2 tbsp earth balance butter

What to do

1. Heat up oven to 350 degrees f. Line a 12 c. Muffin tin with cupcake liners & spray a light cover of non-stick cooking spray.
2. In a small bowl, mix wet ingredients & put to the side.
3. In a bigger bowl, sift all dry ingredients.
4. Gently pour wet ingredients right into dry ingredients & mix to incorporate. Do not overmix.
5. Using a medium ice-cream scoop, divide batter evenly right into lined muffin tin.
6. Bake for 18 – 20 min. Or till a toothpick inserted in middle comes out clean.
7. Allow to cool on a wire rack for a few min. Before removing to cool completely.
8. Heat a saucepan with some water on medium high heat. When water boils, turn down the heat to low. Put a bowl over the saucepan, add chocolate squares & butter. Mix to mix & permit chocolate to completely melt with the help of steam.

9. Once cupcakes are completely cool, dunk each with chocolate ganache & dash on some of your favorite festive dashs.
10. Allow ganache to cool & harden completely before sinking in your fangs.

Cupcakes with caramel

What you need

- 70g salted butter
- 170g plain flour
- 250g caster sugar
- 50g cocoa powder
- 1tbsp baking powder
- A pinch of salt
- 210ml milk
- 2 eggs

For the frosting

- 670g icing sugar
- 210g salted butter (partially melted)
- 70ml milk
- 30g tinned caramel

For the filling...

- 100g tinned caramel

What to do

1. Pre-heat your oven to 180 degrees c
2. Combine all the ingredients & whisk till smooth.
3. Pop right into 12 cupcake cases, they should fill 3/4 of each case.
4. Put in the oven & cook for 22 min.
5. Combine the icing sugar, butter & milk till smooth.
6. Then add in the tinned caramel till smooth & even in colour.
7. Once the cupcakes are completely cooled take a knife & cut a hollow out of each cupcake.
8. Keep the cut out 'top' of the cake.
9. In the hollow, put about a tsp of caramel right into each cake.
10. Place the 'top' back on & repeat for all the cupcakes.

11. Once complete it's time to ice the cupcakes, only scoop on a generous amount of icing & decorate as you wish.

Dark cupcakes

What you need

- 1/4 c. Finely chopped hazelnut pieces
- Sugar cone
- Sugar cones
- 1/4 c. Dark chocolate
- Dark chocolate vermicelli dashs or dashs of choice
- Hot fudge sauce

Nutella frozen custard

- 1 qt of edy's vanilla frozen custard
- Nutella
- Brownie pieces that you took out of the sugar cones
- 1/4 c. Sugar cone crumb topping that you made earlier

What to do

1. Heat up oven to 325 degrees. Mix the brownie mix per package instructions & fold in the chopped hazelnuts. If you are utilizing free standing baking c. Like ours this recipe will make 6 big & 6 small. Put the baking c. On a baking sheet. If you are making 2 sizes, put each size on their own baking sheet since the small size take less time to bake. Utilizing a 1.5 tbsp cookie scoop add 2 scoops of the batter to the big baking c. & 1 scoop to the small. In my oven the small size took about 20 min. & the big took 30 min..
2. Whereas the brownies are baking take 6 sugar cones & cut them about 2.25" of the way down with a clean pair of kitchen scissors. Some pieces may break & that is okay since we will be utilizing them for the sugar cone bits topping. Put to the side the top & small tip of the cone.
3. Take the broken sugar cone pieces & crumble them right into smaller bits. If you don't have around 1/2 c. Of pieces you can break up an additional sugar cone as you will be adding the sugar cone bit topping to the frozen custard & utilizing it as a

garnish on the brownie cupcakes. Spread the sugar cone pieces on a sheet of parchment paper. Put the dark chocolate in a quart size freezer bag & melt in the microwave for 1 minute on 50% power. If the chocolate is not fully melted heat for 20 more sec. On 50% power, repeat till fully melted. Snip off a tiny piece of the corner off the bag & drizzle the chocolate over the sugar cone pieces. Add vermicelli dark chocolate dashs (or dashs of choice) to the chocolate before it sets up & put to the side to let harden. When hardened break up the pieces to create the crumble topping.

4. By this time the brownies might be ready to come out of the oven. Put to the side the small size brownies. Whereas the larger brownie cupcakes are still warm from the oven take the top larger piece of the sugar cone & prudently press it completely down right into the brownie. Lightly give it a little twist like you would do with a cupcake corer. Pull the cone back out of the brownie & push the brownie piece that is now inside the cone out, put to the side for the frozen custard mixture. Put the sugar cone back right into the brownie cupcake. Do this to all of the larger brownie cupcakes. Add a tbsp of hot fudge right into the cavity of the sugar cookie cone in the brownie. The hot fudge does not need to be heated for this step. Now it is time to make the frozen custard mixture to fill the sugar cones that are in your brownies!

5. Slightly soften the frozen custard. Scoop out about 1/3 of the container right into a small mixing bowl. Add about 1/4 c. Of sugar cone crumbles you made earlier, a few tbsp of nutella & the reserved brownie pieces from the sugar cones (broken right into smaller pieces) to the frozen custard. Mix till combined. Scoop the frozen custard mixture right into the cavities of the sugar cones.

6. Fill till you reach the top of the cone & use a knife level the custard to the top of the cone. If the custard has become too soft put the brownie cupcakes in the freezer till they firm up or

till serving. Put the extra frozen custard back in the freezer to use with the small brownie cupcakes.
7. When you are ready to serve your brownie sundae nutella cupcakes pull them out of the freezer. Put a few tbsp of hot fudge sauce in a quart size freezer bag & heat in the microwave for 30 sec. On 50% power.
8. You only need to soften it slightly. Snip the corner of bag off. Squeeze the hot fudge sauce onto the top of the brownie to cover it as shown in one of the pictures above. Add some of the sugar cone topping. For the top of the cone sticking out of the brownie add some dark chocolate vermicelli dashs or more of the sugar cone topping. Top with a ferrero rocher hazelnut chocolate to finish. If you are not eating them straight away put them back in the freezer till 5 to 10 min. Before serving.

Coconut & lemon cupcakes

What you need
Cupcakes

- 3 c. All-purpose flour
- 1 tbsp baking powder
- ½ tsp salt
- 2 sticks unsalted butter
- 2 c. Sugar
- 4 big eggs
- 1 c. Half & half
- 1 tsp. Vanilla
- 1½ tsp. Coconut extract

Frosting

- 1 stick butter, softened
- 4 oz. Cream cheese, softened
- 1 tsp. Vanilla
- 1 tsp. Lemon extract
- 3-4 tbsp. Half & half
- 4 c. Powdered sugar

What to do

1. Heat up oven to 350 degrees. Line twenty-four muffin c. With paper or foil liners, & put to the side.
2. Whisk together flour, baking powder, & salt in a medium bowl, & put to the side.
3. Combine butter & sugar in a big bowl; beat till pale & fluffy, about 2 min.. Add eggs one at a time, mixing well next each addition. Add vanilla & coconut extract. Beat in flour mixture & milk in three alternating batches, beginning & ending with flour mixture. Next each addition, beat till only combined, scraping down sides & bottom of bowl as necessary.
4. Fill prepared muffin c. With about ¼ c. Batter. Bake, rotating pans once, till cupcakes are only golden brown & spring back to

the touch, 18 to 20 min.. Let cupcakes cool about 5 min., next which turn them out onto a cooling rack. Frost as desired.

5. To make frosting: beat butter & cream cheese till smooth & fluffy (about 3-4 min.). Add remaining ingredients & mix till smooth.

Chocolate & coconut cupcakes

What you need
For the cupcakes

- 1 c. Coconut flavored rum
- 1 c. (2 sticks) unsalted butter
- 3/4 c. Unsweetened cocoa powder
- 2 c. All-purpose flour
- 1 1/4 c. Sugar
- 3/4 tsp salt
- 1 1/2 tsp baking soda
- 2 big eggs
- 2/3 c. Greek yogurt

For the frosting

- 1 c. Butter, softened
- 4 1/2 – 4 c. Powdered sugar
- 1/4 c. Coconut rum
- 1 tbsp vanilla

What to do

1. Heat up oven to 350 degrees f.line 2 standard cupcake pans with 24 liners.in a big saucepan over medium heat, simmer coconut rum & butter.slowly whisk cocoa powder right into saucepan till mixture is creamy.
2. Take away from heat & permit to cool.in the meantime , whisk sugar, flour, salt & baking soda in a big bowl.in a separate bowl, beat eggs & greek yogurt with an electric mixer. Slowly add coconut rum & cocoa mixture. Mix on low speed.slowly add flour & sugar mixture, combining on low speed till completely incorporated.fill baking c. Three-fourths full. Bake for about 22 min.. Cool.to make the frosting cream butter till smooth. Steadily add powdered sugar, alternating with rum & vanilla, till desired consistency is reached.

Chocolate cream cheese cupcakes

What you need

- 2 c. Shredded zucchini
- 3 eggs
- 2 c. Granulated sugar
- ¾ vegetable oil
- 2 tsp vanilla
- 2 c. All-purpose flour
- ⅔ c. Unsweetened cocoa powder
- 1 tsp baking soda
- 1 tsp salt
- ½ tsp baking powder

Chocolate cream frosting

- 8 oz package cream cheese, room temp
- ½ c. Unsalted butter, room temp
- 3 c. Powdered sugar
- ½ c. Unsweetened cocoa powder
- ¼ tsp salt
- 1 tsp vanilla

What to do

1. Heat up oven to 325 degrees. Line 24 muffin c. With liners or spray with non stick cooking spray & put to the side.
2. In a big bowl, mix together zucchini, eggs, sugar, oil, & vanilla. Add flour, cocoa powder, baking soda, salt, & baking powder. Spoon the batter right into the prepared pan filling them about half way.
3. Bake for 25 min. Or till a toothpick comes out clean. Cool cupcakes on wire racks.
4. To make the chocolate cream cheese frosting: in a big bowl beat together the cream cheese & butter till creamy. Add powdered sugar, cocoa powder & salt & vanilla. Continue beating till smooth & whipped. Frost cupcakes.

Coconut cupcakes with lemon curd

What you need

Cupcakes

- 2 c. Cake flour
- 1 ½ tsp baking powder
- ¾ tsp salt
- 2 sticks softened butter
- 1 ½ c. Sugar
- Seeds of 1 vanilla bean
- ¾ c. + ⅛ c. Coconut milk
- 1 egg yolk
- 4 egg whites
- 1 c. Shredded, sweetened coconut

Assembly

- 1 batch lemon curd or a scant ¾ c. Lemon curd
- 1 c. Cold heavy cream
- 2 tbsp sugar
- ¼ tsp pure vanilla extract
- 1 c. Unsweetened flaked coconut

What to do

1. Heat up oven to 350 degrees & line a regular muffin tin with liners.
2. Sift flour, baking powder & salt in a medium bowl. Put to the side.
3. Cream butter & sugar in the bottom of a stand mixer till creamy, about two min.. Add vanilla bean. Mix till combined. Add egg yolk, mix till combined.
4. With the mixer on low add in flour & coconut alternating each in three batches.
5. In a separate dry bowl, use an electric mixer to beat the egg whites till medium stiff peaks form.
6. Fold coconut till batter.

7. Gently fold egg whites right into batter, making sure to not deflate.
8. Fill cupcake liners ¾ of the way full & bake for 24-25 min. Turning cupcakes midway through. Depending on how your oven cooks it could be a minute or two less or more, the cupcakes are done when a wooden skewer comes out with a few crumbs attached.
9. Let cool.
10. In the bottom of the same stand mixer fitting with the whisk, add sugar & cream, whisk on a medium-high speed till whipped cream is formed, & be careful to not over mix. Whisk in vanilla. Put to the side in fridge till ready to use.
11. Toast coconut in a small sauté pan over a low heat on the stove. Be careful the oils in the coconut can cause it to burn quickly; the toasting process should only take about 30 sec..
12. When cupcakes are cool, spread about two tsp of lemon curd on the top. Pipe whipped cream on top of lemon curd & next which dash with toasted coconut.

Triple chocolate cupcakes

What you need

For the crust

- 1 1/2 c. Graham cracker crumbs
- 2 tbsp granulated sugar
- 1 tsp kosher salt
- 5 tbsp unsalted butter, melted & cooled

For the double chocolate cupcakes

- 1 c. All-purpose flour
- 1/2 c. Graham flour
- 1 1/4 c. Natural unsweetened cocoa powder
- 1 1/2 tsp baking soda
- 1/2 tsp baking powder
- 3/4 tsp kosher salt
- 2 oz. 70% cocoa chocolate, finely chopped
- 1 c. Boiling water
- 1 c. Buttermilk
- 1/2 tsp pure vanilla extract
- 2 big eggs
- 1/2 c. Vegetable oil
- 2 1/4 c. Granulated sugar

For the chocolate butter frosting

- 4 oz. 70% cacao chocolate, finely chopped
- 4 tbsp (1/2 stick) unsalted butter, cut right into 1-inch cubes
- 1 tsp light corn syrup

For the marshmallow meringue icing

- 1 1/2 c. Granulated sugar
- 1/4 tsp cream of tartar
- 1/4 c. Water

- 3 big egg whites
- 1 tsp pure vanilla extract

What to do

For the double chocolate, double graham cupcakes

1. Center a rack in the oven & heat up to 350 (f). Prepare 2 muffin trays by lining each cavity with cupcake liners.
2. In a medium bowl, use a rubber spatula to mix together 1 1/2 c. Graham cracker crumbs, 2 tbsp granulated sugar, 1 tsp kosher salt & 5 tbsp melted & cooled unsalted butter till evenly coated.
3. Use a 1 tbsp measuring spoon to portion out a tbsp sized scoop of the mixture in the bottom of each baking cup. Use your fingers (or one of these nifty tart tampers) to press down the graham cracker crumbs to the bottom of each liner till they form a solid crust. Bake in the heat uped oven for 5 min. To permit the base to harden, before transferring to wire racks to cool for a minimum of 15 min.. Whereas the graham cracker crusts are cooling, make the chocolate cake batter. Be sure to keep the oven on!
4. To make the chocolate cake batter, whisk together 1 c. All-purpose flour, 1/2 c. Graham flour, 1 1/4 c. Natural unsweetened cocoa powder, 1 1/2 tsp baking soda, 1/2 tsp baking powder & 3/4 tsp kosher salt in medium bowl till fully incorporated. Put to the side.
5. Place 2 oz. Finely chopped 70% cocoa chocolate in a medium, heatproof bowl & pour 1 c. Boiling water over the chocolate. Whisk till the chocolate is melted, & permit the mixture to cool for 15 min..
6. In a liquid measuring cup, whisk together 1 c. Buttermilk & 1/2 tsp pure vanilla extract. Put to the side.
7. In the bowl of a freestanding electric mixer fitted with a whisk attachment, whisk 2 big eggs on medium-high speed till light & foamy, about 2 min.. Reduce the mixer speed to its lowest setting & slowly pour in 1/2 c. Vegetable oil, whisking for 30 to 60 sec. Till combined.

8. With the mixer still on low, slowly pour in the cooled chocolate mixture right into the egg mixture. When the chocolate has been added, slowly pour in the buttermilk & vanilla mixture. Add 2 1/4 c. Granulated sugar & continue to whisk till the batter is smooth & liquid, about 2 min..
9. Stop the mixer. Take away the bowl from the mixer & add the dry ingredients. Use a rubber spatula to mix right into the liquid ingredients till only incorporated, scraping down the sides of the bowl & lifting & folding in from the bottom & middle of the bowl. Whisk till the dry ingredients are only incorporated — at this point, the batter will still look a little lumpy, but that's okay.
10. Pour the batter through a fine-mesh sieve over a big bowl to take away any lumps. Use a rubber spatula to press against any solids left in the sieve to push through as much batter as possible, but no need to overdo it. Disregard the remaining big lumps.
    Use a 1 tbsp sized cookie dough scoop to divide the strained batter evenly between the graham-crusted cupcake liners, filling each c. Up to two-thirds full with batter. Bake in the heat uped oven for 25 to 30 min., or till a skewer inserted right into the middle of a cupcake comes out clean & the cupcake tops spring back when lightly poked. Transfer the pans to a wire rack & permit to cool completely in the pan. When the cupcakes have cooled completely, make the chocolate ganache & marshmallow meringue frostings.

For the chocolate butter frosting

1. In a small, heavy bottomed saucepan over medium-low heat, melt together 4 oz. Finely chopped chocolate, 4 tbsp unsalted butter, & 1 tsp corn syrup, utilizing a rubber spatula to mix continously till completely melted & combined. Take away from heat & permit to cool in room temperature for about 20 min. Till mixture thickens to a spreadable consistency.
2. Once the mixture is spreadable, work quickly & use a small offset icing spatula to spread about 1 1/2 tsp of chocolate on the top of

each cupcake. If the frosting hardens too much & becomes difficult to work with, reheat over medium-low heat, whisking continously till the mixture becomes spreadable again.

For the marshmallow meringue icing

1. In a medium, heavy bottom saucepan over medium-low heat, mix 1 1/2 c. Granulated sugar, 1/4 tsp cream of tartar & 1/4 c. Of water. Whisk continously till the sugar starts to dissolve, continuing to do so till the mixture reaches 240 (f) as measured by a candy thermometer. When the mixture reaches 240 (f), it should be syrupy. Straight away transfer to a heatproof liquid measuring c. & work quickly to ensure that it maintains its temperature.
2. In the bowl of a freestanding electric mixer fitted with a whisk attachment, mix 3 big egg whites & 1 tsp pure vanilla extract. With the mixture on medium speed, slowly pour the fresh sugar syrup down the side of the mixer bowl. When all the syrup is added, turn the mixer speed to medium-high & whisk till the icing becomes thick & holds a firm peak. Continue to whisk till the icing is only slightly warm & very thick, about 10 min. Total. Do not continue to beat for longer than 10 min., otherwise the icing will thicken too much, become cement-like & impossible to spread & pipe.
3. Use straight away by transferring to a piping bag with a big round tip. Pipe a generous dollop of icing onto each cupcake. When the cupcakes have all been frosted, use a culinary chef's torch to lightly toast each dollop to give it that pretty toasted look.

Root beer cupcakes

What you need

- 1 1/2 c. Root beer
- 1/4 c. Butter
- 3/4 c. Cocoa
- 2 c. Brown sugar
- 3/4 c. Sour cream
- 2 eggs
- 1 tsp vanilla extract
- 2 c. All purpose flour
- 2 1/2 tsp baking soda

Bourbon cream buttercream

- 1/2 c. Unsalted butter, softened
- 1/2 c. Shortening
- 4 c. Powdered sugar
- 1/2 tsp salt
- 4 tbsp bourbon cream liquor

What to do

1. Pre heat oven to 325
2. Combine root beer & butter in a saucepan, when butter has melted, take away from heat. In a separate bowl, whisk together sour cream, eggs & vanilla. Add to cooled root beer & whisk till combined. Add in the cocoa & the sugar, mixing well. In a separate bowl, whisk together the flour & the baking soda. Add this to your root beer mixture, whisking till flour is incorporated. Batter will be very runny, but will bake up nicely. Fill cupcake liners about 3/4 full. This made pouring right into my cupcake liners much easier. Bake in heat uped oven for 15-17 min. Or till your cupcakes spring back when touched. Take away from oven & let cool completely before frosting.

For the buttercream

1. Combine softened butter & shortening in a big mixing bowl. Beat till very fluffy, about 10 min.. Add in powdered sugar one c. At a time, mixing well next each addition. Add in the salt. Add in your bourbon cream. This is something you may have to taste as you go along . 4 tbsp to half of my buttercream added a subtle flavor. You may want to add more if you want the bourbon to be more pronounced. Mix buttercream till creamy.

Funfetti cupcakes

What you need

- 2 c. All purpose flour
- 2 tbs baking powder
- 1/2 tsp salt
- 1/2 c. Unsalted butter, melted
- 1 & 1/2 c. Granulated sugar
- 2 eggs
- 1 & 1/2 tsp vanilla extract
- 1 & 1/4 c. Milk
- 1/2 c. Red, white, & pink dashs

What to do

2. Heat up oven to 350f. Line muffin pan with paper cupcake tins (preferably valentine's day ones).
3. In a bowl, mix together flour, baking powder & salt. Put to the side.
4. In a separate bowl, mix melted butter & sugar well. Mixture should be light & fluffy.
5. Add in eggs & vanilla extract & beat well. Whisk in milk.
6. Slowly add in flour mixture to the wet mix. Whisk only till combined.
7. Add dashs right into mixture. Lightly fold in only till dashs are scattered throughout the batter.
8. Pour batter right into lined cupcake pan. Fill cupcake c. 3/4 of the way.
9. Bake cupcakes 15 to 20 min. Or till a toothpick inserted in the middle of the cupcake comes out clean. Permit to cool before frosting.

Flourless chocolate cupcakes

What you need

- 8 oz. Chocolate chips, 60% cacao content or higher
- 14 tbsp (1¾ sticks) butter, chopped
- 2 tbsp currant jelly
- 4 big eggs
- ¼ c. Sugar
- 1 tbsp vanilla extract
- 1 tbsp creme de cassis

For the chantilly cream

- 2 c. Heavy whipping cream
- ¼ c. Sugar
- 3 tbsp creme de cassis
- Fresh cherries & currants to garnish
- Chocolate shavings, to garnish

What to do

1. Heat up the oven to 325 degrees. Line a muffin tin with 12 cupcake wrappers.
2. Place the chocolate, butter, & jelly in a saucepan. Melt over medium/low heat, stirring well, till chocolate is melted & the mixture is well combined. Take away from heat & cool to lukewarm, stirring often, about 10 min..
3. Whereas the chocolate mixture is cooling, whisk the eggs, sugar, creme de cassis, & vanilla in a big bowl till well blended, about 1 minute. Steadily whisk in the cooled chocolate mixture.
4. Divide the batter among baking wrappers.
5. Bake in the heat uped oven for 12-15 min., or till puffy & slightly cracked on top.
6. Take away & let cool on a wire rack. Put in the fridge & chill till firm & cold.

7. Place the heavy cream & ¼ c. Sugar in a bowl & beat with an electric mixer till stiff peaks form. Add the creme de cassis to the cream & beat in only till combined.
8. Place the cream in a piping bag fitted with a big star tip & pipe on top of the chilled cakes.
9. Garnish with 1 cherry each, fresh currants, & chocolate shavings.

Double chocolate cupcakes

What you need
Cupcakes

- ¼ c. Cocoa powder
- 1 c. All-purpose flour
- ½ tsp baking soda
- ½ tsp baking powder
- ¼ tsp salt
- 2 big eggs, room temp
- 1 c. Granulated sugar
- ⅓ c. Melted coconut oil
- 2 tsp vanilla extract
- 1 tsp instant coffee mixed with 1 tsp warm water
- ½ c. Buttermilk
- ½ c. Mini chocolate chips, plus more for topping

Frosting

- 2 tbsp milk
- 1 tbsp matcha powder
- 1 stick (1/2 cup) butter, room temp
- 3 c. Icing sugar

What to do

1. Heat up the oven to 350°f. Line a 12-cup muffin pan with cupcake liners; put to the side. If you have a second muffin pan, line 4 more c. With liners, if not, simply bake the first batch & next which reuse the pan for the remaining of the batter.
2. In a medium bowl, whisk together the cocoa powder, flour, baking soda, baking powder, & salt; put to the side.
3. In a big bowl, whisk together the eggs, sugar, oil, vanilla, & coffee mixture till smooth.

4. Add in half the dry ingredients to the wet ingredients, next which half the buttermilk, mixing till smooth. Repeat with remaining dry ingredients & buttermilk. Add in chocolate chips & mix till only combined.
5. Pour batter right into cupcake liners, filling about ⅔ of the way. Bake 18-20 min. Till a toothpick inserted in the centre comes out clean. Take away from oven & let cool completely.
6. Make frosting: in a small bowl, mix the matcha powder & milk & mix till a smooth paste forms. It is important that you get rid of any clumps as best you can. In a mixing bowl, beat together the butter till smooth. Add in icing sugar & matcha mixture & beat till thickened. Transfer to a piping bag & frost the fully cooled cupcakes. Top with mini chocolate chips, if desired.

Egg nog cupcakes

What you need
Cupcakes

- 1 (16 ounce) box white cake mix
- 1¼ c. Egg nog
- 2 eggs
- ½ tsp ground nutmeg
- ½ tsp vanilla extract

Frosting

- ½ c. Butter, softened to room temperature
- ¼ c. Egg nog
- 1 tsp vanilla
- ½ tsp ground nutmeg
- 4 to 5 c. Powdered sugar

What to do

1. Heat up oven to 350 degrees f.
2. In a big bowl, mix cake mix, egg nog, eggs, nutmeg & vanilla. Whisk together till only combined.
3. Spoon batter right into a mini cupcake pan filled with paper liners or sprayed with nonstick cooking spray. Fill each cupcake ⅔ of the way full.
4. Bake for 8-10 min., or till barely golden brown.
5. Take away from oven & let cool completely.

For the frosting

1. In a big bowl, cream together butter, egg nog, vanilla, & nutmeg.
2. Mix in powdered sugar one c. At a time.
3. Spread or pipe frosting onto cooled cupcakes.

Chocolate & peanut butter cupcakes

What you need

Chocolate cupcakes

- 1/4 c. Cocoa powder
- 1/2 c. Flour
- 1/2 tsp baking powder
- 1/4 tsp baking soda
- 1/8 tsp salt
- 1/2 stick butter, room temperature
- 6 tbsp sugar
- 1 egg
- 1/2 tsp vanilla
  - Tbsp sour cream
- 1 tbsp melted chocolate, cooled

Peanut butter cupcakes

- 1/2 c. & 1 tbsp flour
- 1/4 tsp baking soda
- 1/2 tsp baking powder
- 1/4 tsp salt
  - Tbsp peanut butter
- 2 tbsp vegetable oil
- 1/4 c. Brown sugar
- 1/4 c. Buttermilk
- 1 egg
- 1/4 tsp vanilla

Chocolate buttercream

- 1 stick butter
- 1/2 c. Vegetable shortening
- 3/4 c. Cocoa
- 2-2.5 c. Powdered sugar

Peanut butter cream

- 1 stick butter
- 1/2 c. Vegetable shortening
- 3/4 c. Peanut butter
- 2-4 c. Powdered sugar

What to do
Chocolate cupcakes

1. Heat up the oven to 350º f. Line a muffin tin with 12 cupcake liners.
2. In a small mixing bowl, mix the cocoa powder, flour, baking powder, baking soda & salt. Lightly mix utilizing a spoon.
3. In a larger mixing bowl, mix the butter & sugar, beat utilizing an electric mixer till fluffy. Add in the eggs & vanilla, lightly beat.
4. Add in the sour cream & melted chocolate, mix by hand utilizing a spatula.
5. Add half of the flour mixture to the wet ingredients, do not dump it in, rather take spoonfuls of the flour mixture & lightly shake it over the wet ingredients, as if you were sifting in the flour. Fold in the mixture till no flour remains. Repeat with the other half of the flour, folding it in & scraping the sides & bottom of the bowl to incorporate everything. Put to the side.

Peanut butter cupcakes

1. In a bowl mix the flour, baking soda, baking powder, & salt. In a separate bowl, mix the peanut butter, oil, & brown sugar, beat together utilizing an electric mixer. Add in the egg & vanilla, beat again. Add the flour mixture & buttermilk, alternating between the two & mixing by hand till everything is incorporated.
2. Begin to add the batter right into the pan, alternating between chocolate & peanut butter. Fill the cupcake liners just about completely full with batter.
3. Place the pan in the middle of the oven & bake for 15-17 min. Or till a toothpick inserted in the middle comes out clean.

4. Allow the cupcakes to cool for about 3 min. In the pan, next which take them out & permit them to cool upside down on a cooling rack. This will help create cupcakes with a dome top.
5. Allow the cupcakes to cool completely before adding the frosting.

Chocolate buttercream

1. In a mixing bowl, mix the butter & vegetable shortening, beat utilizing an electric mixer till fluffy. Add in the cocoa powder, & lightly mix by hand with a spatula.
2. Begin to add the powdered sugar, 1 c. At a time, mixing by hand first, next which with the electric mixer. Continue adding powdered sugar till the frosting tastes good to you.

Peanut buttercream

1. In a mixing big bowl, mix the butter & vegetable shortening, beat utilizing an electric mixer till fluffy.
2. Add in the peanut butter, beat utilizing electric mixer.
3. Begin to add the powdered sugar, 1 c. At a time, mixing by hand first, next which with the electric mixer. Continue adding powdered sugar till the frosting tastes good to you.

Frosting

1. In a piping bag fit with a wilton 6b piping tip, do your best to add chocolate buttercream to one side of the bag & peanut butter buttercream to the other. Push the buttercream down right into the bag. Pipe the buttercream onto the cupcakes, starting on the outside edge & working your way right into the center, progressively stacking the frosting as you get to the center.

Chocolate cupcakes with caramel

What you need
Chocolate cupcakes

- 1/2 c. Salted butter
- 1 c. Sugar
- 2 eggs
- 1/2 tsp vanilla extract
- 6 tbsp water
- 6 tbsp cocoa powder
- 1 c. All purpose flour
- 1/2 tsp baking soda
- 6 tbsp kahlua

Kahlua icing

- 1/2 c. Salted butter
- 1/2 c. Shortening*
- 4 c. Powdered sugar
- 4-5 tbsp kahlua
- Caramel sauce
- Sea salt

What to do

2. Heat up oven to 350 degrees.
3. Beat butter & sugar till light in color & fluffy, about 2-3 min..
4. Add eggs, one at a time, beating only till blended.
5. Add vanilla, water & cocoa powder to an additional bowl & whisk till smooth.
6. Add chocolate mixture to batter & mix till combined. Scrape down the sides of the bowl as needed to ensure everything is well combined.
7. Combine flour & baking soda in a separate bowl.
8. Alternate adding the flour mixture & kahlua to the batter. Start by adding half of the dry mix, next which mix well. Add the

kahlua & mix well, scrapes down the sides as needed. Add the remaining flour mixture & beat till smooth.
9. Fill cupcake liners about half way. Bake for 16-18 min., or till a toothpick inserted comes out with a few crumbs.
10. To make icing, beat butter & shortening till smooth.
11. Add 2 c. Of powdered sugar & beat till smooth.
12. Add 4 tbsp kahlua & remaining powdered sugar & beat till smooth. Add additional kahlua if needed to get the right icing consistency.
13. Pipe icing onto cupcakes
14. Drizzle cupcakes with caramel sauce & a dash of sea salt.

Apple cupcakes

What you need

- 1½ c. Cake flour
- 1 c. All-purpose flour
- 3 tsp. Baking powder
- ¼ tsp. Salt
- 1 c. Butter, room temperature
- 1½ c. Brown sugar
- 4 eggs, room temperature
- ½ c. Buttermilk
- 1½ c. Apple sauce
- 1 tsp. Vanilla
- 1½ tsp. Cinnamon
- ½ tsp. Ground ginger
- ¼ tsp. Nutmeg

Filling

- 2 apples, cored & cubed
- 1 tbsp. Brown sugar
- 1 tbsp. Butter
- Salt
- ¼ tsp. Cinnamon
- 1 tsp. All-purpose flour

Topping

- ½ c. Butter, room temperature
- ½ c. Old-fashioned oats
- ¼ c. All-purpose flour
- ½ tsp. Cinnamon

Buttercream

- ¾ c. Butter, room temperature
- 1½ c. Confectioners' sugar

- 1 tsp. Vanilla
- ¼ c. Brown sugar
- 1-2 tbsp. Heavy whipping cream

What to do
Filling

1. Heat butter in a small saute pan over medium heat. When melted, mix in sugar, salt, cinnamon, & apples. Mix continously till apples are tender, about 5 min.. Mix in flour & cook for an additional minute or two. Take away from heat & cool.

Topping

1. Combine all the topping ingredients right into a bowl & mix till well combined.

Cake

2. In the bowl of a stand mixer, add the butter & sugar. Beat till light & fluffy, about 5 min. Beat in the eggs one at a time, making sure to mix well before adding the next. Add vanilla & applesauce: mix well.
3. Sift together the flours, baking powder, cinnamon, ginger, nutmeg, & salt.
4. With the mixer on low, add in the flour mixture & buttermilk alternatively, always starting & ending with the dry ingredients. Mix till only combined.
5. Heat up the oven to 350f.
6. Line a cupcake tray with cupcake liners. Add a bit of batter to the bottom of each liner, maybe ⅓ of the way. Evenly put the filling right into each liner. Top with remaining batter. This should make about 12 cupcakes. Spread out the topping onto each cupcake.
7. Place tray right into the oven & bake for 18-20 min., or till toothpick comes out clean. Permit to cool slightly in tray & next which move cupcakes to wire rack to finish cooling.

8. If decorating with buttercream, add the butter to the bowl of a stand mixer. Cream, on medium speed, till pale & fluffy (about 5 min..)
9. Sift in confectioners' sugar & add brown sugar.
10. Pour in vanilla & heavy whipping cream, mixing till combined. Mix on medium/high speed till whipped & fluffy, a good 3-4 min..
11. Decorate cupcakes & serve.

Mint ice cream cupcakes

What you need
Cupcakes

- 24 chocolate cupcakes, baked & cooled
- 1/2 carton (about .75 quart) mint chip ice cream
- Mint chip frosting
- Mini chocolate chips, for garnish

Mint frosting

- 12 tbsp unsalted butter, softened
- 3 c. Powdered sugar
- 1 tsp vanilla
- 1/4-1/2 tsp peppermint extract
- 4-6 tbsp heavy whipping cream
- 4-5 drops green food coloring, optional
- 1/2 c. Mini chocolate chips

What to do

1. Start with 24 cupcakes that have been baked & completely cooled. You can use a chocolate box mix, or your favorite from scratch recipe.
2. Place the cupcakes on a cookie sheet lined with wax paper. Make room for a second cookie sheet lined with wax paper in your freezer.
3. To prep the cupcakes: use a pairing knife to cut a big circle in the top of the cupcake. Cut down just about to the bottom of the cupcake, next which lift out the cut part. You should end up with a cone shaped chunk of cake. Slice the cone off of each of the cupcake pieces. (you need to make the piece of cake smaller, because the cupcake will be filled with ice cream.) See this post for photo instructions.
4. Prepare all the cupcakes for the ice cream, next which put your second cookie sheet in the freezer. Work in batches of 3-4 cupcakes, filling with ice cream, next which placing on the cookie

sheet that's in the freezer. That way the ice cream won't melt out of the cupcakes.
5. Scoop about 1-2 tbsp of ice cream right into the middle of each cupcake. Put the top back on & press lightly . Put the cupcake on the cookie sheet in the freezer. Continue till all the cupcakes are filled & in the freezer.
6. Cover the cupcakes with plastic wrap (leaving them on the cookie sheet) & freeze for at least 4 hours before serving. You can put them in a single layer in big ziploc bags & freeze for up to 1 month before serving.
7. To make the frosting: beat butter with a hand or a stand mixer till smooth. Mix in powdered sugar slowly, next which add vanilla & peppermint extract. Start with 1/4 tsp peppermint extract next which taste & add more as desired. Mix in 1 tbsp of heavy whipping cream at a time, mixing well, till you've reached your desired consistency.
8. When ready to serve, have your frosting ready. Take away a cupcake from the freezer, frost as desired, & serve straight away. Top with additional mini chocolate chips for garnish.

Classic cupcakes with chocolate buttercream

What you need
Cupcakes

- 1/2 c. Unsalted butter (1 stick), melted
- 1 big egg plus 1 egg yolk
- 1 c. Granulated sugar
- 6 oz. (about 1/2 cup) greek yogurt
- 2 tsp vanilla extract
- 1 1/2 c. All-purpose flour
- 1 1/2 tsp baking powder
- 1/4 tsp salt, optional & to taste

Chocolate buttercream frosting

- 1/2 c. Unsalted butter (1 stick), softened
- 1/2 heaping c. Unsweetened natural cocoa powder, sifted
- 2 1/2 to 3 c. Confectioners' sugar, sifted is ideal
- 1 tsp vanilla extract
- Splash cream or milk, only as needed for consistency
- Chocolate dashs, optional for garnishing

What to do

1. Heat up oven to 350f. Line a non-stick 12-cup regular muffin pan with paper liners; put to the side.
2. Cupcakes - in a large, microwave-safe bowl, melt the butter, about 1 minute on high power.
3. Allow the butter to cool momentarily, & add the egg plus yolk, sugar, yogurt, vanilla, & whisk to combine.
4. Stir in the flour, baking powder, optional salt, & mix till only combined & free from big lumps; don't overmix or cupcakes will be tough.

5. Using a medium 2-inch cookie scoop, put about 2 tbsp of batter per cupcake right into each of the 12 cavities so they're solidly ¾ full
6. Bake for 18 to 19 min., or till tops are golden, set, slightly domed, & springy to the touch. A toothpick inserted in the middle should come out clean or with a few moist crumbs, but no batter. Permit cupcakes to cool in pan for 5 to 10 min. Before transferring to a wire rack to cool completely. Whereas they cool, make the frosting.
7. Frosting - to the bowl of a stand mixer fitted with the paddle attachment, add the butter & beat on medium-high speed till pale, light & fluffy, about 5 min.. Stop to scrape down the sides of the bowl as necessary.
8. Add the cocoa, 2 1/2 c. Confectioners' sugar, vanilla, & beat on medium-high speed till fluffy, about 5 min.. Stop to scrape down the sides of the bowl as necessary.
9. Based on texture & taste preferences, optionally add ½ c. Additional sugar. Transfer frosting to a piping bag & frost the cooled cupcakes.
10. Optionally, garnish each cupcake with a pinch of dashs.

Avocado cupcakes

What you need

Milk chocolate cupcakes

- 1 c. Cake flour
- ⅔ c. Sugar
- ⅓ c. Cocoa powder
- 1 pinch of baking soda
- 1 pinch of salt
- ¾ c. Water
- ⅓ c. Oil
- 1 egg, beaten
- 1 tsp vinegar

Avocado buttercream

- ½ an avocado
- ½ tbsp butter, softened
- 1¼ c. Powdered sugar
- ½ tsp vanilla

What to do

1. Whisk the dry ingredients together till well mixed.
2. Add the wet ingredients & mix till moistened. The batter will be thinner than typical cake batter.
3. Pour right into a lined muffin pan, filling each cupcake about ¾ of the way full. They pop straight up, so you can fill them up closer to the top if you want.
4. Bake at 350 for about 12 min..
5. Avocado buttercream
6. With an electric mixer, blend the avocado & butter together. Add the vanilla & powdered sugar. If it's too thick, add a tbs. Of milk. If it's too thin, add more sugar.
7. To put the frosting neatly on the cupcakes, scoop it right into a snack-size plastic bag, cut off the tip, & squeeze out the frosting right into nice little spirals on top of the cupcakes.

Cakes

Caramel cheesecake

What you need

- Butter 70g, melted
- Digestive biscuits 150g
- Full-fat soft cheese 400g
- Double cream 100ml
- Dulce de leche 200g, plus more to serve
- Eggs 2, beaten

Directions

1. Heat the oven to 170c/fan 150c/gas 31/2. To make the base, mix the butter & biscuits till they looks like damp breadcrumbs. Butter & line the base of a 22cm springform tin, pack the biscuit mixture right into the base & chill.
2. For the filling, mix the cheese, cream, dulce de leche & eggs to a smooth paste. Put this mix in the tin with the biscuit base & cook for 45 min. Till it is set, but still has a slight wobble. Cool to room temperature, next which chill till ready to serve. Spread more dulce de leche on top.

The new 2015 brownies recipe

What you need

- ¼ c. (1/2 stick) unsalted butter
- ¼ c. Unsweetened applesauce
- ¾ c. White sugar
- 2 big eggs
- ½ c. Unsweetened cocoa powder
- ½ tsp salt
- ½ tsp baking powder
- ½ tbsp vanilla extract
- ¾ c. Unbleached all-purpose flour
- ¼ c. Semisweet chocolate chips

Directions

1. Heat up oven to 350 f.
2. In medium bowl, add cocoa, applesauce, eggs, salt, baking powder, & vanilla & whisk till all blended & smooth. Add chocolate chips on top, but do not mix in yet.
3. In a separate small bowl, microwave butter till melted (30 sec.). Add sugar, & microwave again for 30 sec..
4. Pour melted butter & sugar over chocolate chips sitting on cocoa mixture & stir.
5. Add flour & mix till everything is well blended & smooth.
6. Pour melted butter & sugar over chocolate chips sitting on cocoa mixture & stir.
7. Add flour & mix till everything is well blended & smooth.

The ultimate blueberry cake

What you need

- 1 (15.25 oz) box of yellow cake mix
- 4 c. Of fresh blueberries
- 3 tbsp cornstarch
- 3/4 c. White granulated sugar
- 1/2 c. Butter (1 stick) cut right into 1/2 in. Chunks

Directions

1. Heat up oven to 350f. Grease a 9 x 13 in. Baking pan. Add 3 c. Of blueberries to the pan, spreading evenly across. Dash cornstarch evenly across. Dash sugar evenly across.
2. Dash cake mix on top of blueberries, trying to spread evenly across. Spread butter chunks evenly on top. Dash remaining 1 c. Of blueberries on top.
3. Bake for 45-55 min. Or till cake mix is golden brown & no raw cake mix remains. Let cake cool for about 30 min. Before serving & eating.

Apple cake with caramel

What you need
Apple cake

- 3 granny smith apples, peeled & cored
- 2 c. All purpose flour
- 1 tbsp baking powder
- 1 tbsp cinnamon
- 1 tsp nutmeg
- 1 tsp salt
- ½ c. (1 stick) unsalted butter, softened
- ½ c. Light brown sugar
- ⅓ c. Honey
- ½ c. Sour cream
- ½ c. Unsweetened almond milk
- 2 big eggs
- 2 tsp vanilla

Caramel

- 1 c. Granulated sugar
- 6 tbsp unsalted butter, cut right into pieces
- ½ heavy cream
- 1 tsp salt

What to do

1. Heat up oven to 350 degrees. Lightly grease an 8 in. Springform pan.
2. Slice all three apples, with two of the apple chop them in till you have a big dice.
3. In a bowl, mix the flour, baking powder, cinnamon, nutmeg & salt. Put to the side.
4. In a stand mixer, beat the butter till smooth. Add the sugar & honey & beat till fluffy.
5. Next add the sour cream & beat till combined, followed by each egg, one at a time, mixing well next each addition.

6. Scrape down your bowl, add vanilla & beat an additional time.
7. Finally, beat in the milk. The batter may appear to be curdled, but that's perfectly normal.
8. Stir in the flour mixture, beating till you get a smooth, creamy, beige batter.
9. Stir in the chopped apples & spread right into the prepared pan. Arrange the remaining apple slices over top, overlapping them slightly, in a circular patter over the batter.
10. Put the pan on the top rack of the oven for 40-50 min.. When a toothpick or skewer is inserted & comes out dry, the cake is done.
11. Allow the cake to cool completely.
12. Heat sugar in a medium saucepan over medium heat, stirring continously with a rubber spatula, the sugar will start to form hard clumps but will eventually melt right into a thick brown amber liquid. Be careful not to burn.
13. Once the sugar has completely melted, straight away add the butter. The butter will bubble rapidly so be careful. Mix the butter right into the caramel till it is completely melted, about 2 min..
14. Very slowly, pour the heavy cream right into your pan. Again, this will bubble & splatter so be careful. Permit the mixture to boil for one minute.
15. Take away from the heat & mix in salt.
16. Allow to cool slightly before drizzling over the apple cake. If done over the entire cake, serve straight away. If serving over a longer period of time, drizzle over each slice individually as served.

Flourless chocolate blender cake

What you need

- 1 extra-large or 2 small ripe banana(s), peeled
- 1 big egg
- Heaping 1/2 c. Creamy peanut butter
- 3 tbsp honey
- 1 tbsp vanilla extract
- 1/4 tsp baking soda
- Pinch salt, optional & to taste
- Heaping 1/2 c. Mini semi-sweet chocolate chips, plus more for sprinkling on top

Directions

1. Heat up oven to 350f & spray a 9-inch round cake pan with cooking spray; put to the side.
2. To the canister of a blender, add all ingredients excluding chocolate chips & blend on high speed till smoothy & creamy, about 1 minute.
3. Add chocolate chips & mix in by hand; don't use the blender because it will pulverize them.
4. Turn batter out right into prepared pan, smoothing the top lightly with a spatula if necessary.
5. Evenly dash with a tbsp or two of extra chocolate chips.
6. Bake for about 25 min., or till the cake is set in the center, springy to the touch, & a toothpick inserted right into the middle comes out clean, or with a few moist crumbs, but no batter. Due to variances in moisture levels in bananas, peanut butter, oven & climate variances, baking times will range. Start watching closely at 20 min., & always bake till done. Permit cake to cool in pan for about 15 min., or till it's firmed up & is cool enough to take away from pan.

The ultimate banana cake

What you need

For the cake

- 1 1/2 c. Sugar
- 1/2 c. (1 stick) unsalted butter, softened
- 2 big eggs
- 1 tsp vanilla extract
- 3 medium ripe bananas
- 2/3 c. Milk
- 1 tsp baking soda
- 1/8 tsp salt
- 2 1/4 c. All-purpose flour

For the cream cheese frosting

- 2 oz. Cream cheese, softened
- 3/4 c. Confectioners' sugar
- 6 tbsp unsalted butter, melted
- 1/2 tsp vanilla extract

Toppings

- Caramel sauce
- 1/4 c. Semisweet chocolate chips, melted or chocolate syrup
- 1/4 c. Mini chocolate chips
- 1/4 c. Salted peanuts
- 1/2 jar maraschino cherries, cut in half
- Dashs

Directions

1. Heat up oven to 350 degrees f. Spray an 8-x-8-inch baking pan with nonstick spray.
2. In a stand mixer, mix sugar, butter, eggs, & vanilla. Mix on medium speed for 3 min. Or till well incorporated.

3. In the meantime , smash 3 big bananas (use a potato masher) & add to the mix.
4. Slowly add milk, soda, salt, & flour & mix till well combined.
5. Pour batter right into the prepared baking pan & put right into oven. Bake for 30 min. Or till a toothpick inserted in the middle comes out clean. Let cake cool completely.
6. Once cake is cooled, prepare the cream cheese frosting by mixing together the cream cheese, confectioners' sugar, butter & vanilla till smooth & creamy. Spread evenly over the top. Drizzle caramel sauce over the cream cheese frosting (as much as desired), followed by melted chocolate or chocolate syrup. Add cherries, mini chocolate chips, peanuts & dashs. Put in the fridge for 2 hours or till cream cheese frosting is set. Cut right into squares & serve.

Coffee & chocolate cake

What you need
For the cake

- 2 c. Cake flour
- ¾ c. Cocoa
- 1½ tsp baking soda
- ¾ tsp salt
- ¾ c. Butter, room temperature
- 2 c. Golden brown sugar
- 3 big eggs
- 1½ tsp vanilla extract
- 1 c. Buttermilk
- 4 tsp instant espresso powder dissolved in ¾ c. Hot water

For the peanut butter frosting

- 1½ c. Butter, softened
- 1½ c. Creamy peanut butter
- 4½ c. Powdered sugar
- 4 tsp dark rum
- 3 tsp vanilla
- 6 tbsp heavy cream

For the rum drizzle

- ¾ c. Brown sugar
- ½ c. Dark rum
- 1 tbsp unsalted butter

Directions
Cake layers

1. Position rack in middle of oven; heat up to 325. Generously butter two 9-inch cake pans; dust with cocoa, tapping out excess. Line bottom of pan with parchment paper.

2. Sift 2 c. Cake flour, cocoa, baking soda & salt right into medium bowl.
3. Using electric mixer, beat butter in big bowl till smooth. Add brown sugar & beat till well blended, about 2 min..
4. Add eggs, 1 at a time, beating well next each addition. Mix in vanilla.
5. Add flour mixture in 3 additions alternately with buttermilk in 2 additions, beating only till blended next each addition.
6. Steadily add hot espresso-water mixture, beating only till smooth.
7. Divide batter between pans; smooth tops. Bake cakes till tester inserted right into middle comes out clean, about 40 min.. Cool cakes in pans on rack 15 min.. Run small knife around sides of pans to loosen cakes. Invert cakes onto racks; lift pans off cakes & take away parchment. Put wire rack atop each cake, invert again so top side is up.
8. Cool completely.
9. Mark each cake layer with toothpicks midway up the sides; use the toothpicks as a guide to cut each cake layer in half.

Frosting

1. In the bowl of a stand mixer, cream together the peanut butter & butter for 2-3 min..
2. Add the powdered sugar, scrape the sides of the bowl & mix on high for one minute.
3. Add the rum & vanilla & mix in.
4. Add the heavy cream & beat till smooth; scraping the sides. Beat for 3 min. On high. Use straight away

Rum drizzle

1. Put all of the ingredients right into a medium size saucepan. Heat till bubbly & cook for one minute. Cool completely.
2. Putting it all together:
3. Spread a tbsp of frosting in the middle of your cake plate to help hold cake in place. Brush crumbs from one cake layer & put in the middle of the plate. Drizzle one tbsp of rum drizzle over cake

layer & spread 1 & ½ c. Of frosting on cake, smoothing to edges. Repeat with all layers
4. Swirl frosting over top of cake & either pipe rosettes in the middle of the cake on the top or dollop additional frosting & swirl in center.
5. Gently pour rum drizzle over cake; letting pool on top & drip down the sides. Serve.

Lemon & cheese cream cake

What you need

For the cake

- 2 c. Sugar
- 2 1/2 c. Cake flour
- 1 1/2 tsp baking powder
- 1 1/2 tsp baking soda
- 1 tsp kosher salt
- 1 tbsp pure vanilla extract
- 2 eggs
- 1/2 c. Oil
- 1 c. Milk
- 1 c. Boiling water
- 2 1/2 tsp lemon extract
- Zest & juice of 1 lemon

For the frosting

- 1 c. Unsalted butter, room temperature
- 8 oz. Cream cheese, room temperature
- 1 tsp pure vanilla extract
- 1 1/2 tsp lemon extract
- 3 1/2 c. Powdered sugar

For the middle bit

- 1/2 c. Baker's choice of jam

For the candied lemon topping

- Lemon, cut in 1/4 in. Slices
- 1/2 c. Sugar
- 1/2 c. Water

Directions

1. In a small saucepan, mix the sugar & water together till the mixture becomes clear.
2. Drop in your slices of lemon & permit to cook in the syrup for 1 minute before taking the mixture off of the heat.
3. Refrigerate till you are ready to frost your cake heat oven to 350°f. Grease & flour two 9-inch round baking pans.
4. In a big bowl, mix all dry ingredients. Add eggs, milk, oil, vanilla, lemon extract, & lemon zest & juice.
5. Beat with a hand mixer on medium speed for 2 min.. Mix in boiling water (batter will be thin). Pour right into 2 prepared cake tins.
6. Bake for 30-35 min., or till a knife comes out clean in the center.
7. In a big bowl, beat the cream cheese, butter, vanilla, lemon extract, & salt with a hand mixer on medium high speed.
8. Add in the powdered sugar in 3 additions, beating in between each time.
9. Place a dollop of frosting on a cake stand (this will hold the cake & prevent it from sliding). Put a layer of cake on the stand, frost the top with the lemon cream cheese frosting, next which a thick layer of jam.
10. Place the second layer of cake on top. Frost the sides before frosting the top. Add on your candied lemon babies.

Basic chocolate pudding cake

What you need

- 2 1/2 c. All-purpose flour
- 2 1/4 c. Packed light brown sugar, divided
- 3 tsp baking powder
- 1 tsp baking soda
- 1/2 tsp salt
- 1 c. Chocolate chips
- 2 tbsp unsalted butter
- 2 oz. Unsweetened chocolate
- 2 c. Buttermilk
- 1 tsp vanilla extract
- 1/2 c. Plus 2 tbsp unsweetened
- 2 1/2 c. Boiling water

Directions

1. Heat up the oven to 350 degrees f. Grease a 9 x 13-inch baking pan & put to the side.
2. In a big mixing bowl, mix flour, 1 c. Of the brown sugar, baking powder, baking soda, & salt. Whisk till well combined. If there are lumps of brown sugar, use your hands to break them up. Mix in chocolate chips & put to the side.
3. In a small saucepan, melt the butter & chocolate together over medium-low heat.
4. In a separate small saucepan, heat buttermilk over low heat till barely warmed. You don't want it to bubble or boil. Take away from heat.
5. Take away chocolate & butter mixture from heat & mix in the vanilla. Pour mixture over dry ingredients. Add the buttermilk & mix till combined. Spread right into the prepared pan.
6. Combine the remaining 1 1/4 c. Brown sugar with the cocoa in a small bowl. Whisk till smooth, utilizing your hands to break up any brown sugar clumps. Dash mixture evenly over the chocolate cake batter.

7. Pour the boiling water evenly over the cake.
8. Prudently transfer the pan to the oven. Bake for 30-35 min. Or till the middle is firm to the touch.
9. Take away cake from oven & cool on a cooling rack for at least 30 min. Before serving. To serve, invert each serving on a plate so that the fudge sauce on the bottom becomes a topping. Spoon any extra sauce in the pan over the top. You can serve the cake at room temperature or warm. Top with ice cream, if desired.

Three colors cake

What you need

- 101 g all-purpose flour
- 31 g unsweetened cocoa powder
- 2.5 g baking soda
- 0.5 g baking powder
- 1 g kosher salt
- 56 g eggs
- 126 g granulated sugar
- 2 g vanilla paste
- 86 g mayonnaise
- 105 g water, at room temperature

Graham streusel

- 50 g almond flour
- 50 g graham crumbs
- 50 g light brown sugar
- 25 g all-purpose flour
- 1 g vanilla powder
- 60 g unsalted butter, cold, cut right into 1/2 in. Dice

Chocolate cream

- 233 g heavy cream
- 100 g whole milk
- 66 g granulated sugar
- 10 g unsweetened cocoa powder
- 1 g salt
- 66 g egg yolks
- 125 g dark chocolate, melted

Meringue

- 50 g egg whites
- 75 g granulated sugar

- 1 g vanilla paste

Directions

1. To start, line three 3 in. Diameter & 1.75 in. Tall ring molds with acetate & put on a silpat lined baking sheet. Put to the side.
2. For the cake, heat up the oven to 325 f. Line a half sheet pan with a silpat or spray lightly with nonstick spray, line with parchment paper, & spray the parchment.
3. Sift the flour, cocoa powder, baking soda, & baking powder right into a medium bowl. Add the salt & mix to combine.
4. Place the eggs, sugar, & vanilla paste in the bowl of a stand mixer fitted with the whisk attachment & mix on medium-low speed for about 1 minute to combine. Increase the speed to medium & whip for 5 min., till the mixture is thick & pale yellow. Scrape down the sides & bottom of the bowl, next which whip on medium-high speed for an additional 5 min., or till the mixture has thickened. When the whisk is lifted, the mixture should form a slowly dissolving ribbon.
5. Add the mayonnaise & whip to combine. Take away the bowl from the mixer stand & fold in the dry ingredients & water in 2 additions each.
6. Pour the batter right into the prepared pan and, utilizing an offset spatula, spread it in an even layer, making sure that it reaches right into the corners. Bake for 10 min., till a skewer inserted right into the centre comes out sean & the cake springs back when lightly touched. Set on a cooling rack & cool completely.
7. Lay a piece of parchment on the back of a sheet pan. Run a knife around the edges of the cake to loosen it & invert it onto the parchment. Take away the silpat or parchment from the top of the cake. Put in the freezer for at least 30 min..
8. Cut out three 3-inch diameter rounds from the cake whereas it is still frozen & put in the ring molds. Wrap the remainder of the cake in plastic wrap & freeze for up to 2 weeks (this is extra).
9. For the streusel, heat up the oven to 325 f. Line a baking sheet with parchment paper.

10. Combine the almond flour, graham crumbs, sugar, vanilla powder, & flour in a small bowl. Whisk to combine. Add the butter & quickly break it up with your fingertips till the mixture resembles coarse meal. Spread the streusel on the baking sheet in an even layer & freeze for 10 min..
11. Bake for 12 to 15 min., stirring the streusel every 4 min.. Take away from the oven & cool completely. Spoon 40 g of streusel right into each ring hold & lightly press right into the holds store the remainder in an airtight container at room temperature for up to 4 days or freeze for up to 2 weeks.
12. For the custard, mix the milk & cream in a medium saucepan set of medium-high heat. In a small bowl, whisk together the egg yolks, sugar, & cocoa powder till slightly paler in colour.
13. When the milk mixture has come to a boil, slowly pour a small amount right into the yolk mixture, whisking continuously. Continue tempering the yolks with the milk mixture, next which transfer all of back right into the saucepan. Cook over medium-low heat, stirring continuously with a rubber spatula, till the mixture has thickened enough to cover the back of a spoon & a thermometer reads 82 c.
14. Take away from heat & strain through a fine-mesh sieve right into a bowl set over an ice bath. Whereas the mixture is still warm, add the melted chocolate & emulsify with an immersion blender. Put a piece of plastic wrap directly on the surface of the custard & refrigerate for at least 3 hours, or overnight.
15. Fill a piping bag with the chocolate custard & pipe right into the molds till it reaches the top of the molds. Smooth the top with an offset spatula & freeze for 4 hours, or overnight.
16. Take away the rings from the cakes, but keep the acetate on. Add a second layer of acetate 0.5 in. Higher than the original acetate over top the original acetate. Put the rings back on.
17. For the meringue, mix the egg whites & sugar in the bowl of a stand mixer set over a saucepan of barely simmering water. Whisking continuously , bring the mixture to 60 c, next which transfer to the stand mixer & whip on high speed till stiff peaks form, about 8 min.. Add the vanilla paste & whip for 1 minute to combine.

18. Pipe the meringue right into the rings till it reaches the top of the second layer of acetate. Smooth the top with an offset spatula & freeze for 30 min..
19. Place right into the fridge 4 hours before serving but take away the rings & both layers of acetate whereas frozen. When ready to serve, use a handheld torch to toast the meringue whereas being careful not to scorch the custard.

Chocolate buttercream brownies cake

What you need

- 1 c. Chocolate chocolate drink mix
- ¾ c. Butter, softened
- 1½ c. Flour
- 2½ c. Sugar
- 4 eggs
- 1 tb vanilla
- ½ american heritage chocolate bar
- 1 tsp. Salt

Frosting

- 6 tb unsalted butter, softened
- ¼ c. Unsweetened cocoa powder
- ¼ tsp. Salt
- 1¼ c. Powdered sugar
- 1 tb milk
- ½ tsp. Vanilla extract

Directions

1. Combine chocolate drink mix, flour, sugar & salt in a bowl & mix. Add softened butter, eggs & vanilla & beat on low till well combined. Fold in ½ c. Chocolate bar (grated) & mix well.
2. Spread right into a greased 9x13. Bake at 350 for 30-35 min.. Let cool completely.
3. For frosting, mix butter, cocoa, vanilla & salt in a bowl till well combined. Slowly add powdered sugar & milk & beat till well combined. Spread over cooled brownies. Dash with mini m&ms.

Apple cake with caramel v2

Ingredietns
Apple spice cake

- 1 c. Flour
- 1/2 tsp baking soda
- 1 tsp baking powder
- 1/4 tsp salt
- 1/2 tsp cinnamon
- 1/4 tsp cloves
- 1/4 tsp allspice
- 1/2 stick butter, room temperature
- 1/2 c. Brown sugar
- 1 egg
- 3/4 c. Unsweetened applesauce

Vanilla buttercream

- 2 stick butter, room temperature
- 1/2 c. Vegetable shortening
- 1 tsp vanilla paste (or extract or vanilla bean pods)
- 5-7 c. Powdered sugar

Caramel drizzle

- 1/4 c. Heavy cream
- 1 tbsp butter, unsalted
- 1/4 tsp salt
- 1/2 tsp vanilla extract
- 6 tbsp sugar
- 1 tbsp light corn syrup
- 1 tbsp water

Directions

1. Heat up the oven to 350º f.

2. Using butter, grease the bottom & sides of an 6 in. Round cake pan or springform pan & line the bottom with a round piece of parchment paper. To ensure even baking, put a bake even strip around the pan. You can make your own homemade bake even strip by cutting a towel or shirt to fit the size of your pan. Get the fabric really wet, next which squeeze out the dripping water but do not squeeze it too dry. Secure the fabric around the pan with a safety pin.
3. In a small bowl mix the flour, baking soda, baking powder, salt, cinnamon, cloves, & allspice. Mix well.
4. In a larger bowl, mix the butter & brown sugar. Beat utilizing an electric mixer till creamy, about 1 minute.
5. Add in the egg, beat again with the mixer.
6. Add in the applesauce, mix by hand with a spatula.
7. Steadily add in the flour mixture, mixing by hand till it's incorporated.
8. Scrape the batter right into the prepared cake pan, utilizing a spatula to evenly spread it out.
9. Bake for 23-25 min., or till a toothpick inserted in the middle comes out clean.
10. Once the cake is done, permit it to cool in the pan on a cooling rack for 10 min.. Next 10 min., prudently take away the cake from the pan. If utilizing a springform pan, take away the sides & bottom. Permit the cake to cool completely on a cooling rack. When cool, take away the parchment paper round from the bottom of the cake. If you need to level the top of your cake, do so now utilizing either a cake lever or knife. Ensure the cake is completely cooled, next which wrap the cake in plastic wrap & put it in the fridge. This cake is good for up to one week like this.
11. In a mixing big bowl, mix the butter & vegetable shortening, beat utilizing an electric mixer till fluffy, 2 min..
12. Add in the vanilla paste, beat utilizing electric mixer.
13. Begin to add the powdered sugar, about 1-2 c. At a time, mixing by hand first, next which with the electric mixer. Continue adding powdered sugar till the frosting tastes good to you.
14. Spread a small amount of buttercream on a 6 in. Round cardboard cake circle. Put your first layer of cake on top of the

cardboard. Put buttercream on top of the first layer & spread it as even as possible with an offset spatula. Decide how much or how little frosting you want in-between each layer, you can measure the frosting, i'd use 1/3 to 1/2 c. In between each layer.
15. Repeat this process for each layer of cake. When all of the layers are stacked & frosted, spread some frosting on the top of the cake.
16. Next, go back & fill in the gaps between the cake layers with more frosting. The frosting between the layers does not need to look perfect. Use a small offset spatula to get the frosting in between the layers & to spread it around the cake. Don't completely cover the cake layers as they are suppose to still be visible.
17. Place the entire cake in the freezer or fridge for 20 min. To harden the buttercream.
18. Once the caramel sauce is cooled, use a spoon to drizzle the caramel around the middle & sides of the cake, allowing it to drip down the sides.
19. For decoration, add cinnamon sticks or an additional garnish to the top of the cake.

Chocolate cheesecake with cookie dough (no bake)

What you need
Crust

- 4 tbsp butter, melted
- 2 1/2 c. Chocolate cookie crumbs
- Filling
- 4 (8-ounce) blocks cream cheese, softened to room temperature
- 1 c. Sugar
- 4 big eggs
- 1 tsp all-purpose flour
- 1 tsp vanilla
- 1 c. Sour cream

Cookie dough

- ½ c. Butter, softened
- ½ c. Sugar
- ½ c. Packed light brown sugar
- 2 tbsp water or milk
- 2 tsp vanilla extract
- 1 c. All-purpose flour
- 1/4 tsp salt
- 1 c. Mini chocolate chips
- An additional 1 c. Mini chocolate chips to fold right into the batter with the cookie dough balls

Garnish

- 1 c. Heavy whipping cream, whipped to stiff peaks
- Mini chocolate chips, for sprinkling

Directions

1. In a medium bowl, mix the butter & sugars for the cookie dough. Add the water (or milk), vanilla & blend. Mix in the flour, salt & the chocolate chips. The dough will be fairly soft. Lightly roll the

dough right into small balls & put them on a wax paper lined plate or baking sheet. Put them in the freezer to harden whereas making the remaining of the cheesecake.

2. Lightly grease the bottom & sides of a 10-inch springform pan. In a medium bowl, mix the butter with the chocolate cookie crumbs. Press onto the bottom & about midway up the sides of the prepared pan.
3. Using an electric mixer on high speed, beat the cream cheese, sugar, eggs & flour till smooth. Add the vanilla & sour cream & mix only till blended.
4. Pour half the batter right into the prepared crust. Lightly mix in the cookie dough balls & the additional 1 c. Mini chocolate chips right into the remaining batter. Pour right into the pan, spreading the batter to the sides of the pan & evening it out across the top. Wrap your springform pan tightly in a couple layers of foil. Put the pan directly right into a bigger pan that's filled about midway full of water. Obviously, you don't want the water to be higher than the foil, or the water will seep right into your cheesecake, & that would be bad news for all.
5. Bake the cheesecake at 325 degrees for one hour. Turn off the oven & prop the door open several inches. Let the cake sit in the oven for an additional 30 min.. Take away the cake from the oven & let it cool completely on a wire rack. Refrigerate till chilled to serve, cut right into slices & top with whipped cream & mini chocolate chips.

Caramel & chocolate cupcakes

What you need

Chocolate cupcakes

- 1/2 c. Salted butter
- 1 c. Sugar
- 2 eggs
- 1/2 tsp vanilla extract
- 6 tbsp water
- 6 tbsp cocoa powder
- 1 c. All purpose flour
- 1/2 tsp baking soda
- 6 tbsp kahlua

Kahlua icing

- 1/2 c. Salted butter
- 1/2 c. Shortening
- 4 c. Powdered sugar
- 4-5 tbsp kahlua

Caramel sauce

- A pinch of salt
- Sugar

Directions

1. Heat up oven to 350 degrees.
2. Beat butter & sugar till light in color & fluffy, about 2-3 min..
3. Add eggs, one at a time, beating only till blended.
4. Add vanilla, water & cocoa powder to an additional bowl & whisk till smooth.
5. Add chocolate mixture to batter & mix till combined. Scrape down the sides of the bowl as needed to ensure everything is well combined.
6. Combine flour & baking soda in a separate bowl.

7. Alternate adding the flour mixture & kahlua to the batter. Start by adding half of the dry mix, next which mix well. Add the kahlua & mix well, scrapes down the sides as needed. Add the remaining flour mixture & beat till smooth.
8. Fill cupcake liners about half way. Bake for 16-18 min., or till a toothpick inserted comes out with a few crumbs.
9. To make icing, beat butter & shortening till smooth.
10. Add 2 c. Of powdered sugar & beat till smooth.
11. Add 4 tbsp kahlua & remaining powdered sugar & beat till smooth. Add additional kahlua if needed to get the right icing consistency.
12. Pipe icing onto cupcakes.
13. Drizzle cupcakes with caramel sauce & a dash of sea salt.

Basic cream cake

What you need

For the cake

- 1 1/3 c. All-purpose flour
- 1/2 c. Unsweetened cocoa powder
- 3/4 tsp baking soda
- 1/2 tsp baking powder
- 1/4 tsp fine salt
- 1 1/4 sticks (10 tbsp) unsalted butter, room temperature
- 1/2 c. Packed light brown sugar
- 1/2 c. Granulated sugar
- 3 big eggs, room temperature
- 1 tsp vanilla extract
- 2 oz. Bittersweet chocolate, melted & cooled
- 1/2 c. Buttermilk, room temperature
- 1/2 c. Boiling water
- 2/3 c. Mini chocolate chips
- 1 tbsp all-purpose flour

For the frosting

- 8 oz. Cream cheese, room temperature
- Pinch of salt
- 1/2 c. Granulated sugar
- 1 tsp vanilla extract
- 2 c. Heavy cream, cold
- 3 c. Crushed oreos

Directions

1. Begin by making the cake. Heat up oven to 350 degrees f. Butter & flour three 8 in. Cake pans. Or use my favorite method: spray the pans with cooking spray, line the bottoms with parchment paper, & next which spray the parchment paper.
2. In a medium sized bowl, sift together the flour, cocoa powder, baking soda, baking powder, & salt.

3. In a big bowl utilizing an electric mixer, beat the butter on medium speed till creamy. Add the sugars & beat for an additional couple min., till light & fluffy. Add the eggs one at a time, beating next each addition till incorporated. Next which beat in the vanilla. Lower the mixer speed to low, & mix in the melted chocolate.
4. Add the dry ingredients & the buttermilk alternately, beginning & ending with the dry ingredients (do the dry ingredients in 3 batches & the buttermilk in 2). Beat next each addition only till incorporated. Use a rubber spatula to scrape down the sides & bottom of the bowl. Still mixing on low speed, add in the boiling water.
5. Toss the chocolate chips with the tbsp of flour, next which use a spatula to mix the chocolate chips in.
6. Divide the batter evenly among the three cake pans, & if necessary use a spatula to spread the batter out in the pans.
7. Bake for 15 to 18 min., till a toothpick inserted right into the middle comes out clean. Let the cakes cool in the pans for about 5 min., & next which take away them from the pans & put them on wire racks to complete cooling. When the cakes are completely cooled, wrap them separately in plastic wrap & put them in the freezer for at least an hour.

Frosting

1. In a big bowl mix the cream cheese, salt, & sugar. Cream together utilizing an electric mixer till smooth & creamy. Next which mix in the vanilla.
2. In a separate big bowl, use an electric mixer to beat the cream right into stiff peaks. Next which use a rubber spatula to lightly fold the cream right into the cream cheese mixture. Next which fold in the crushed oreos.
3. To frost the cake, put one cake layer on the bottom of your cake round or cake plate. Use an offset spatula to spread the top with a layer of frosting. Stack the second layer, next which an additional layer of frosting, next which the final layer. (it's best, if you can, to find the most flat layer for the top, & if your layers have risen quite a bit you can use a serrated knife to cut a bit off to make them flatter.) Next which spread the top & the sides with frosting. To make the icing smooth, run your spatula under hot water & lightly run it over the frosting.

4. Store the cake in the fridge till serving.

Chocolate bundt cake with biscuits dough (no bake)

What you need

- ¼ dough from chocolate chip cookies
- 1 c m&m's® milk chocolate harvest candies
- 1 c unsalted butter, softened
- 2 c sugar
- 2 eggs
- 4 tbsp cocoa powder
- 2 tsp vanilla extract
- 1 c sour cream
- 2 tsp baking soda
- 2½ c all-purpose flour
- ¼ tsp kosher salt
- 1 c boiling water
- 1x cream cheese

Directions

1. Prepare chocolate chip cookies as directed in the original recipe, swapping out the chocolate chips for the 1 c. Of m&m's®. Reserve ¼ of the dough, & wrap the remaining in plastic & put in the fridge for later use.
2. Heat up oven to 325 degrees. Grease a bundt pan with shortening or butter, next which cover in an even layer of cocoa powder. Tap out the excess & put to the side.
3. In a big mixing bowl beat the butter & sugar till light & fluffy, around 5 min.. Beat in the eggs, one at time, till fully incorporated, next which mix in the cocoa powder, vanilla extract, & sour cream.
4. Whisk together the flour, baking soda, & salt & slowly add to the mixture.
5. Gently beat in the boiling water on low speed. Pour the batter right into the prepared bundt pan.

6. Roll the cookie dough right into small balls & plop them right into the cake batter in the bundt cake, pressing down only slightly.
7. Bake for 60 min., or till a toothpick inserted right into the middle of the cake comes out clean.
8. Allow the cake to cool for 10 min. In the pan before flipping out onto a cooling rack to cool completely.
9. Take away the lid & foil from the icing, next which put in the microwave & heat for 15 second intervals till smooth & pourable. Slowly pour over cooled bundt cake, permit to set.

Pumpkin mousse sweet cake

What you need
For the crust

- 30-40 ginger snap cookies- crushed right into crumbs
- 3 tbsp of butter, melted
- Pinch of salt

For the filling

- 1 1/2 c. Heavy cream
- 12 oz cream cheese, softened
- 1 c. Pumpkin puree
- 1 1/2 tsp pumpkin pie spice
- 1 1/4 c. Powdered sugar
- 1/4 c. Chopped pecans
- 1/4 c. Toffee bits
- An extra pinch of cookie crumbs, pecans & toffee for garnish

Directions

1. Heat up the oven to 350f. In a big bowl, mix together the cookie crumbs, melted butter & salt. Mix to moisten & next which press right into the bottom of a 7-inch spring form pan or a 9 in. Pie dish.
2. Freeze crust for 10 min. & next which bake for 10 min.. Permit to cool on a wire rack whereas you prep the filling.
3. Whip the heavy cream in a stand mixer with a whisk attachment till medium-stiff peaks form. Scrape the whipped cream right into a separate bowl & wipe the mixer bowl out. (no need to wash it.)
4. Switch to the paddle attachment & beat the cream cheese till smooth & creamy. Add the pumpkin, pumpkin pie spice, & powdered sugar, mixing till smooth.
5. Take away the bowl from the mixer & steadily fold in about 2/3 of the whipped cream, saving the remaining for the topping. Mixture will be thick & creamy.

6. Fold in the chopped pecans & toffee bits. Spread the filling right into the cooled crust. Cover with plastic wrap & chill overnight or till filling has firmed up.
7. Spread the remaining whipped cream over the torte & garnish with a crushed gingersnap, chopped pecans, or toffee.
8. Chill till right before serving

Easy coconut & chocolate cake with rum

What you need

- 2 cans coconut milk
- 4 c. Maple syrup and/or agave nectar
- 5 tbsp vanilla
- 8 oz. Dark chocolate, around 70%
- 3 c. Unsweetened coconut flakes
- 1-1/2 c. Pecans
- 1 c. Coconut oil
- 2 tbsp rum
- 2 tbsp arrowroot powder
- 2-1/2 tsp salt
- 1-3/4 c. Brown rice flour
- 3/4 c. Garbanzo bean flour
- 1-1/3 c. Cocoa powder
- 1 tbsp baking soda

Chocolate cake

- 1-3/4 c. Brown rice flour
- 3/4 c. Garbanzo bean flour
- 1-1/3 c. Cocoa powder
- 1 tbsp baking soda
- 1-1/2 tsp salt
- 1 c. Coconut oil
- 2 c. Maple syrup
- 2 c. Water
- 1 tbsp vanilla

Coconut filling

- 1 can + 1 c. Coconut milk
- 1-1/4 c. Maple syrup or agave nectar
- 3/4 tsp. Salt
- 2 tbsp arrowroot powder

- 2 tbsp vanilla
- 3 c. Coconut flakes, toasted
- 1-1/2 c. Pecans

Rum syrup

- 1/2 c. Agave nectar
- 1/4 c. Water
- 2 tbsp rum
- 1 tbsp vanilla

Chocolate ganache

- 3/4 c. Coconut milk
- 1/4 c. Agave or maple syrup
- 1 tbsp vanilla
- 8 oz. Dark chocolate, chopped

Directions

1. Heat up the oven to 350f.
2. Grease two 9-inch cake pans & line the bottoms with parchment paper.
3. In a big bowl, whisk together the maple syrup, water, vanilla, & coconut oil. In a medium bowl, sift together the remaining ingredients & whisk together thoroughly. In a big bowl, whisk together the wet ingredients. Slowly whisk the dry ingredients right into the wet till there are no lumps.
4. Pour the batter right into the pans & bake for about 25-28 min., or till somewhat firm. Set the cakes on the counter to cool. When they are no longer hot, chill them in the fridge till you are ready to assemble the cake. Whereas the cakes are baking & cooling, make the coconut filling, rum syrup, & chocolate frosting.
5. To toast the coconut, spread evenly over a cookie sheet & bake for about 5 min. At 350f. Take it out, mix it around with a spatula, & put back in the oven, checking & stirring every few min., till evenly golden brown.

6. Whereas the coconut is toasting, spread the pecans over an additional cookie sheet & bake for 7-8 min., till well browned & fragrant. Take away from oven & let cool for a few min., next which transfer to a cutting board & chop.
7. In a stainless steel saucepan, bring the coconut milk, agave, & salt nearly to a boil, next which reduce heat to medium-low & simmer uncovered for around 10 min.. Try not to boil it, because the coconut milk can lose some of its flavor. Mix together the arrowroot & vanilla & whisk in. Cook for an additional 5 min. Or so, till thickened, whisking often to activate the arrowroot. Take away from heat & mix in the pecans & coconut. It will thicken slightly as it cools.
8. For the syrup, bring all ingredients to a boil in a small saucepan & simmer for around 10 min., till it resembles a thin syrup. It will thicken slightly upon cooling.
9. For the ganache, put the chocolate in a heat resistant bowl. In a small saucepan, heat the coconut milk, agave, & vanilla till it is about to boil. Pour over the chocolate & let it stand a minute. Mix with a spatula till smooth, slowly as to not create air bubbles. Let sit till room temperature, refrigerating if it is not firm enough to spread as frosting.
10. With a plastic spatula or utensil, loosen the cake around the edges of the pan. Take away the cake layers (this is easer if you refrigerate or freeze them for a short whereas beforehand) & put several toothpicks around the perimeter of the cake, midway down. Utilizing these as a guide, cut the cake in half horizontally with unflavored dental floss, wrapping it around the cake & tugging the ends toward each other till cut all the way through.
11. Set the first layer on a cake plate & with a pastry brush, douse liberally with the rum syrup. Spread a little less than 1/4 of the coconut frosting over the layer, being sure to reach the sides. Set an additional layer on top & repeat, brushing each layer with syrup & coconut filling. Be sure to save enough coconut filling for the top; it's okay if there is more frosting on top than in the other layers, but too little frosting on top would be a problem.
12. With a frosting spatula, ice the sides with the chocolate frosting, saving a little to pipe around the edges. Run the spatula under

hot water, dry, & use it to smooth the chocolate icing around the sides. With a piping bag & tip, pipe a decorative border of chocolate icing around the top & bottom edges of the cake.

Easy snack cake with lots of banana chunks & chocolate

What you need

Cake

- 2 c. All purpose flour
- 1 1/2 tsp baking powder
- 1/2 tsp salt
- 3/4 c. Unsalted butter, room temperature
- 1 c. Sugar
- 2 eggs
- 1 tsp vanilla
- 1/2 c. Milk
- 1 c. Mashed bananas
- 1 1/2 c. Chocolate chunks

Frosting

- 1 c. Butter, room temperature
- 3 c. Powdered sugar
- 1/3 c. Unsweetened cocoa
- 1 tsp vanilla
- 1 tbsp milk

Directions

1. Heat up oven to 350 f. Grease & flour a 9 x 13 in. Baking dish.
2. In a medium bowl, whisk together flour, baking powder & salt till combined. Put to the side.
3. In a mixing bowl, cream butter & sugar. Add eggs & vanilla & mix till combined. Add milk, continuing to mix till combined. With the mixer on low, slowly add flour & mix till only combined. Mix in mashed bananas. Mix in chocolate chunks.
4. Pour batter right into prepared dish & bake for 30-35 min. Or till done.
5. Take away from oven & cool completely.
6. For frosting: utilizing a mixer, beat butter & vanilla till smooth. Sift powdered sugar & cocoa together & slowly add to mixer

whereas on low. Increase to medium & beat till completely incorporated. Add milk a tsp at a time till desired creaminess.

Simple ducle de leche cake with banana layers

What you need

Topping

- 1 can (14 oz) sweetened condensed milk

Layered banana cake

- 3/4 c. Unsalted butter, room temperature
- 1 1/2 c. Extra fine granulated sugar
- 3 big eggs, room temperature
- 3/4 c. Plain yogurt
- 2 big ripe bananas, mashed
- 2 tsp vanilla extract
- 2 1/2 c. All-purpose flour
- 2 tsp baking powder
- 1/2 tsp baking soda
- 1/2 tsp salt

Dulce de leche frosting

- 16 oz. Cream cheese, room temperature
- 1 can (14 oz) sweetened condensed milk
- 2 c. Confectioners powdered sugar
- 1/2 tsp salt

Directions

1. Start by making the dulce de leche. Put two 14 ounce cans of sweetened condensed milk (labels take awayd) on their sides right into a big pot of boiling water. Lower heat & simmer for 2 1/2 hours. Ensure water covers top of can at all times (pouring in more water every 30 min. Or so). Permit cans to cool to room temperature before opening. This last step is very important because if you open a hot can the dulce de leche will gush out & burn you.

2. Whereas dulce de leche is cooling, make banana layer cake. Heat up oven to 350°f. Grease three 8-inch cake pans. Put to the side.
3. In a big bowl, cream butter & sugar on medium speed. Add in eggs, yogurt, mashed bananas, & vanilla extract, mixing well.
4. In a separate bowl, mix flour, baking powder, baking soda, & salt. Slowly fold right into wet ingredients, mixing till combined.
5. Scoop batter evenly right into prepared pans & bake for roughly 35 min., till each cake is golden brown & a knife comes out clean when inserted right into the center. Permit to cool for at least 10 min. Before removing from pan & cooling completely on a wire rack.
6. Whereas cakes are cooling, prepare dulce de leche frosting. Whip cream cheese, 1 can of prepared dulce de leche, & powdered sugar till smooth. Frost top of each cake layer & stack. Frost sides & top completely. Put in freezer for 5-10 min. To cool frosting.
7. In a small microwave-safe bowl, mix 1/2 of remaining can of dulce de leche with salt, next which heat in microwave for 25 sec.. Take away cake from fridge & drizzle warmed dulce de leche over top of cake.

Apple & coffee cake

What you need
Cake

- ½ c. Unsalted butter + more to grease pan
- 1½ c. Light brown sugar, lightly packed
- 2 big eggs
- 2 c. Flour
- 1 tsp baking soda
- 1½ tsp cinnamon
- 1 tsp allspice
- 1 tsp ground ginger
- ½ tsp ground cardamom
- ½ tsp salt
- 1 c. Plain greek yogurt
- 1 tsp vanilla extract
- 2 c. Peeled, cored & chopped apples

Crumble

- ½ c. Light brown sugar, lightly packed
- ½ c. Flour
- ½ tsp cinnamon
- ¼ tsp allspice
- 4 tbsp unsalted butter, softened

Caramel drizzle

- 1 c. Light brown sugar, lightly packed
- ½ c. Half-and-half
- 4 tbsp salted butter
- 1 tsp vanilla extract

Directions

1. Heat up oven to 350 degrees. Grease a 9"x13" glass baking dish with butter.

2. In a big bowl, cream together the butter & brown sugar till light & fluffy. Add the eggs one at a time, beating well next adding each. Fold in the yogurt & vanilla.
3. In a medium bowl, mix flour, baking soda, cinnamon, allspice, ginger, cardamom & salt. Slowly add dry ingredients to wet ingredients till fully combined. Fold in apples. Spread batter evenly across the greased baking dish.
4. In a small bowl, mix crumble ingredients. Dash over the batter in the baking dish. Bake for 35 min..
5. Whereas the cake is baking, prep the caramel sauce. Mix the brown sugar, half-and-half, butter & vanilla in a small saucepan. Cook over medium-low heat, stirring slowly, till the sugar dissolves & the mixture thickens. This should take around 8-10 min.. Take away from heat & pour sauce right into a jar. Refrigerate till cooled.
6. Once the cake is out of the oven, drizzle caramel over the cake. Serve cake warm.

The big cake: chocolate, buttercream frosting & ganache

What you need

Triple layer chocolate cake

- 2¼ c. Plain flour
- 2¼ c. White sugar
- 1½ c. Unsweetened cocoa powder
- 2¼ tsp baking soda
- 2¼ tsp baking powder
- 1½ tsp salt
- 3 eggs, at room temperature
- 1½ c. Buttermilk
- ¾ c. Canola oil
- 2 tsp vanilla extract
- 1 c. + 2 tbsp hot coffee
- ¾ c. Semi-sweet chocolate chunks or chips

Salted caramel

- ½ c. Water
- 1½ c. Caster sugar (330g)
- 90g unsalted butter, cubed
- ¾ c. Cream
- ½ -1 tsp table salt
- 1 tsp vanilla extract

Caramel popcorn

- ½ c. Salted caramel
- A few c. Of plain popcorn (1/4-1/3 c. Of kernels)
- ¼ tsp baking soda

Salted caramel cream cheese buttercream

- 225g unsalted butter, softened at room temperature
- 120g philadelphia cream cheese
- ½ c. Salted caramel, at room temperature

- 1 tsp vanilla
- 3.5-4 c. Icing sugar (430-480g)

Chocolate ganache

- 200g dark chocolate, very finely chopped
- ½ c. Cream

Directions

1. Triple layer chocolate cake
2. Heat up the oven to 175°c. Grease & line three x 20cm round cake tins with baking paper.
3. In a bowl, sift together the flour, sugar, cocoa, baking soda, baking powder & salt. Put to the side.
4. In a separate bowl, beat together the eggs, buttermilk, canola oil & vanilla till smooth.
5. Steadily add the dry ingredients to the wet ingredients on a low speed till just about combined. Add the hot coffee & mix till only combined. Lightly fold in the chocolate chunks.
6. Divide the batter among the three cake tins & bake for 20-25 min. Or till the tops are only set & a skewer comes out only clean. Take away from the oven to cool. Next 20 min. Or so, take away from the tins & put cakes on cooling rakes or paper-lined flat plates to cool completely. The cakes need to be completely cool before you start frosting - normally a couple of hours.
7. Make the salted caramel & caramel popcorn in the few days before you assemble the cake, & make the buttercream straight away prior to assembly.
8. For the caramel, heat the butter & cream in a small saucepan over a low heat till the butter is melted & the mixture is combined. Take away from the heat.
9. Place the sugar & water in a big pot over a low heat, stirring till the sugar is dissolved. Stop stirring & cook on a high heat till the mixture reaches a dark amber colour (usually about 10 min. & when it reaches ~175°c/350°f on a candy thermometer).

10. Quickly whisk in the cream & butter mixture, but be careful here as it boils up vigorously with a lot of steam, so you may want to wear an oven mitt or much like protect your hand.
11. Take away from the heat & add the salt & vanilla extract, stirring to combine. Leave to cool & next which taste to adjust the salt.
12. Put to the side in a jar or similar - you will be utilizing this caramel in the popcorn, the buttercream & to drip over the completed cake.
13. Heat up the oven to 150°c & line a baking tray with baking paper. Make the popcorn according to packet instructions, in a popcorn machine or in a pot
14. Place popped popcorn in a big bowl.
15. Heat the caramel till just about boiling. Add the baking soda, mix as it fluffs up & quickly pour over the popcorn. Toss the caramel through the popcorn till evenly coated & next which spread out over the baking tray in an even layer. Bake for 10 min., turning when next 5 min.. Leave to cool. Store in an airtight container.
16. Using a stand mixer fitted with a paddle attachment or a handheld electric mixer, beat the softened butter till pale & creamy, about five min..
17. Add the cream cheese, caramel & vanilla & beat at low speed till fully incorporated. Steadily increase speed & continue beating till light & fluffy, scraping down the sides of the bowl with a spatula, about 3-4 min..
18. Add the icing sugar in three lots, beating on low speed till combined. Beat on medium high speed till smooth & fluffy whereas scraping down the sides (about 2 min.)
19. Make the salted caramel & the salted caramel popcorn. Only before assembly, make the salted caramel cream cheese buttercream.
20. If your cakes have domed at all, cut off the top with a serrated knife to flatten.
21. Place the first layer, flat side up (upside-down) on a cake stand. Cut out few strips of baking paper & slide under the edges of the cake (see picture above) to catch any drips, so when you have completed icing the cake you can pull them out & end up with a clean-edged cake stand/plate.

22. With a knife or offset spatula, spread the top with caramel buttercream (use only under a cup, or enough to make a layer a similar size to in the picture). It doesn't matter if the buttercream goes over the edge a little as it will be incorporated right into the frosting on the sides of the cake. Put the second layer on top & spread evenly with frosting. Repeat with the third layer, but this time also frost the sides of the cake with the remaining frosting.
23. If you are at all worried about the structural stability of your, cut 3-4 wooden skewers to the height of your cake & poke them through the three layers to stop them from sliding over each other.
24. Place in the fridge to set slightly whereas you make the chocolate ganache.
25. Place very finely chopped chocolate a small bowl. Bring cream to boiling point & pour over the chocolate, making sure the chocolate is all covered. Leave for five min. Next which mix with a fork till smooth & glossy.
26. Once you have made the chocolate ganache, take away the cake from the fridge & pour the ganache over the top of the cake. Use a knife or offset spatula to spread it over the top, creating drips down the sides.
27. Leave to set for 10-15 min.. At this point you can take away the baking paper strips from the cake stand.
28. Just before serving, stack the caramel popcorn on the top of the cake, interspersing handfuls of popcorn with drizzles of extra salted caramel to stick it all together. You will probably end up with extra popcorn.
29. Drizzle any extra salted caramel over the sides of the cake.

Pumkin cake v2

What you need

- 1 box yellow cake mix
- 1 can (16 oz.) Pumpkin
- 1 can (12 oz.) Evaporated milk
- 3 eggs
- 1 1/2 c. Sugar
- 4 tsp pumpkin pie spice
- 1/2 tsp salt
- 1/2 c. Chopped pecans
- 1/2 c. Chopped walnuts
- 1 c. Melted butter
- Whipped topping

Directions

1. Heat up oven to 350f.
2. Grease bottom of 9x13 pan.
3. Combine pumpkin, evaporated milk, eggs, sugar, pumpkin pie spice & salt in bowl next which pour it right into your pan.
4. Dash your dry yellow cake mix evenly over pumpkin mixture.
5. Dash chopped pecans & walnuts over the cake mix.
6. Drizzle melted butter evenly over everything.
7. Bake your pumpkin crunch cake for 55 min. Or till top is turning golden brown. Cool completely, cut & serve with whipped topping. Refrigerate leftovers.

The simple recipe: chocolate cake newbie level

What you need

Cake

- 1 c. All-purpose flour
- ½ c. Whole-wheat or white whole-wheat flour
- 1 ½ c. Unsweetened cocoa powder
- ½ c. White sugar
- ½ c. Brown sugar, packed
- ½ tsp baking soda
- ½ tsp baking powder
- ¾ tsp salt
- 1 c. Sour cream
- ½ c. Milk
- 4 eggs, beaten
- ½ c. Butter, melted
- ¼ c. Maple syrup
- 1 tsp vanilla extract
- 1 c. Semisweet chocolate chips

For the frosting

- 2 c. Chocolate chips
- 1 c. Sour cream, at room temperature

Directions

1. Heat up the oven to 350° f. Butter a 9- x 9-inch baking pan, line it with parchment paper, & butter the paper, too. In a big bowl, mix together all of the dry ingredients (flour through salt). In an additional bowl, mix together the wet ingredients (sour cream through vanilla extract). Make a well in the middle of the dry ingredients, add the wet ingredients, & fold with a rubber spatula till everything is only incorporated. Fold in the chocolate chips. Bake the cake for about 50 min., or till the middle is set & a tester comes out clean.

2. Once the cake has cooled completely, melt the chocolate chips in a double boiler or in the microwave. Mix the melted chocolate chips & the room temperature sour cream utilizing either a whisk, a stand mixer, or hand beaters. Let the frosting cool slightly so that it thickens a bit. If it becomes too thick & clumpy for your liking, lightly melt it in a double boiler or the microwave & whisk till smooth. Use a rubber or offset spatula to frost the cake.

Strawberry cheesecake (no bake)

What you need

- 200g gluten free digestive biscuits
- 100g unsalted butter, melted
- 500g philadelphia cream cheese
- 1 tsp vanilla extract
- 170g icing sugar
- 135g pack of strawberry or raspberry jelly cubes
- 100ml boiling water
- 200ml evaporated milk
- 400g strawberries
- Zest of 1 orange

Directions

1. Put the biscuits right into a big bowl & crush right into crumbs utilizing the end of a rolling pin, next which mix in the melted butter till thoroughly combined. Pour right into a 20cm diameter loose bottomed cake tin & push down so you have a tightly packed, level layer covering the bottom of the cake tin. Put in the fridge whilst you start on the vanilla layer.
2. In a bowl, add 300g of the cream cheese & mix with a whisk till the cream cheese has loosened to a smooth consistency. Add the vanilla extract & 100g of the icing sugar next which whisk again till combined. Take about 4 or 5 strawberries & chop right into chunks, next which add them to the mixture & mix in lightly . Take the biscuit base out of the fridge & spread this vanilla layer on top. Put back in the fridge.
3. Next make the mousse layer. Chop the jelly right into chunks & mix with 100ml of boiling water till dissolved. If the chunks aren't dissolving well, next which put it in the microwave for 30 sec. Or so & mix again. Put to the side to cool slightly. Add the remaining 200g of cream cheese to a big bowl & mix utilizing the whisk till it's smooth. Whisk in the remaining icing sugar, next which whisk in the evaporated milk. Finally add the jelly mixture

& whisk in. Pour this mixture onto the top of the cheesecake & put back in the fridge to set for at least an hour.
4. Once the mousse layer has set, you can decorate with the strawberries. Take the cheesecake out of the fridge & prudently slide out of the cake tin & onto a plate. Slice the strawberries right into thin slices. Arrange the strawberries in a circle around the cheesecake, starting from the outside & working your way in. Overlay the strawberries slightly so you're not left with any gaps. Dash the top with the orange zest & serve.

Blueberry cheesecake v2

What you need

Crust

- 2 c. Raw nuts
- 1 c. Dates or raisins
- Pinch of salt

Orange cheesecake

- 3 c. Cashews
- 3/4 c. Fresh orange juice
- 1/2 c. Agave/maple syrup
- 1/2 c. Melted coconut oil
- Juice of one lemon
- Zest of all the oranges you juiced
- Pinch of salt

Blueberry layer

- 2 c. Organic blueberries
- 1/4 c. Of the orange cheesecake mixture

Directions

1. To make the crust: process the nuts & dates/raisins in your food processor till the nuts have become crumbs & the mixture sticks together when you press it. Press right into the bottom of a spring-form pan & put in the fridge.
2. To make the orange cheesecake: blend all ingredients (excluding orange zest) in your high speed blender till very smooth, next which add in the orange zest with a spoon. Reserve 1/4 c. Of this mixture for the blueberry topping – pour the remaining onto your crust & put in the freezer.
3. To make the blueberry layer: blend the blueberries & the 1/4 c. Of cheesecake mixture in your food processor or blender till creamy but still with small pieces of blueberry for texture.

Spread this over your cheesecake & keep in the freezer or fridge overnight.

Dark cake

What you need

- ½ cup/50g unsweetened cocoa powder
- ½ cup/100g light brown sugar, packed
- 1 tsp instant coffee
- 1 cup/250 ml hot water
- 1 stick/125g softened butter, plus some for greasing
- 1 tbsp vegetable oil
- ¾ cup/150g superfine/caster sugar
- 1½ cups/225g all-purpose/plain flour
- ½ tsp baking powder
- ½ tsp baking soda
- 1 tbsp vanilla extract
- 2 eggs

For the frosting

- ½ c. Milk
- 2 tbsp light brown sugar
- 1½ sticks (3/4 cup) butter, cubed
- 11 oz. Dark chocolate, chopped

Directions

1. Heat up the oven to 350 degrees f/180 c.
2. In a mixing bowl whisk together the coco powder, instant coffee, brown sugar & hot water. Put to the side.
3. In a separate bowl, mix the flour, baking powder, & baking soda together & put to the side.
4. Cream the butter & sugar together, beating well till pale & fluffy.
5. Add the oil & the vanilla extract.
6. Add eggs, one at a time with a c. Of the flour mixture in between eggs.
7. Mix in the remaining of the dried ingredients for the cake & fold in the cocoa mixture.

8. Divide the batter evenly between the two greased 9-inch round pans & bake for about 25-30 min., or till a cake tester comes out clean.
9. Take the pans out & put them on a wire rack for 5 to 10 min., before turning the cakes out to cool.
10. For the frosting: put the milk, 2 tbsp dark brown sugar & butter in a pan over medium heat & bring to a simmer
11. Place the chopped chocolate in a heat proof bowl. Add the simmering milk mixture & leave to sit for 5 min. Or till the chocolate softens enough to whisk & next which whisk till smooth & glossy.
12. Let it stand for about 1 hour, whisking now & again often to keep it from becoming too stiff.
13. Frost the cooled cakes starting with topping one with a half a c. Of icing & placing the other on top (bottom side up). Use the remaining frosting to frost the remaining of the cake. If the frosting is quite soft when you've iced the cake, you can put it in the fridge till its set.

Chocolate cheesecake v2

What you need
Cookie dough

- 1/2 c. Butter
- 1/3 c. White sugar
- 1/3 c. Dark brown sugar
- 1 1/2 tsp vanilla extract
- 1 c. Plus 2 tbsp flour
- Pinch salt
- 1 c. Chocolate chips

Cookie crumb crust

- 1 1/3 c. Graham cracker crumbs
- 3 tbsp sugar
- 1/3 c. Melted butter

Vanilla cheesecake

- 2/3 c. Sugar
- 2 eggs
- 2 tsp vanilla extract
- 2 eight ounce packages oz. Cream cheese
- 1/2 c. Whipping cream

Chocolate ganache

- 1/3 c. Whipping cream
- 1 1/3 c. Chocolate chips

Vanilla whipped cream

- 1 c. Whipping cream
- 3 rounded tbsp icing sugar (powdered sugar)
- 1 tsp pure vanilla extract

Directions

1. For the dough, mix the sugar, butter, vanilla extract & fold in only till a dough forms. Add the flour & salt. Finally mix in the chocolate chips.
2. Chill the dough in the fridge for at least an hour.
3. Break off small nuggets of the dough about the size of the top of your forefinger. Put them on a parchment lined tray & keep chilled in the fridge. About 3/4 of these dough nuggets will go right into the cheesecake batter. Reserve the other 1/4 to garnish the cheesecake next it is baked, cooled & glazed.
4. For the crumb crust, in a small bowl, mix the graham cracker crumbs, sugar & the melted butter.
5. Press right into the bottom of a lightly greased or parchment lined 9 in. Spring form pan. (grease bottom only!) Parchment paper is ideal here because it makes it very easy to release the cheesecake from the bottom of the pan.
6. For the vanilla cheesecake, cream together the cream cheese, sugar, the eggs(one at at time), vanilla extract. Finally blend in a ½ c. Of whipping cream.
7. Fold in 3/4 of the chilled cookie dough pieces. Pour over the prepared base & bake at 300 degrees f for 60 – 70 min.. The cheesecake does not have to brown at all in order to be fully baked; the surface of the cheesecake should lose any shine when the cake is properly baked. It can still be slightly wobbly only at the middle at this point.
8. Take away the cake from the oven & run a sharp knife completely around the edge of the pan. This will permit for the cheesecake to shrink as it cools & hopefully not crack (allow the cheesecake to cool thoroughly on a wire rack at room temperature. (not in the fridge). Refrigerate next fully cooled.
9. Top with chocolate ganache & vanilla whipped cream as well as the reserved cookie dough pieces.
10. In a small saucepan, heat just about to boiling:
11. Take away from heat & pour in

12. Let stand for 5 min., next which mix till smooth. Pour evenly over the cheesecake when it is still in the pan. Return to the fridge to let the chocolate set.
13. Beat to firm peaks & use to garnish the edges of the cheesecake. If you don't have a piping bag only cut a half in. Opening off the corner of a big ziploc bag & use that to squeeze the whipped cream onto the cheesecake.

Simple lava chocolate cake

What you need

- 4 oz. Semi-sweet baking chocolate, chopped
- 6 t. Butter, cubed
- ⅓ c. Granulated sugar
- 2 eggs
- 4 t. All-purpose flour
- 2 tsp knees peanut butter
- 1 + ½ t. Unsweetened cocoa powder

Directions

1. Heat up oven to 425 degrees. Spray 2 8 oz. Ramekins with non-stick cooking spray. Put 1 tbsp of cocoa powder in the first ramekin. Swirl the cocoa powder all around the ramekin & tap out the extra in the second ramekin. Add in the remaining ½ tbsp of cocoa powder & discard the excess cocoa powder when ramekin is covered.
2. In a medium-sized microwave-safe bowl, add in the chopped semi-sweet chocolate & butter. Microwave in 30 second intervals & mix next each 30 sec.. Do this 3 to 4 times till the chocolate is smooth & completely melted.
3. Put to the side & let cool for 10 min..
4. Add in the granulated sugar & eggs & whisk till thoroughly incorporated.
5. Add in the all-purpose flour. Utilizing a spatula, mix till the flour is barely combined.
6. Pour batter right into the 2 ramekins.
7. Place a big tsp of the peanut butter in the middle of each ramekin. Ensure to press it down a little & cover it with the cake batter.
8. Place the two ramekins on a quarter sheet pan & put in the oven. Bake for about 14 min.. The outside of the cakes will be baked & the middle will still be very jiggly.

9. Serve straight away. If you're feeling crazy, add a scoop of ice cream to the cake.

Oreo cake

What you need

Chocolate layer cake

- 3/4 c. Unsweetened cocoa powder (not dutch process)
- 1 & 1/2 c. Granulated sugar
- 1 & 1/2 c. Cake flour1
- 1 tsp baking soda
- 1/4 tsp salt
- 2 big eggs, at room temperature2
- 1/4 c. Vegetable or canola oil
- 1 c. Full fat sour cream or full fat greek yogurt, at room temperature
- 2 tsp vanilla extract
- 1/2 c. Hot coffee or hot water
- 1 c. Milk chocolate chopped
- 1 15.25 ounce package oreos

Oreo cream

- 1/4 c. Unsalted butter, softened to room temperature
- 1/4 c. Shortening3
- 2 & 1/2 c. Confectioners' sugar
- 2 tbsp milk or cream
- 2 tsp vanilla extract

Chocolate buttercream

- 3/4 c. Unsalted butter, softened to room temperature
- 1/2 c. Unsweetened cocoa powder
- 1 tsp vanilla extract
- 4 c. Confectioners' sugar
- 1/4 c. Milk or cream
- 16 additional oreo cookies, pulsed right into a fine crumb

Directions

1. Position oven rack in the middle of the oven. Heat up to 350°f (177°c). Generously spray two 9-inch cake pans with nonstick spray. Line the bottom of the pan with oreos in a single layer. Put to the side.
2. In a big bowl, utilizing a handheld or stand mixer fitted with a paddle attachment, blend the cocoa powder, sugar, cake flour, baking soda, & salt together on low speed for 30 sec.. Add the eggs, oil, sour cream, & vanilla & mix for 1 minute on medium-low speed.
3. Take away the bowl from the mixer & add the coffee & chocolate chips; mix to combine. Some of the chocolate chips will melt as you stir. Try to avoid over mixing the batter.
4. Pour the batter right into the prepared cake pans over the oreos. Bake for 28-32 min. Or till a toothpick inserted in the middle of the cakes comes out clean. Permit cakes to cool completely in the pan on a wire rack.
5. Whereas the cake cools, make the oreo cream filling. In a big bowl, utilizing a handheld or stand mixer fitted with a paddle attachment, cream the butter & shortening together on high speed till fluffy. Add the confectioners' sugar, 1 c. At a time, alternating with the milk/cream & vanilla. The filling will be very thick, but you may add more milk/cream if you prefer. Put to the side in the fridge.
6. Whereas the cake cools, make the chocolate buttercream. In a big bowl, utilizing a handheld or stand mixer fitted with a paddle attachment, cream the butter on high speed till fluffy, about 1 minute. Beat in the cocoa powder & vanilla on low speed, next which add the confectioners' sugar 1 c. At a time, alternating with the milk/cream. The buttercream will be thick. Put to the side in the fridge.
7. Once the cakes are cooled, assemble the cake. Put 1 cooled layer on a cake stand or big plate, oreo cookie side down. Utilizing an offset spatula or knife, cover the top with a 1-inch thick layer of oreo cream filling. Top with the 2nd cake, oreo cookie side up. Cover the tall layer cake with chocolate buttercream. Working

quickly, cover the cake in oreo crumbs. This will get a little messy, but only pat them up the sides with your hands & all over the top of the cake.
8. Slice & serve cake. Leftover cake can be covered & stored in the fridge for up to 3 days.
9. Make ahead tip: the cake layers can be baked, cooled, & covered tightly at room temperature overnight. Likewise, the frosting & filling can be prepared next which covered & refrigerated overnight. Assemble & frost the cake the next day when you are ready to serve. Frosted cake can be frozen up to 2 months if you have room in the freezer. Thaw overnight in the fridge & bring to room temperature before serving.

Upside-down meyer cake

What you need

- ¾ c. Butter, softened
- ⅔ c. Packed brown sugar
- 3-4 meyer lemons
- Zest of 2 big meyer lemons
- 1 c. Granulated sugar
- 2 eggs
- 1 c. All-purpose flour
- ¾ c. Cornmeal
- 2 tsp baking powder
- ¼ tsp salt
- ½ c. Milk
- 1 tsp vanilla extract

Directions

1. Heat up oven to 350°. Spray the inside of a 9-inch springform pan with oil & line the bottom with parchment paper. Spray the inside of the paper; put to the side.
2. In a small saucepan over medium heat, bring brown sugar & ¼ c. Of the butter to a boil, stirring continuously . Pour mixture right into prepared pan & spread evenly.
3. Thinly slice meyer lemons*, removing any seeds & discarding the ends. Layer lemon slices in pan, starting with one in the centre & working outwards. Slices should overlap by about half.
4. In a small bowl, mix together flour, cornmeal, baking powder, & salt; put to the side.
5. In an additional small bowl, mix milk & vanilla; put to the side.
6. Add ⅓ of flour mixture to butter mixture, scraping the sides of the bowl as needed. Add half the milk, mixing till well combined. Continue alternating adding the flour & milk all mixed. Pour batter right into pan & spread evenly.

7. Bake till cake has browned & springs back to the touch, 50-55 min.. Let cool in pan for about 2 hours before running a knife around the edges of the pan & releasing the cake.
8. Flip, cut with a serrated knife, & serve.

Lemon & blueberry cheesecake

What you need

Blueberry sauce

- 2 c. Fresh blueberries
- ½ c. Water
- ½ c. Sugar
- 2 tbsp cornstarch, mixed with 2 tbsp cold water
- 1 tbsp vanilla extract

For the crust

- 2 c. Graham cracker crumbs
- 8 tbsp unsalted butter, melted
- 2 tbsp granulated sugar

Cheesecake filling

- 4 packages (8 oz.) Cream cheese, softened
- 1 c. Sour cream
- 2 tbsp cornstarch
- 3 eggs
- 1⅓ c. Sugar
- ½ c. Graham cracker crumbs
- Juice of one meyer lemon

- Zest from one meyer lemon

What to do

Preparing the blueberry sauce

1. The sauce can be made whereas the cake is cooking or many days in advance.
2. In a big saucepan over medium heat, mix blueberries, water & sugar. Mix frequently, but careful not to crush the berries, bring to a low boil.
3. In a small bowl, mix the cornstarch with cold water till combined.
4. Slowly mix the cornstarch right into the blueberries, careful not to crush them. Simmer till the homemade blueberry sauce is thick enough to cover the back of a metal spoon, about 10 min..
5. Take away from heat & lightly mix in vanilla.
6. Let the sauce cool at room temperature. Measure ½ c. For your recipe, store the remaining in jars in the fridge.

   ii.

Preparing the crust

1. In a big bowl, mix the crumbs with melted butter & granulated sugar with a rubber spatula till combined.
2. Press the mixture right into the bottom of a 9inch spring form cake pan & slightly up the sides. Ensure it is tight & compact.
3. Chill the crust for 15 min..

Cheesecake filling

1. Heat up oven to 325f.
2. In the bowl of an electric mixer fitted with the whisk attachment beat cream cheese on medium speed till fluffy. Add the sugar, cornstarch, lemon juice, lemon zest & beat till combined.
3. Add eggs, one at a time, beating till only combined next each addition. On low speed beat in sour cream only till combined.
4. Take away crust from the fridge & pour the batter right into the crust.

5. In circles pour the blueberry sauce over the cheesecake & with the edge of a spatula create swirls & mix the blueberry sauce right into the cheesecake filling. Prudently not to over mix.
6. Bake for about 1¼ hours or till middle is just about set. Cool on a wire rack for 15 min.. Dash graham crackers on top & loosen sides of pan & continue cooling on wire rack till the cheesecake is at room temperature.
7. Transfer to the fridge. Refrigerate overnight or at least 6 hours before serving.
8. The cheesecake can be served with warm blueberry sauce.
9. Store in fridge.

Chocolate brownie cake with mascarpone

What you need
For the brownie layers

- 1 c. Unsalted butter, melted
- 2 c. Granulated sugar
- 4 big eggs
- 1 c. All-purpose flour
- ½ c. Unsweetened cocoa powder
- ½ tsp salt
- ½ tsp baking soda

For the coconut filling

- 1 c. Walnuts, measure next which grind
- 1 c. Coconut flakes
- ½ c. Heavy cream
- ½ c. Sugar
- 1 egg yolk
- 3 tbsp. Butter, room temperature

For the vanilla buttercream

- 3 sticks of butter, softened
- 8 oz mascarpone cheese, chilled
- 2½ c. Powdered sugar
- 1 vanilla bean
- Pinch of salt

For the chocolate ganache

- 8 oz. Semisweet chocolate, chopped
- 2 tbsp. Light corn syrup
- 3 tbsp unsalted butter
- 1 c. Heavy cream

What to do

1. Heat up oven to 350°f.
2. Grease bottom of 3 8inch round pans with melted butter or cooking spray.
3. In the bowl of an electric mixer, whisk together melted butter & sugar till smooth. Add in each egg one at a time on low speed & whisk till well combined.
4. Using a big rubber spatula, lightly mix in flour, cocoa, baking soda & salt.
5. Spread batter right into the pans & bake for 25-30 min. Till set.
6. Take away & let cool completely before assembling the cake.

For the coconut filling

1. Place the butter, walnuts & coconut in a big bowl & put to the side.
2. In a medium sauce pan, on low/medium heat, mix together the heavy cream, sugar & egg yolk till the mixture starts to thicken & coats the back of a spoon (180 degrees f.). Pour the hot custard straight away onto the walnut-coconut mixture & mix till the butter is melted. Cool completely to room temperature before topping the brownie layers.

For the vanilla mascarpone buttercream

1. Place softened butter & mascarpone right into the bowl of an electric stand mixer that has been fitted with the whisk attachment. Turn the mixer on a medium setting & cream till it smooth & combined, 2 - 3 min..
2. Add sugar, ½ a c. At a time. Add vanilla beans & a pinch of salt & whisk till well-incorporated.
3. If the frosting is too thick add heavy cream one tbsp at a time till it has reached the desired consistency.

For the chocolate ganache

1. Place the chocolate, corn syrup & butter in a medium bowl. Heat the cream in a small saucepan over medium heat till it only starts

to boil. Take away from heat & pour over the chocolate. Let stand one minute, next which mix till smooth. Cool to room temperature.

Assemble the cake

1. Take away the cooled brownie layers from the pans. Set the first cake layer on a cake plate.
2. Top with a half of the coconut walnut filling, spread it evenly. Top the coconut wittier with ⅓ of the frosting, also spread evenly. Repeat the process with the second brownie cake layer. Third (top) layer, is covered in frosting only, no coconut mixture.
3. Pour the chocolate ganache on top of the cake, distribute evenly & also ice the sides of the cake whereas the ganache is dripping down.
4. Decorate with frosting if you have any remaining & chocolate dashs.
5. Chill the cake for at least 2 hours before serving.

Dark & white chocolate truffle cake

What you need

Cake layers

- 6 oz. Bittersweet chocolate, finely chopped
- 1 stick unsalted butter
- ½ c. Unsweetened cocoa powder
- 1 c. Water
- ⅔ c. Mascarpone cheese, room temperature
- 3 big eggs
- 3 big egg yolks
- 1 c. Granulated sugar
- 1 c. Light brown sugar
- 1¼ c. All-purpose flour
- 1 tbsp baking soda
- 2 tsp baking powder
- 1 tsp salt

White chocolate whipped ganache

- 1 pound white chocolate, chopped
- ¾ c. Heavy cream
- 2 tbsp unsalted butter
- 2 c. Powdered sugar

Milk chocolate whipped ganache

- 1⅓ c. Heavy cream
- 10 oz. Milk chocolate, chopped
- 3 c. Powdered sugar

Dark chocolate frosting

- 4 oz. Dark chocolate, chopped
- 3 tbsp granulated sugar
- ¼ c. Corn syrup
- 6 tbsp unsweetened cocoa powder

- ¼ c. Plus 2 tbsp water
- 1 pound (4 sticks) unsalted butter, softened
- ¾ c. Powdered sugar

Cake truffles

- 1½ c. Milk chocolate ganache
- Cake edges & top
- 10 oz. Dark chocolate

What to do
Cake layers

1. Heat up the oven to 350°.
2. Spray with non stick baking spray a 18x13 in. Sheet cake pan & line with parchment paper, spray the parchment paper with baking spray. Put to the side.
3. In a medium saucepan, melt the chopped chocolate with the butter over very low heat, stirring lightly . When chocolate has completely melted, take away the mixture from the heat & let cool slightly.
4. In a small saucepan, mix cocoa powder with the water & bring to a boil, whisking continously . Let it cool slightly & next which whisk the mixture right into the melted chocolate. Whisk in the mascarpone cream cheese.
5. In a big bowl or in the bowl of an electric mixer fitted with the whisk attachment, beat the whole eggs, egg yolks & both sugars at medium speed till pale & fluffy, about 5 min.. Beat in the chocolate mixture.
6. In a medium bowl, whisk together the dry ingredients: flour, baking soda, baking powder & salt. Utilizing a spatula, lightly fold in the dry ingredients right into the cake batter till fully incorporated.
7. Transfer the batter to the prepared pan & bake the cake in the lower third of the oven for 25 to 30 min., till the centers spring back when lightly pressed.
8. Let the cake cool completely in the pans.

White chocolate whipped ganache

1. In a medium bowl set over a medium saucepan of simmering water, melt the white chocolate. Take away from the heat & put to the side.
2. Discard the water from the sauce pan add the heavy cream & butter to the saucepan & heat till the butter is melted & small bubbles appear around the edges.
3. Whisk the hot cream mixture right into the white chocolate. Lumps will start to appear, don't be afraid, continue to quickly mix till the mixtures mix & the lumps disappear. Set the bowl in a cool put for at least 1 hour.
4. Once the ganache has cooled down, utilizing a hand mixer or an electric mixer whisk in the powdered sugar. When you did this cool the mixture for a few min. Only & start layering it on the cake as if placed in the fridge it will stiffen.

Milk chocolate whipped ganache

1. In a medium saucepan, heat the cream till small bubbles appear around the edges. Put the chopped chocolate in a heatproof bowl & pour the hot cream on top. Let stand for 2 to 3 min., till the chocolate has melted, next which whisk till shiny & smooth. Set the bowl in a cool put for at least 1 hour.
2. Once the ganache has cooled down, measure 1½ c. Of chocolate ganache & put to the side for the cake truffles.
3. Using a hand mixer or an electric mixer whisk in the powdered sugar right into the remaining chocolate ganache. When you did this cool the mixture for a few min. Only & start layering it on the cake as if placed in the fridge it will stiffen.

Dark chocolate frosting

1. In a medium saucepan, melt the chocolate over very low heat, stirring frequently. In a small saucepan, whisk together the granulated sugar, corn syrup, cocoa & water & bring to a boil, whisking continously . Take away from the heat & whisk in the melted chocolate. Let cool completely, about 30 min..
2. In the bowl of an electric mixer fitted with a wire whisk, beat the butter at medium speed till light & fluffy. Add the cooled chocolate

mixture. With a spatula scrape the bowl & whisk till fully combined. With the mixer on low speed, beat in the confectioners' sugar, scraping & beating till fully combined.

Cake arrangement

1. Cut out a 5-by-11-inch cardboard rectangle.
2. Prudently transfer the cake from the pan to a working area. You will need someone's help on this one, as its easier if you prudently hold the parchment paper with the cake up & someone is pulling the pan.
3. Once the cake was transferred on a working area, put the cardboard one in. From the left corner & cut a rectangle. Repeat moving to the right, you will end up with 3 rectangles. Utilizing a cake leveler, level the top of the rectangles.
4. Transfer the cake edges & take awayd tops to a medium bowl & crumble with your hands. Put to the side as that is what we will be utilizing for the cake truffles. Utilizing a cake lifter, transfer one of the rectangles to a flat rectangle platter, that is our first layer.
5. Spoon dollops of milk chocolate whipped ganache onto the cake & spread it evenly, make the layer as thick as you want, you must have only a little chocolate whipped ganache leftover.
6. Top with an additional cake rectangle & top it with white chocolate whipped ganache. Top with the final layer, if you have chocolate whipped ganache left spread it on the top layer.
7. Coat the sides & top of the cake with a thick layer of chocolate frosting & refrigerate to set the frosting.
8. Cake truffles:
9. Mix cake truffles with chocolate ganache in a bowl utilizing a fork till well combined, you can make small golf ball sized cake balls & put them on parchment paper & refrigerate till firm.
10. Or you can use a silicone petit four cakes or truffles form, press the cake truffle batter which is soft at this point right into the form, refrigerate for a few hours & when ready take away from silicone form & top the cake.
11. In a medium bowl set over a medium saucepan of simmering water, melt the dark chocolate. Take away from the heat & put to the side for a few min. To cool down. Pour the melted chocolate over the cake truffles & cake.

12. When serving the cake run a knife thru how water before slicing it whereas the cake is cold, & let the slices come to room temperature before serving.

Peanut butter cheesecake with brownie bottom layer

What you need
For the brownies

- 1 package of brownie mix
- 15 peanut butter eggs or cups
- For the cheesecake:
- 16oz cream cheese, at room temperature
- 3 eggs
- 1 c. Of sugar
- 2 c. Creamy peanut butter
- 1 tbsp. Vanilla extract

For the chocolate ganache

- 1 semi sweet chocolate bar
- ½ c. Of heavy cream

Toppings

- 2 small packages of peanut m&ms
- 1 small package of mini peanut butter cups

What to do

1. Heat up the oven to 325 degrees f, butter a 9" springform pan & put to the side.
2. To make the brownies: follow the instructions on the box, when the batter is prepared pour it right into the pan & cover with a layer of peanut butter c.
3. To make the cheesecake: beat the cream cheese & peanut butter together on medium speed till smooth. Add the sugar, vanilla extract & continue to beat on medium speed till well combined. Reduce the speed to low & add the eggs one at a time, beating till combined next each addition. Utilizing a spatula, scrape the bowl & mix on low for an additional 30 sec.. Pour the cheesecake filling on top of the brownies & pb cups.

4. Bake for 45 min. To one hour or till the sides of the cheesecake are set & the middle only slightly jiggles. Turn of the oven, open the door slightly & let the cheesecake cool inside for one hour. Transfer the cake to a wire cooling rack & cool at room temperature for 2 hours.
5. To make the ganache: chop the chocolate & put in a medium bowl. In a sauce pan, on medium heat, bring the heavy cream to a boil, pour over chocolate & mix well till the chocolate is melted & well combined with the heavy cream. Pour the mixture on top of the cheesecake, utilizing a spatula distribute it evenly. Decorate with mini peanut butter c. & peanut m&m's.
6. Refrigerate the cheesecake before serving for at least 4 hours or overnight, till thoroughly chilled.

Dark & white cake with mascarpone & caramel buttercream

What you need
For cake layers

- 1 vanilla cake mix
- 1 triple chocolate cake mix
- 6 eggs
- 2 c. Water
- ⅔ c. Vegetable oil
- 4 tbsp butter, melted (to grease the pans)

For vanilla mascarpone buttercream

- 2 sticks unsalted butter, softened
- 4 oz chilled mascarpone cheese
- 2 vanilla beans
- 2 c. Confectioners sugar, sifted
- 2 tbsp. Heavy cream
- 1 c. Fresh strawberries, washed & sliced

For caramel buttercream

- 2 sticks unsalted butter, softened
- 3 c. Confectioners sugar, sifted
- ½ c. Caramel sauce

What to do
For cake layers

1. Heat up oven to 350°f.
2. Grease sides & bottom of 4 8inch foil pans with butter. Flour lightly.
3. Open the vanilla mix, & empty the box mix right into a medium bowl. Add 3 eggs, 1 c. Water & ⅓ c. Of vegetable oil. Mix utilizing a spatula till well incorporated. Divide the mixture equally right into 2 pans. Put to the side.

4. Open the chocolate mix, & empty the box mix right into a medium bowl. Add 3 eggs, 1 c. Water & ⅓ c. Of vegetable oil. Mix utilizing a spatula till well incorporated. Divide the mixture equally right into 2 pans. Bake for 25-30min or till a toothpick inserted in the middle of the cake comes out clean, or with only a few moist crumbs attached to it, the cake is done.
5. Let the cakes completely cool, when cooled utilizing a sharp kitchen knife level the surface of the cakes.

For vanilla mascarpone buttercream

1. Place softened butter right into the bowl of a stand mixer that has been fitted with the paddle attachment. Turn the mixer on a medium setting & cream the butter till it is smooth & has lightened in color, about 2 min..
2. Add the mascarpone cheese, specs from vanilla beans & sugar ½ c. At a time, beating 15 sec on medium next each addition.
3. Add heavy cream one tbsp. At a time, beating on medium till desired consistency is achieved.
4. Set the bowl aside & let the frosting chill for 30 min..

For the caramel buttercream

1. Place softened butter right into the bowl of a stand mixer that has been fitted with the paddle attachment. Turn the mixer on a medium setting & cream the butter till it is smooth & has lightened in color, about 2 min..
2. Add sugar ½ c. At a time, & mix on medium till well incorporated.
3. Add caramel, & mix till desired consistency is achieved.

Assemble the cake

1. On a cake stand, start with a leveled vanilla layer, top with vanilla mascarpone buttercream & fresh strawberries, followed by a chocolate layer topped with caramel buttercream, an additional vanilla layer topped with vanilla mascarpone buttercream & fresh strawberries. Finish with a top layer of chocolate cake, cover the entire cake in caramel buttercream. Decorate with vanilla mascarpone buttercream & dashs.

Brownie chocolate cake with vanilla buttercream

What you need

For the brownie layers

- 2 packages brownie mix
- 4 eggs
- ½ c. Of water
- ¾ c. Vegetable oil

For the coconut filling

- 1 c. Heavy cream
- 1 c. Granulated sugar
- 3 egg yolks
- 5 tbsp. Unsalted butter, cut right into small pieces
- 1 c. Pecans, grinded
- 1½ c. Unsweetened coconut

For the vanilla buttercream

- 1 c. Unsalted butter/2 sticks, softened
- 4 c. Confectioner's sugar
- 1 vanilla bean
- 3 tbsp. Heavy cream
- Pinch of salt

For the chocolate ganache

- 8 oz. Semisweet chocolate, chopped
- 2 tbsp. Light corn syrup
- 3 tbsp unsalted butter
- 1 c. Heavy cream

What to do

For the brownie layers

1. Heat up oven to 350°f , 325°f.

2. Grease bottom of 3 8inch round pans with shortening or cooking spray.
3. In a big bowl mix brownie mix, eggs, oil & water. Mix till well blended. Spread evenly right into the greased pans & bake straight away.
4. Brownies are done when toothpick inserted 1 in. From edge of pan comes out clean. About 25 min.. Cool completely in pan on wire rack before assembling the cake.

For the coconut filling

1. Place the butter, pecans & coconut in a big bowl & put to the side.
2. In a medium sauce pan, on low/medium heat, mix together the heavy cream, sugar & egg yolks till the mixture starts to thicken & coats the back of a spoon (180 degrees f.). Pour the hot custard straight away right into the pecan-coconut mixture & mix till the butter is melted. Cool completely to room temperature before topping the brownie layers.

For the vanilla buttercream

1. Place softened butter right into the bowl of a stand mixer that has been fitted with the paddle attachment. Turn the mixer on a medium setting & cream the butter till it is smooth, 2 - 3 min..
2. Add sugar, ½ a c. At a time.
3. Add vanilla beans & a pinch of salt & mix till well-incorporated.
4. Add heavy cream a tbsp at a time till the frosting has reached the preferred consistency.

For the chocolate ganache

1. Place the chocolate, corn syrup & butter in a medium bowl. Heat the cream in a small saucepan over medium heat till it only starts to boil. Take away from heat & pour over the chocolate. Let stand one minute, next which mix till smooth. Cool to room temperature.

Assemble the cake

1. Take away the brownie layers from the pans. Set the first cake layer on a cake plate.
2. Spread with a generous amount of buttercream first & add top the buttercream with ¾ c. Of the coconut filling over the cake layer, making sure to reach to the edges.
3. Set an additional cake layer on top & repeat with all three layers including the top one.
4. Ice the sides with the chocolate ganache, add coconut topping to the middle, & create a border with ferrero chocolates.

French cake with blueberries

What you need
Custard cake filling

- 2 c. (500 grams) heavy cream
- 3½ tbsp (50 grams) butter
- 1 tsp vanilla extract
- ¾ c. (100 grams) all-purpose white flour
- 1¼ c. (250 grams) white granulated sugar
- 2 whole big eggs + 2 egg yolks
- ½ tsp salt
- Zest of one lemon
- 1¾ c. (550 grams) of blueberries
- Extra butter for the mold

Biscoff crust

- 3 c. (750 grams) biscoff crumbs
- 10 tbsp (140 grams) unsalted butter, melted
- ⅔ c. (85 grams) granulated sugar
- Blueberry sauce:
- 6 c. Fresh blueberries (frozen work too)
- 1½ c. (375 ml) water
- 1½ c. (300 grams) sugar
- 6 tbsp cornstarch, mixed with 6 tbsp cold water
- 2 tbsp vanilla extract

Mascarpone lemon buttercream

- 1 sticks (113 grams) of butter, softened
- 5 oz. (140 grams) mascarpone cheese, chilled
- 2½ c. (225 grams) powdered sugar
- Zest of one lemon
- Pinch of salt

What to do

Custard cake filling

1. In a big bowl, whisk by hand till well combined eggs, egg yolks, flour, sugar, lemon zest & salt. Put to the side.
2. In a small sauce pan, put heavy cream on medium heat till it starts to boil, take away from heat & mix in vanilla extract.
3. Slowly pour ⅓ of the heavy cream right into the egg mixture & whisk continously. Do not pour all the heavy cream at once, since the high temperature will make the eggs cook.
4. Slowly pour the ½ of the remaining heavy cream, whisk till combined. Repeat with the remaining boiled heavy cream.
5. Cover the bowl with a plastic wrap & let it cool on the counter for 20 min., before transferring to the fridge for one hour.

Biscoff crust

1. Heat up oven to 350f.
2. In a food processor or blender to grind the biscoff cookies till you get 3 c. Of crumbs.
3. Mix the crumbs with melted butter & granulated sugar with a rubber spatula in a medium bowl till combined.
4. Press the mixture right into the bottom of a 10inch spring form cake pan & slightly up the sides. Ensure it is tight & compact, otherwise the custard will leak.
5. Pre-bake the crust for 7 min. At 350°f (177°c), before adding the custard filling.
6. Note: for a no-bake dessert, chill the crust for 2 hours before utilizing in your recipe.
7. Butter the edges of the spring form pan. Put the blueberries on the biscoff crust.
8. Take away the custard from the fridge & pour it right into the pan. Bake for 50 min., till golden brown.
9. Take away cake from the oven & put on a wire rack to cool completely.
10. Blueberry sauce:
11. The sauce can be made whereas the cake is cooking or many days in advance.

12. In a big saucepan over medium heat, mix blueberries, water & sugar. Mix frequently, but careful not to crush the berries, bring to a low boil.
13. In a small bowl, mix the cornstarch with cold water till combined.
14. Slowly mix the cornstarch right into the blueberries, careful not to crush them. Simmer till the homemade blueberry sauce is thick enough to cover the back of a metal spoon, about 10 min..
15. Take away from heat & lightly mix in vanilla.
16. If making the buttercream frosting, let the sauce cool completely before topping the cake.
17. Note: this makes a lot of sauce, save the remaining for other recipes, or cut it in half.
18. Mascarpone lemon buttercream:
19. Place softened butter & mascarpone right into the bowl of an electric stand mixer that has been fitted with the whisk attachment. Turn the mixer on a medium setting & cream till it smooth & combined, 2 - 3 min..
20. Add sugar, ½ a c. At a time. Add lemon zest & a pinch of salt & whisk till well-incorporated.
21. If the frosting is too thick add heavy cream one tbsp at a time till it has reached the desired consistency.
22. Top the cooled cake with the lemon mascarpone buttercream, & pour the cooled blueberry sauce on top of the frosting.

Strawberry cream crepe cake

What you need

For crepes

- 4 big eggs
- 1½ c. Milk
- 1 c. Water
- 2 c. Flour
- 6 tbsp melted butter
- 4 tbsp sugar
- 1 tsp vanilla extract or 3 vanilla beans
- Butter - cover the pan between making each crepe
- 3 - 4 c. Of fresh strawberries, sliced

For the mascarpone buttercream

- 1 stick of butter, softened at room temperature
- 6 oz mascarpone cheese, chilled
- 2 c. Powdered sugar
- 1 vanilla bean
- Pinch of salt

For the chocolate ganache

- 8 oz. Semisweet chocolate, chopped
- 2 tbsp. Light corn syrup
- 3 tbsp unsalted butter
- 1 c. Heavy cream

What to do

For the crepes

1. Place all the liquid ingredients in a blender & mix on low - medium speed. If you don't have a blender only whisk by had till well combined. Add flour one c. At a time & mix/whisk till well combined. Put batter in the fridge for at least 1 hour.

2. Place an 8-inch non-stick pan on low heat & when hot & add a little butter to cover it (less than half of a tbsp).
3. Pour ⅓ c. Of crepe batter right into the middle of the pan & swirl to spread evenly. Cook for roughly 30 sec. Or till the edges of the crepe appear loosened from the pan.
4. Flip the crepe & cook for an additional 10 sec., till slightly golden brown.
5. Take away crepe & stack on a plate. Continue with the remaining batter & stack crepes on the plate.
6. When done cooking cover the crepes with a kitchen towel to avoid the edges from drying out.

For the mascarpone buttercream

1. Place softened butter & mascarpone right into the bowl of an electric stand mixer that has been fitted with the whisk attachment. Turn the mixer on a medium setting & cream till it smooth & combined, 2 - 3 min..
2. Add sugar, ½ a c. At a time. Add vanilla beans & a pinch of salt & whisk till well-incorporated.
3. If the frosting is too thick add heavy cream one tbsp at a time till it has reached the desired consistency.
4. Refrigerate for 30 min. Before assembling the cake.

For the chocolate ganache

1. Place the chocolate, corn syrup & butter in a medium bowl. Heat the cream in a small saucepan over medium heat till it only starts to boil. Take away from heat & pour over the chocolate. Let stand one minute, next which mix till smooth. Cool to room temperature before assembling the cake.

Assemble the cake

1. Take one crepe from the stack, put on a flat surface, utilizing a soup spoon, take 1 - 2 spoons of chocolate ganache, put it in the middle

of the crepe & cover it avoiding the edges, it should be covered in chocolate ½ in. From the edges.
2. In a line, put the strawberries in the middle of the crème on top of the chocolate ganache, from one edge to the other.
3. From your side, flip the bottom of the crepe to cover the strawberries, secure with your hand only where the strawberries are (like you would do when rolling sushi) & roll right into a tube.
4. Place the filled crepe on the bottom of a glass baking pan, starting from one side, not the middle.
5. Repeat this technic with the remaining of the crepes till the bottom of the pan is covered. This is your first layer.
6. Now, cover your crepe layer with a good amount of mascarpone buttercream, even it out. Start filling the remaining of the crepes & stacking them on top of the cream, your second layer must be smaller than the first one, aiming for a pyramid.
7. Once you are done with your layers, pour the leftover chocolate ganache on top of the cake.
8. Refrigerate the cake for at least 3-4 hours or overnight before serving.

Strawberry, champagne & rose cake

What you need
For the sponge

- 125g unsalted butter, softened
- 400g caster sugar
- 350g plain flour
- 3 tsp baking powder
- ¼ tsp salt
- 350ml milk
- 3 medium eggs
- 1 tsp vanilla extract

For the syrup

- 140g caster sugar
- 1 tsp rose water

For the decoration

- 400g white chocolate
- 5 waitrose british strawberries
- Dr oetker hot pink gel food colour
- Waitrose cooks' homebaking freeze dried strawberries & cooks' what you need rose petals

For the buttercream filling

- 250g unsalted butter, softened
- 500g icing sugar
- 125ml champagne or prosecco
- 6 tbsp waitrose duchy
- Organic strawberry preserve

What to do

1. Grease & line 3 x 20cm round baking tins with baking parchment, & heat up the oven to 170ºc, gas mark 3.

2. Place the butter, sugar, flour, baking powder & salt right into the bowl of a stand mixer with paddle attachment. Mix on low till all the butter is rubbed right into the dry mixture & it has a sandy texture.
3. In a small jug, beat together the milk, eggs & vanilla. Keeping the mixer on a low speed, pour the mixture down the side of the flour & butter bowl. When all the liquid has been added, beat on a high speed for 2 min. Till it is light & fluffy.
4. Divide the mixture evenly between the prepared tins & bake in the heat uped oven for 25-30 min. Till golden brown.
5. Whereas the cake is baking, put the sugar right into a saucepan with 100ml of water & bring to the boil. Simmer for 2 min., next which take away from the heat & mix in the rose water.
6. When the cakes are cooked, leave them to cool in the tins for 10 min., next which liberally brush with the cooled rose syrup. Leave to cool completely.

Chocolate decorations

1. Melt the chocolate over a bowl of simmering water till smooth. Dip the strawberries right into the chocolate & put them onto baking parchment to set.

Shards

1. Take a quarter of the remaining white chocolate & mix in the food colouring till it is one uniform colour, next which transfer this mixture right into a piping bag.
2. Pour the remaining of the white chocolate right into a large, lined baking tray, next which drizzle with the pink chocolate & scatter over dried strawberries & rose petals.
3. Leave to set at room temperature for 30 min., next which score 12 big triangles right into it with a sharp knife. Chill till completely solid.

For the buttercream

1. Beat the soft butter & icing sugar in a stand mixer till it clumps together.
2. Add the champagne, a few tbsp at a time, till the icing loosens up & becomes fluffy. Beat on a high speed for 3-4 min. To get air in.

Assemble the cake

1. Place the bottom layer of sponge onto a big plate.
2. Spread the top with buttercream & 3 tbsp strawberry jam, repeat with the second layer of sponge, next which add the third on top.
3. Cover the whole cake with a thin layer of buttercream, next which put in the fridge for 20 min. To solidify. Then, utilizing a big palette knife, cover the chilled cake with more buttercream to achieve a smooth, clean finish.
4. Arrange the chocolate shards & strawberries on top, next which dash over some dried berries & rose petals.

Chocolate & pomegranate layer cake

What you need

For the layers

- 200g plain flour
- 70g cocoa powder
- 1 tsp bicarbonate of soda
- 1 tsp baking powder
- ¼ tsp salt
- 120ml sunflower oil
- 340g caster sugar
- 2 medium eggs
- 200ml pomegranate juice

For the ganache

- 200g butter
- 280g dark chocolate (60-70% cocoa solids), chopped
- 2 tbsp golden syrup
- 250ml double cream
- 110g pack pomegranate seeds, to decorate

Intructions

1. Heat up the oven to 180°c, gas mark 4. Grease & line the bases of 3 x 20cm tins with baking parchment.
2. Combine the flour, cocoa powder, bicarbonate of soda, baking powder & salt together in a bowl. In a separate bowl, whisk together the oil, sugar & eggs till smooth.
3. Add the pomegranate juice & the flour mixture to the oil, sugar & egg mixture. Pour in half the juice, & next which add half the flour, next which the remaining juice & the remaining flour. Ensure you mix well next each addition to avoid any lumps.

4. Divide the mixture between the 3 tins & bake in the heat uped oven for 20-25 min., or till the cakes are springy to touch and, when inserted, a skewer comes out clean. Leave to cool in the tins for 10 min., next which transfer to a wire rack to cool completely.

For the ganache

1. Place the butter, chocolate & golden syrup right into a heatproof bowl over a pan of boiling water. Mix till the mixture is melted & smooth – about 7-8 min.. Pour in the double cream & mix till combined, next which put right into the fridge & chill till cool but not set – about 35-40 min.. Use an electric hand whisk to whip the ganache till it turns from dark to pale brown – about 2-3 min..

Assemble the cake

1. Place one layer of the sponge on to a plate & spread with quarter of the ganache. Top with the second layer of sponge & an additional quarter of the ganache.
2. Add the final layer of sponge. Crumb cover the top & sides of the completed cake with a thin layer of ganache.
3. Place in the fridge for around 30 min. To set. Cover the cake with the remaining ganache & next which top with the pomegranate seeds.

Chocolate cinnamon cake

What you need

- 225 g organic butter
- 225 g organic golden caster sugar
- 4 range medium eggs
- 175 g organic self raising flour
- 1 tsp baking powder
- 50 g cocoa powder
- 1 tsp ground cinnamon
- ½ x 265g jar
- 150ml double cream, whipped
- Extra cocoa for dusting

What to do

1. Heat up the oven to 180c, gas mark 4.
2. Place the butter, sugar & eggs together in a big mixing bowl. Sift in the flour, baking powder, cocoa & cinnamon & beat till thoroughly mixed.
3. Spoon right into 2 greased & base-lined round 20cm sandwich tins & levels the surface.
4. Bake for 30 min. Till well risen & a metal skewer emerges clean from the centre of the cakes.
5. Turn out & cool on wire racks.
6. Sandwich the 2 cakes together with the damson jam & whipped cream & dust with cocoa.

Chocolate ganache cake

What you need
For the filling

- 150g country life butter
- 150g sugar
- 200g plain chocolate, broken right into small chunks
- 200g ground almonds
- 6 medium free range eggs, separated
- 4 tbsp brandy or milk

For the ganache

- 200g plain chocolate
- 200ml double cream

What to do

1. Heat up the oven to 150°c, gas mark 2. Base line 2 x 20cm sandwich tins with non-stick baking parchment.
2. Melt the butter, sugar & chocolate in a pan till melted. Cool slightly & fold in the almonds, egg yolks & brandy or milk.
3. Whisk the egg whites till they hold stiff peaks & fold right into the chocolate mixture. Pour right into the tins & bake for 40-45 min. Till firm. Cool slightly before turning out onto wire racks. Discard the paper & permit to cool.
4. In the meantime, make the ganache by melting the chocolate & cream in a bowl over a pan of simmering water till melted. Whisk till glossy & thickened & permit to cool.
5. Place one half of the cake upside down on a serving plate, spread with ¼ of the ganache & put the other cake on top. Spread the remaining of the ganache on the top & sides with a palate or round bladed knife till smooth & shiny.

Chocolate pistachio cake

What you need

- 100g pack pistachio nuts
- 200g bar white chocolate, chopped
- 450ml essential waitrose double cream
- 250g tub ricotta cheese
- 2 tsp vanilla bean paste or extract
- 330g double chocolate loaf
- 3 tbsp kirsch, optional
- 200g bar plain chocolate, chopped
- 2 tbsp golden syrup

What to do

1. Put the nuts in a heatproof bowl & cover with boiling water. Leave to stand for 30 sec., next which drain well & tip the nuts onto several sheets of kitchen paper. Cover with more layers of paper & rub under the palms of your hands to release the skins.
2. Peel away the skins. Roughly chop the nuts, either by hand or in a food processor.
3. Put the white chocolate & 100ml of the cream in a heatproof bowl over a pan of lightly simmering water. Leave till melted, stirring often. Take away from the heat & beat in the ricotta & vanilla.
4. Slice the cake as thinly as possible. Arrange a third of the slices in a base-lined 20cm spring-release or shallow, loose-based cake tin, cutting the slices to fit. Drizzle with 1 tbsp of the kirsch, if using.
5. Whip a further 200ml of the cream till firm, & mix right into the white chocolate mixture, along with all but 2 tbsp of the nuts.
6. Spread half the mixture in the tin & level the surface. Arrange half the remaining cake slices on top & drizzle with an additional tbsp of the kirsch. Spread with the remaining filling, next which the remaining cake slices & kirsch.
7. Cover & chill for at least 2 hours.

8. Melt the plain chocolate in a heatproof bowl over a saucepan of simmering water.
9. Take away from the heat & add the golden syrup, next which the remaining 150ml of cream, stirring till smooth. Leave till cooled but not thickened. Run a knife around the edges of the cake & release the cake from the sides of the tin.
10. Invert onto a serving plate & peel away the lining paper.
11. Spread the chocolate mixture over the top & sides with a palette knife & scatter with the reserved nuts.

Flourless chocolate praline cake

What you need

- 175g unsalted butter, softened, plus extra for greasing
- 100g whole blanched hazelnuts
- 175g caster sugar
- 200g dark chocolate (70% cocoa), chopped
- 5 eggs, separated
- ½ tsp salt

What to do

1. Heat up the oven to 180°c, gas mark 4.
2. Grease a 23cm cake tin & line with baking parchment.
3. Put the hazelnuts in a roasting tray & roast for 10 min. Till golden. Put to the side and, when cool, blitz in a food processor with 25g sugar till finely ground.
4. In the meantime, melt the chocolate in a bowl set over a pan of barely simmering water.
5. Using electric beaters, cream the butter & 100g sugar in a bowl for 5 min., till pale & fluffy. Beat in the egg yolks one at a time, next which the melted chocolate & salt. Fold through the ground hazelnuts.
6. Reduce the oven to 160°c, gas mark 2.
7. In a separate bowl, whisk the egg whites to stiff peaks. Whisk in the remaining 50g sugar till stiff & glossy. Mix $1/3$ the egg white right into the chocolate mixture to loosen, next which prudently fold in the remaining egg white, a third at a time, trying to retain as much air as possible. Prudently tip right into the tin, lightly smooth the top & bake for 50-55 min. Till only set.
8. Cool in the tin for 20 min., next which take away the sides (leave the base on) & cool completely on a wire rack.

Flourless chocolate & almond cake

What you need
For the cake

- 265g waitrose belgian dark chocolate
- 6 eggs, 5 separated + 1 whole
- 210g caster sugar
- 150g ground almonds

For the toppin

- 3 tbsp apricot jam
- 120ml double cream
- 120g waitrose belgian dark chocolate

What to do
Cake layers & filling

1. Pre-heat your oven to 180°c, gas mark 4.
2. Grease & base line a 21cm round loose bottom cake tin.
3. Melt the chocolate in a bowl over a pan of simmering water & next which permit to cool a little.
4. Whisk the egg whites in a big bowl till stiff.
5. In an additional bowl utilizing an electric whisk, beat the egg, egg yolks & sugar together till thick & pale. The mixture should leave a trail on the surface when the beaters are lifted.
6. Whisk the ground almonds, melted chocolate & 1tbsp of egg white right into the egg yolk mixture. Utilizing a metal spoon prudently fold the remaining egg whites right into the chocolate mixture. Pour the mixture right into the prepared tin.
7. Bake for 45-50 min., till the crust that forms on top of the cake is firm & the sides shrink away from the tin.
8. Leave the cake to cool in the tin for at least 10 min.. Next which turn it out, upside down onto a clean tea towel on a wire rack.
9. Take away the parchment from the cake & leave to cool completely. Turn the cake the right way up on the rack & take away the tea towel.

10. Gently heat the jam & brush it evenly over the top & sides of the cake.

Topping

1. Melt the cream & chocolate in a bowl over a pan of simmering water. Mix often till smooth & glossy. Permit to cool so the topping starts to thicken, but don't let it set.
2. Pour onto the centre of the cake & permit it flow over the top & the sides of the cake.
3. Use a palette knife to spread around the sides & completely cover the cake. Leave to set before serving.

Black forest cake

What you need

For the sponge

- 8 big eggs
- 2 big egg yolks
- 200g golden caster sugar
- 1 tbsp vanilla bean paste
- 90g cocoa powder
- Pinch of salt

For the chocolate icing

- 35g cocoa powder
- 120g golden syrup
- Pinch salt
- 100g plain chocolate, finely chopped
- 25g unsalted butter

For the filling & topping

- 250g jar opies black cherries with kirsch
- 4 tbsp kirsch
- 600ml double cream
- 50g icing sugar, sifted
- 2 tsp vanilla bean paste
- 8-10 whole cherries with stems
- 25g pack dark chocolate curls

What to do

1. Heat up the oven to 180°c, gas mark 4.
2. Grease & line two 23cm round cake tins with baking parchment.

3. Separate the eggs & mix the yolks (plus extra yolks), sugar & vanilla bean paste in a big bowl. Use an electric hand whisk to whisk till pale & doubled in volume. Sift over the cocoa powder & fold in. In a clean bowl, whisk the egg whites & salt to stiff peaks next which prudently fold right into the egg yolk mixture.
4. Divide between the lined tins & bake for 30 min.. Cool on a wire rack. Cut each cake in half horizontally.
5. For the icing, put the cocoa powder, syrup & salt right into a saucepan with 125ml hot water, whisk till smooth next which bring to the boil. Reduce the heat to a simmer & cook for 2 min., whisking continuously , till smooth & glossy. Take away from the heat & whisk in the chocolate & butter till smooth. Put to the side to cool.
6. Drain the cherries, reserving the syrup, & put to the side. Pour the syrup right into a saucepan, bring to the boil & reduce by two thirds. Take away from the heat & mix in the kirsch.
7. Whip the cream, icing sugar & vanilla to soft peaks next which fold in the drained cherries.

Assemble the cake

1. put a small spoonful of cream onto a serving plate or cake stand & lay a sponge on top. Spoon over a quarter of the kirsch syrup, spread over a thin layer of the chocolate icing & top with a third of the cream. Repeat this layer with the next two sponges. Top with the final sponge, soak with the remaining syrup & spread over the remaining icing. Top with the fresh cherries & chocolate curls. Chill for 1 hour before serving.

Velvet mocha cheesecake

What you need

- 85 g unsalted butter
- 250 g double chocolate cookies, crushed
- 4 eggs
- 150 g caster sugar
- 1 vanilla pod, split
- 400 g full fat cream cheese
- 300 g light cream cheese
- 2 tbsp cornflour, sifted
- 300 ml creme fraiche
- 2 tbsp hot coffee
- 350g dark chocolate, 300g melted, 50g chopped
- 5 tbsp golden syrup
- 2 tbsp cocoa powder
- 2 tsp instant coffee granules

What to do

- Heat up the oven to 180c/gas 4.
- Melt 70g butter & mix with the crushed cookies; press right into a base-lined 23cm springform tin. Bake for 10 min. Till only firm. Leave to cool slightly, next which wrap the tin in two big sheets of tinfoil, double-wrapping it around the outsides (it needs to be watertight), but leaving the top open.
- To make the cheesecake, whisk the eggs with the sugar for several min., till thick & airy. Scrape in the vanilla pod seeds; beat in all the cream cheese, the cornflour, crème fraîche, coffee & melted chocolate; pour right into the tin.
- Set the cake tin in a big roasting tin or dish. Pour boiling water right into the roasting dish to reach midway up the cake tin. Bake for about 1 hour 20 min. Till only firm. Turn the oven off & leave for 15 min.
- In the meantime, make the sauce. In a pan, melt the syrup, 15g butter, cocoa, coffee granules & chopped chocolate over a very

low heat with 80ml water. Whisk together till smooth. Keep in the fridge for up to 1 week & warm through lightly before serving
- Chill the cheesecake overnight, or for up to 4 days, before serving with a drizzle of chocolate sauce

Flourless chocolate cake

What you need

- 250g soft unsalted butter, plus extra for greasing
- 100g roasted chopped hazelnuts
- 365g light brown muscovado sugar
- 300g 70% dark chocolate, broken right into pieces
- 50g ground almonds
- 85g cocoa powder
- 6 big eggs, lightly whisked
- 1 tsp vanilla bean paste or 1 vanilla pod, split and
- Seeds scraped out
- 1 heaped tsp sea salt
- 190g fresh raspberries, to serve

What to do

1. Heat up the oven to 180°c, gas mark 4.
2. Grease & line the sides & bottom of a 23cm loose-bottomed cake tin.
3. Grind the hazelnuts with 1 tsp of the sugar in a small food processor to a fine powder.
4. Gently melt the butter & chocolate in a big bowl over a pan of simmering water. Take away from the heat & mix to combine. Add the sugar, lightly whisk till there are no lumps, next which fold in the ground almonds & hazelnuts & cocoa powder. Steadily add the eggs, vanilla paste & salt, giving it all a good stir.
5. Pour the batter right into the prepared tin & bake in the oven for 35 min.. Take away & leave to cool for 20 min. In the tin before prudently removing from the tin to cool.
6. Top with fresh raspberries. Serve in slivers with a dollop of crème fraîche, if you like, & an espresso or glass of amaretto on the side.

What to do

1. Make the cake: heat up the oven to 350 f. Spray three 6-inch round cake pans (or two 8 in. Pans) with baking spray & line bottoms with parchment paper.
2. In the bowl of a stand mixer, beat together the eggs, sugar & vanilla till it has tripled in volume - about 10 min.. Mixture should be thick, creamy & pale. Add the lemon zest.
3. Sift the flour & salt (preferably three times) right into a separate bowl or a big parchment paper on the counter. Mix right into stand mixer utilizing a plastic or metal spoon, preferably in batches.
4. Add the melted butter & lightly fold it in to the cake batter mix.
5. Divide the batter evenly between the pans & lightly smooth the tops. Tap the cake pans on the counter to take away any air bubbles.
6. Bake in heat uped oven for 21-25 min. Or till the sponges are evenly golden & come away from the sides of the baking pans.
7. Allow the cakes to cool in their pans for 10 min.. Next 10 min., turn them onto the wire rack prudently & permit the cakes to cool completely.
8. in the meantime, make the whipped cream: in a small pan, mix gelatin & cold water & permit to sit for 5 min. Till thick. Put over low heat, stirring continously, only till the gelatin dissolves.
9. Take away from heat & permit to cool slightly (but do not let it to set).
10. Using a stand mixer, whip the heavy cream with the icing sugar till soft peaks form.
11. Whereas slowly beating, add the gelatin to the whipping cream. Whip at high speed till stiff peaks form.

Assemble the cake

1. Place your first layer of cake on top of a cardboard circle, serving plate or cake stand.
2. Spoon a generous layer of whipped cream & spread evenly utilizing an offset spatula.

3. Place an even layer of sliced strawberries & berries on top of the whipped cream.
4. Add the second layer of cake & repeat till all of the layers are on the cake.
5. For the top layer, spread on with a generous layer of whipped cream & spread evenly utilizing an offset spatula.
6. Garnish with fresh strawberries, blueberries & blackberries. Dust with powdered sugar.

Cheesecake brownies

What you need

- 1 boxed brownie mix or homemade brownie recipe
- 8 oz. Cream cheese, softened
- 2 tbsp butter, softened
- 1 tbsp cornstarch
- 14 oz. Sweetened condensed milk
- 1 egg
- 1 tsp vanilla extract
- 16 ounce container chocolate frosting

What to do

1. Heat up oven to 350of. Grease a 9x13 baking dish with nonstick cooking spray.
2. Prepare brownie mix according to directions on package. Pour batter in the baking dish.
3. Beat the cream cheese, butter, & cornstarch till fluffy. Steadily beat in the sweetened condensed milk, egg, & vanilla till smooth. Pour cream cheese mixture over the brownie batter.
4. Bake for 45 min.. Permit to cool. Spread frosting over top. Store covered in the fridge.

Mudslide cake

What you need

For cake

- 2 c. Granulated sugar
- 2 big eggs, room temperature
- 1 c. Hot water
- 1/2 c. Unsweetened cocoa powder
- 1 tsp instant coffee
- 1 tsp salt
- 2 1/2 c. Sifted all-purpose flour
- 2 tsp baking soda
- 1 tsp baking powder
- 1 c. Vegetable oil
- 1 c. Buttermilk, room temperature
- 1 tbsp vanilla extract

For filling

- 1/2 tsp gelatin
- 2 c. Heavy cream, cold
- 1/2 c. Confectioners sugar
- 4-5 tbsp bourbon, to taste
- For ganache
- 6 oz. Chopped semisweet chocolate
- 1/2 c. Heavy cream, room temperature

For garnish

- 1 c. Chopped or crumbled chocolate wafer or sandwich cookies

What to do

1. Heat up oven to 350 degrees f. Line the bottoms of 3 9-inch round cake pans with parchment paper; butter parchment & sides of pan.
2. In a big mixing bowl or the bowl of a stand mixer fitted with a whisk attachment, beat sugar & eggs on high speed for 2 to 3 min. Till lightened in color.

3. Combine the hot water, cocoa powder, instant coffee, & salt; mix to combine. With mixer on low speed, slowly pour right into mixer bowl. Continue to mix on low speed till incorporated.
4. Add flour, baking soda, & baking powder & mix on low speed till only incorporated. Mix in oil, buttermilk, & vanilla, scraping down the sides of the bowl as necessary. Do not overmix. The batter will be quite thin.
5. Divide batter among prepared pans. Bake for 22 to 25 min. Or till a toothpick inserted near the middle comes out clean.
6. Let cool on wire racks. If necessary, run a thin metal knife around the edges of the pans to loosen, next which invert onto wire racks. Cakes should come out cleanly. Let cool completely. At this point you can wrap cakes in plastic wrap & seal inside zip-top bags, store in the freezer overnight or till ready to use.
7. To prepare whipped cream, fill a small dish with 2 tbsp cold water. Dash over gelatin & let sit for 5 min. To soften. Microwave for 5 sec. To melt, stirring lightly to smooth out any chunks, next which put to the side to cool.
8. In a cold metal mixing bowl, whip cream on high speed till frothy. Add sugar & cooled gelatin & continue to whisk till cream holds soft peaks. Add bourbon to taste & whisk till cream holds stiff peaks. Refrigerate till ready to use.
9. To prepare ganache, mix chopped chocolate & cream in a microwave-safe bowl. Microwave on half power for 15 sec. At a time, stirring well next each interval. Continue to microwave till chocolate is only melted; the residual heat of the mixture should be enough to melt it completely. Let cool till slightly thickened but still pourable. If the ganache is on the thick side, whisk in a tbsp or two of butter, cut right into small cubes, to thin out the ganache as desired.
10. To assemble, put one layer on a cake stand or serving plate. Top with 1/3 of whipped cream, spreading to within 3/4" of the edge. Drizzle with 1/3 of ganache, & dash with crumbled cookies. Repeat with second & third layers, finishing with the remaining whipped cream, ganache, & crushed cookies. Refrigerate till ready to serve.

Vegan cake

What you need

- 1 1/2 c. Almond milk
- 2 tsp apple cider vinegar
- 1 c. Plus 2 tbsp vegan granulated sugar
- 1/3 c. Plus 2 tbsp vegetable oil
- 1 tbsp vanilla bean paste
- 1/4 tsp almond extract
- 2 c. Unbleached all-purpose flour
- 3 tbsp cornstarch
- 3/4 tsp baking soda
- 1 tsp baking powder
- 3/4 tsp salt

Frosting

- 3/4 c. Non-hydrogenated margarine
- 3/4 c. Non-hydrogenated shortening
- 3 1/2 c. Vegan powdered sugar
- 1 tbsp pure vanilla extract
- Pinch of salt
- 1/4 c. Almond milk

What to do

1. Heat up oven to 350 degrees, grease (2) 9-inch cake pans. In a big bowl, whisk together almond milk & vinegar & let stand 4 or 5 min..
2. Whisk in sugar, oil, almond & vanilla paste, & mix till frothy. Sift together flour, cornstarch, baking soda, baking powder, & salt.
3. Add the flour mixture to the almond & vanilla mixture & blend till flour disappears. Don't over mix! Pour half of the batter right into each 9 in. Pan & bake for about 25 min., or till a toothpick inserted right into the middle of the cake comes out clean. Cool completely before frosting.

4. In a mixer, add margarine & shortening & beat at medium speed for about 2.
5. Stir in powdered sugar, add vanilla extract & salt & beat on medium for 1 minute. Add almond milk slowly till only spreadable.

To assemble

1. Place first layer on stand, cardboard round or platter & frost.
2. Add second layer & frost evenly & flat.
3. Decorate with raspberries, blueberries, lingonberries, & baby strawberries & a bit of mint.

Gluten free brownies

What you need

- 23 oz almond flour
- 1 tsp salt
- 1 tbsp cocoa powder
- 6 oz. Dark chocolate, coarsely chopped
- 1 c. (4 oz.) Coconut oil
- 1 c. Coconut sugar
- 2 eggs
- 1 tsp vanilla extract
- 1 c. Dark chocolate chips

What to do

1. Heat up oven to 350of. Line with parchment & lightly grease an 8x8" baking pan.
2. In a medium bowl, whisk the almond flour, salt, & cocoa powder together.
3. Put the chocolate & coconut oil in a big glass bowl & microwave for 30 sec.. Stir, & repeat till the chocolate & coconut oil are completely melted & smooth. Add the coconut sugar. Whisk till completely combined. The mixture should be room temperature.
4. Add 2 eggs to the chocolate mixture & whisk till combined. Add the vanilla & stir.
5. Dash the flour mixture over the chocolate mixture. Utilizing a rubber spatula, fold the flour mixture right into the chocolate till only a bit of the flour mixture is visible. Fold in the chocolate chips.
6. Bake in heat uped oven for 28-32 min. Or till a toothpick comes out with moist crumbs attached.
7. Cool brownies completely.

m&m's brownies

What you need

- 1/2 c. Butter, softened
- 2 c. Brown sugar
- 2 eggs
- 2 tsp almond extract
- 1/2 tsp salt
- 2 tsp baking powder
- 1 3/4 c. Flour
- 1/2 c. Dark cocoa powder
- 1 1/2 c. Mini m&m's candies, divided

What to do

1. Beat the butter & sugar till creamy. Add the eggs & extract & beat again.
2. Stir together the salt, baking powder, flour, & cocoa powder. Slowly beat right into the butter mixture till combined. Add 1 c. Mini m&m's & mix lightly.
3. Spoon right into a greased 9x13 glass baking dish. Top with the remaining candies. Bake at 350 degrees for 25 min.. Take away & let cool completely before cutting.

cinnamon cheesecake bars

What you need

Cake

- 1 big egg
- 1 c. Light brown sugar
- 1 c. Natural sweetener/or sugar of choice
- 1 c. Pure pumpkin puree, canned or homemade
- 1 c. Oil
- 1 tbsp honey
- 1 tbsp vanilla extract
- 11 c. Plain flour
- 1 tbsp baking powder
- 11 tsp ground cinnamon
- Pinch of salt
- 1 c. White chocolate chips

Cheesecake

- 1x 250g | 8.8oz packet low fat/fat free cream cheese, at room temp
- 2 tbsp flour
- 1 tsp ground cinnamon
- 4 tbsp natural sweetener/sugar of choice

What to do

1. Heat up oven to 180c | 350f. Grease a 9x11-inch baking pan with cooking spray; line with baking/parchment paper & put to the side.
2. In a big bowl, whisk the egg, brown sugar, sweetener/sugar, pumpkin, oil, honey & vanilla till smooth & creamy.
3. Add the flour, baking powder, cinnamon & salt, & mix till only combined.
4. Fold through chocolate chips, put to the side & make the cheesecake layer

Cheesecake

1. Combine cream cheese, flour, cinnamon & sweetener/sugar in a medium sized bowl, & beat till smooth.

Assemble

2. Pour the cake batter right into prepared pan & evenly smooth the top lightly with a spatula.
3. Pour the cheesecake mixture over the top, & utilizing the back of a knife, swirl small amounts of the blondie batter lightly right into the cheesecake mix till a marble effect is created on the top.
4. Bake for about 38 - 45 min., or till done. A toothpick inserted in the middle should come out mostly clean/slightly dirty, with a few moist crumbs but no batter. Permit cake to cool in pan for at least 30 min. Before slicing & serving.

Pumpkin & chocolate cake

What you need

Pumpkin layer

- 1 c. Sugar
- 1 c. Canola oil
- 2 big eggs
- 1 c. All-purpose flour
- 1 tsp baking soda
- 1 tsp ground cinnamon
- 1 tsp baking powder
- 1 tsp salt
- 1 c. Pumpkin purée

Chocolate layer

- 6 tbsp unsweetened cocoa powder, plus more for pans
- Cup all-purpose flour
- Cup sugar
- 1 tsp + pinch baking soda
- Tsp + pinch baking powder
- Tsp + pinch salt
- 1 big eggs
- Tbsp buttermilk
- 6 tbsp water
- Tbsp canola oil
- 1 tsp vanilla extract

Whipped brown sugar icing

- 7 tbsp all-purpose flour
- 1 1 c. Milk
- 1 1 tbsp pure vanilla extract
- 1 1 c. Salted butter, at room temperature
- 1 1 c. Brown sugar, packed
- Pinch of salt

What to do

1. Heat up oven to 350of. Butter 2 – 8" layer round pans. Dust one with flour & one with cocoa.

Pumpkin layer

1. Combine sugar, canola oil & eggs in a mixing bowl; mix well.
2. Whisk flour, baking soda, cinnamon, baking powder & salt in an additional bowl.
3. Stir right into oil mixture; beating well. Mix in pumpkin.
4. Pour right into the flour prepared pan. Bake for 35-40 min.. Cool completely before turning out.

Chocolate layer

1. Combine cocoa, flour, sugar, baking soda, baking powder & salt right into the bowl of a mixer. Beat on low till combined.
2. Add eggs, buttermilk, water, oil & vanilla. Increase speed to medium & beat till very smooth, about 3 min..
3. Pour right into cocoa prepared pan. Bake till set about 30-35 min.. Let cool completely before turning out.
4. When both layers are fully cooled, take the one pumpkin layer & cut it in half, next which the one chocolate layer & cut it in half so you have 4 sections of cake. Frost with whipped brown sugar icing alternating one chocolate section, pumpkin, chocolate & finish with pumpkin.

Whipped brown sugar icing

1. In a small saucepan, whisk flour right into milk & heat, stirring continously , till it thickens.
2. Take away from heat & let it cool to room temperature. Mix in vanilla.
3. Whereas the mixture is cooling, cream the butter, sugar, & salt together till light & fluffy on medium high, about 3 min.. Add the completely cooled milk mixture.
4. Beat for 5 min. On medium-high to high till it looks like whipped cream.

Chocolate bundt cake

What you need

- 1/4 dough from chocolate chip cookies
- 1 c m&m's milk chocolate harvest candies
- 1 c unsalted butter, softened
- 2 c sugar
- 2 eggs
- Tbsp cocoa powder
- 2 tsp vanilla extract
- 1 c sour cream
- 2 tsp baking soda
- 2 1/2 c all-purpose flour
- 1/4 tsp kosher salt
- 1 c boiling water
- 1 container cream cheese icing

What to do

1. Prepare chocolate chip cookies as directed in the original recipe, swapping out the chocolate chips for the 1 c. Of m&m's. Reserve 1/4 of the dough, & wrap the remaining in plastic & put in the fridge for later use.
2. Heat up oven to 325 degrees. Grease a bundt pan with shortening or butter, next which cover in an even layer of cocoa powder. Tap out the excess & put to the side.
3. In a big mixing bowl beat the butter & sugar till light & fluffy, around 5 min.. Beat in the eggs, one at time, till fully incorporated, next which mix in the cocoa powder, vanilla extract, & sour cream.
4. Whisk together the flour, baking soda, & salt & slowly add to the mixture.
5. Gently beat in the boiling water on low speed. Pour the batter right into the prepared bundt pan.
6. Roll the cookie dough right into small balls & plop them right into the cake batter in the bundt cake, pressing down only slightly.
7. Bake for 60 min., or till a toothpick inserted right into the middle of the cake comes out clean.
8. Allow the cake to cool for 10 min. In the pan before flipping out onto a cooling rack to cool completely.

9. Take away the lid & foil from the icing, next which put in the microwave & heat for 15 second intervals till smooth & pourable. Slowly pour over cooled bundt cake, permit to set.

Angel cake

What you need

- 13 c. Sugar, divided
- 1 tsp salt
- 1 c. Cake flour, sifted
- 12 egg whites
- 1 c. Warm water
- 1 tsp vanilla extract
- Tsp cream of tartar
- 1 can of vanilla frosting, optional

What to do

1. Heat up oven to 350 degrees f.
2. In medium mixing bowl, mix half of the sugar with the salt & cake flour.
3. In a big mixing bowl, use a balloon whisk to thoroughly mix egg white, water, vanilla, & cream of tartar. Next 2 min., switch to a hand mixer. Slowly add the remaining half of the sugar sugar, beating continuously at medium speed.
4. Once you have achieved medium peaks, dash enough of the flour mixture to dust the top of the fluffy egg whites. Utilizing a rubber spatula to lightly fold in the flour mixture till just about fully incorporated.
5. Repeat till all of the flour mixture is incorporated right into the egg whites. You want to mix in the flour in as few folds as possible.
6. Prudently spoon mixture evenly right into an ungreased tube pan. Bake for 35 min..
7. Check that the cake is done by inserting a wooden skewer right into the cake midway between the middle tube & the outer wall..
8. Cool upside down in the pan on cooling rack for at least an hour. Run a knife around the outer wall of the pan to release the cake. Next which run the knife around the middle tube & under the cake to finish releasing the cake from the pan.

Red velvet cake

What you need
Cake batter

- 31 c. All-purpose flour
- 2 c. Sugar
- 3 tbsp unsweetened cocoa powder
- 2 tsp baking soda
- 3 tsp salt
- 13 c. Buttermilk
- Cups vegetable oil
- 3 big eggs
- 1 tsp distilled white vinegar
- 1 bottle liquid red food coloring

Frosting

- 1 pound cream cheese, room temperature
- 1 c. Butter, softened
- Cups confectioners' sugar

Bloody ganache

- 12 oz. White chocolate bark
- 2 tbsp heavy cream
- Red food coloring

What to do

1. To make cake, heat up oven to 350 degrees & spray 3 9-inch cake pans with baking spray with flour.
2. In a big mixing bowl mix flour, sugar, cocoa powder, baking soda, & salt.
3. In a medium bowl, whisk together buttermilk, vegetable oil, eggs, & vinegar.
4. With the mixer on low, add the buttermilk mixture to the flour mixture. When all buttermilk mixture has been added, turn to medium speed & beat till smooth.
5. Add food coloring & beat till mixed evenly.
6. Divide batter evenly between the prepared pans & bake about 22 to 25 min.. Let cool in pans for 10 min. & next which take away to wire rack to cool completely.

7. For frosting, beat cream cheese & butter with an electric mixer till smooth. Steadily beat in confectioners' sugar.
8. Spread frosting between layers of cakes & on top & sides.
9. Refrigerate cake to firm up frosting before adding bloody ganache.
10. Melt white chocolate bark with cream cheese in a heavy-bottomed pan over low heat, stirring continuously.
11. Once melted, add food coloring to get desired color. Drizzle on top of cake to resemble blood.

Lemon & blueberry cheesecake

What you need
Blueberry sauce

- 2 c. Fresh blueberries
- ½ c. Water
- ½ c. Sugar
- 2 tbsp cornstarch, mixed with 2 tbsp cold water
- 1 tbsp vanilla extract

Crust

- 2 c. Graham cracker crumbs
- 8 tbsp unsalted butter, melted
- 2 tbsp granulated sugar

Cheesecake filling

- 4 packages (8 oz.) Cream cheese, softened
- 1 c. Sour cream
- 2 tbsp cornstarch
- 3 eggs
- 1⅓ c. Sugar
- ½ c. Graham cracker crumbs
- Juice of one meyer lemon
- Zest from one meyer lemon

What to do
Blueberry sauce

1. The sauce can be made whereas the cake is cooking or many days in advance.
2. In a big saucepan over medium heat, mix blueberries, water & sugar. Mix frequently, but careful not to crush the berries, bring to a low boil.
3. In a small bowl, mix the cornstarch with cold water till combined.

4. Slowly mix the cornstarch right into the blueberries, careful not to crush them. Simmer till the homemade blueberry sauce is thick enough to cover the back of a metal spoon, about 10 min..
5. Take away from heat & lightly mix in vanilla.
6. Let the sauce cool at room temperature. Measure ½ c. For your recipe, store the remaining in jars in the fridge.

Crust

4. In a big bowl, mix the crumbs with melted butter & granulated sugar with a rubber spatula till combined.
5. Press the mixture right into the bottom of a 9inch spring form cake pan & slightly up the sides. Ensure it is tight & compact.
6. Chill the crust for 15 min..

Cheesecake filling

10. Heat up oven to 325f.
11. In the bowl of an electric mixer fitted with the whisk attachment beat cream cheese on medium speed till fluffy. Add the sugar, cornstarch, lemon juice, lemon zest & beat till combined.
12. Add eggs, one at a time, beating till only combined next each addition. On low speed beat in sour cream only till combined.
13. Take away crust from the fridge & pour the batter right into the crust.
14. In circles pour the blueberry sauce over the cheesecake & with the edge of a spatula create swirls & mix the blueberry sauce right into the cheesecake filling. Prudently not to over mix.
15. Bake for about 1¼ hours or till middle is just about set. Cool on a wire rack for 15 min.. Dash graham crackers on top & loosen sides of pan & continue cooling on wire rack till the cheesecake is at room temperature.
16. Transfer to the fridge. Refrigerate overnight or at least 6 hours before serving.
17. The cheesecake can be served with warm blueberry sauce.
18. Store in fridge.

Chocolate brownie cake with mascarpone

What you need
For the brownie layers

- 1 c. Unsalted butter, melted
- 2 c. Granulated sugar
- 4 big eggs
- 1 c. All-purpose flour
- ½ c. Unsweetened cocoa powder
- ½ tsp salt
- ½ tsp baking soda

For the coconut filling

- 1 c. Walnuts, measure next which grind
- 1 c. Coconut flakes
- ½ c. Heavy cream
- ½ c. Sugar
- 1 egg yolk
- 3 tbsp. Butter, room temperature

For the vanilla buttercream

- 3 sticks of butter, softened
- 8 oz mascarpone cheese, chilled
- 2½ c. Powdered sugar
- 1 vanilla bean
- Pinch of salt

For the chocolate ganache

- 8 oz. Semisweet chocolate, chopped
- 2 tbsp. Light corn syrup
- 3 tbsp unsalted butter
- 1 c. Heavy cream

What to do

7. Heat up oven to 350°f.
8. Grease bottom of 3 8inch round pans with melted butter or cooking spray.
9. In the bowl of an electric mixer, whisk together melted butter & sugar till smooth. Add in each egg one at a time on low speed & whisk till well combined.
10. Using a big rubber spatula, lightly mix in flour, cocoa, baking soda & salt.
11. Spread batter right into the pans & bake for 25-30 min. Till set.
12. Take away & let cool completely before assembling the cake.

For the coconut filling

3. Place the butter, walnuts & coconut in a big bowl & put to the side.
4. In a medium sauce pan, on low/medium heat, mix together the heavy cream, sugar & egg yolk till the mixture starts to thicken & coats the back of a spoon (180 degrees f.). Pour the hot custard straight away onto the walnut-coconut mixture & mix till the butter is melted. Cool completely to room temperature before topping the brownie layers.

For the vanilla mascarpone buttercream

4. Place softened butter & mascarpone right into the bowl of an electric stand mixer that has been fitted with the whisk attachment. Turn the mixer on a medium setting & cream till it smooth & combined, 2 - 3 min..
5. Add sugar, ½ a c. At a time. Add vanilla beans & a pinch of salt & whisk till well-incorporated.
6. If the frosting is too thick add heavy cream one tbsp at a time till it has reached the desired consistency.

For the chocolate ganache

2. Place the chocolate, corn syrup & butter in a medium bowl. Heat the cream in a small saucepan over medium heat till it only starts

to boil. Take away from heat & pour over the chocolate. Let stand one minute, next which mix till smooth. Cool to room temperature.

Assemble the cake

6. Take away the cooled brownie layers from the pans. Set the first cake layer on a cake plate.
7. Top with a half of the coconut walnut filling, spread it evenly. Top the coconut wittier with ⅓ of the frosting, also spread evenly. Repeat the process with the second brownie cake layer. Third (top) layer, is covered in frosting only, no coconut mixture.
8. Pour the chocolate ganache on top of the cake, distribute evenly & also ice the sides of the cake whereas the ganache is dripping down.
9. Decorate with frosting if you have any remaining & chocolate dashs.
10. Chill the cake for at least 2 hours before serving.

Coffee cake

What you need

- ½ c. Coconut oil
- Eggs
- 1 c. Brown sugar
- 1 tsp. Vanilla
- 1 c. Cooked oatmeal
- Cup white whole wheat flour
- Cup all-purpose flour
- 1 tsp. Cloves
- 1 tsp. Salt
- 1 tsp. Cinnamon
- 1 tsp. Baking soda
- 1 tbsp. Coconut oil
- 1 c. Chopped pecans
- 1 c. Brown sugar

What to do

1. Heat up oven to 350o f. Spray an 8x8" pan with cooking spray.
2. Stir together the coconut oil, eggs, truvia, vanilla & cooked oatmeal.
3. In a separate bowl, mix together flour, cloves, salt, cinnamon & baking soda. Mix dry ingredients with wet ingredients & mix till combined. Pour right into prepared pan.
4. Mix 1 tbsp. Coconut oil, pecans & brown sugar in a small bowl & dash over the top of cake. Bake for 25-30 min.. Cut right into squares & serve.

chocolate cake with caramel & mascarpone

What you need

- 150g of flour
- 30g of cocoa powdered pantaguel
- 1/4 tsp of baking powder
- 1/4 tsp of baking soda
- 1/4 tsp of salt
- 100g of softened butter
- 145g of brown sugar
- 1 egg
- 1 egg yolk
- 75g of melted chocolate
- 1/2 tsp of vanilla extract
- 125ml of milk

For the caramel

- 100g yellow sugar
- 60ml of cream
- Tbsp of unsalted butter
- 1 tsp of vanilla extract
- Pinch of salt

Marscarpone cream & caramel

- 250g mascarpone cheese
- 63g powdered sugar
- 100ml fresh cream
- Caramel

Chocolate shavings

- 100g chocolate

What to do

1. Pre-heat the oven at 175oc & prepare two trays with 15cm with a parchment paper base, spread with butter & dash a little of the powdered cocoa.

2. Mix in a bowl the sieved flour with the cocoa, baking powder, baking soda & salt. Reserve.
3. On an additional bowl, beat the butter with the sugar till it becomes a soft cream.
4. Add the egg & the egg yolk to the butter mixture, whisk well & next which add the melted chocolate & the vanilla. Mix well.
5. Alternating between the flour & the milk, keep involving the liquid mixture, ending with the flour.
6. Divide the mixture on the two trays. Seeing as it is a thick mixture, it will be necessary to smooth it out with a spoon.
7. Bring it to the oven for 30-35mins or till the toothpick comes out clean.
8. Take it out of the oven & let it rest for 10mins before taking it out of the tray & letting it cool completely.

Caramel

1. On a small pan, bring it to medium heat with the sugar, the butter & the cream.
2. Keep stirring non-stop with a spoon, let it shimmer for 3min. Don't stop stirring to avoid it from sticking to the end of the pan.
3. Take it out of the heat & add the vanilla & the salt. Careful because it might me too hot & start to create bubbles.
4. Pour it on a glass bottle & let it cool down at ambient temperature.

Marscarpone cream & caramel

1. Whisk the mascarpone with the sugar & caramel till it becomes a soft & smooth cream.
2. Add the cream & whisk it for 5 more min. Till it becomes smooth again.

Chocolate shavings

1. Put a tray in the fridge, minimum 15min.
2. To season the chocolate, you're going to need to melt half of the black chocolate in bain-marie & the other half, break right into very small pieces.
3. When the chocolate is melted, add the chocolate pieces & mix till it all melts.
4. Pour the chocolate over the tray & spread out a thin layer with the help of a spatula.
5. Wait some min. Till the chocolate dries out, if needed, bring the tray right into the fridge again for less than 5min.

6 With the help of a metallic spatula or a knife, make little rolls.

assembly

1. Put one of the cakes over a base, take out the top & spread a little bit of the cream, some chocolate shaving & some powdered cocoa.
2. On top of it, put the other half of the cake.
3. Spread the remainingo f the cream, chocolate shaving & more powdered cocoa.

Upside-down tea cake

What you need

Upside-down bits

- 300 g kumquats
- Tbsp coconut oil, melted (30 ml)
- 1 c coconut sugar, lightly packed (40 g)
- 1 tbsp boiling water (15 ml)

Cake

- 1 c coconut oil, semi-firm (115 g)
- 1 c coconut sugar, lightly packed (80 g)
- Eggs, at room temperature
- 1 c almond milk (115 ml)
- 1 c orange juice (60 ml)
- 1 tsp vanilla paste
- C whole spelt flour (260 g)
- 2 tbsp arrowroot flour (16 g)
- 2 tsp baking powder
- 1 tsp baking soda
- 1 tsp sea salt

Topping

- Handful flaked almonds
- Handful shredded coconut

What to do

1. Heat up oven to 180°c (350°f). Grease sides of an 8 in. / 20 cm cake tin with a bit of coconut oil.
2. Slice a very thin bit off the end of each kumquat & discard. Cut each kumquat in half — or big ones in thirds — & take away seeds.

Prepare the upside-down bits

1. Drizzle melted coconut oil right into base tin.
2. Combine boiling water & sugar & mix lightly , next which drizzle over coconut oil.

3. Place kumquat slices over caramel mixture, packing them very tightly together.

Make the cake batter

1. In a big bowl use a spatula to cream coconut oil & sugar together till smooth. Add eggs & beat well.
2. Combine orange juice, almond milk & vanilla in a jug. Mix dry ingredients in a separate bowl.
3. Stir a third of the dry ingredients right into the egg mixture followed by half the wet ingredients. Repeat next which end with dry ingredients. Tip batter over kumquats & smooth top.
4. Bake approximately 25 min. Till cake pulls away from the edges & a skewer inserted right into the centre comes out clean. Cool in pan for 5 min., run a knife around the edge next which shake lightly to loosen fruit & tip onto serving plate. Put to the side to cool completely.

Make the topping

1. Toast almonds in oven in a dry pan till only golden, tip right into a plate.
2. Repeat with coconut & mix with almonds.
3. Dash over cake to serve.

Pumpkin carrot cake

What you need
Cake

- Large eggs
- 1 c. Pumpkin puree
- 3/4 c. Granulated sugar
- 1/4 c. Light brown sugar, packed
- 1/2 c. Canola or vegetable oil
- 1 tbsp pumpkin pie spice
- Tsp vanilla extract
- 1 tsp cinnamon
- 1/4 tsp ground cloves
- 1 c. Grated carrots, loosely packed
- 1 c. All-purpose flour
- 1 tsp baking powder
- 1/2 tsp baking soda
- 1/2 tsp salt, or to taste
- 1 c. Raisins, optional (or 1 c. Chopped nuts, or 1/2 c. Raisins & 1/2 c. Chopped nuts)

Frosting

- Ounces cream cheese, softened
- 1/4 c. (half of 1 stick) unsalted butter, softened
- 1 1/2 c. Confectioners' sugar, sifted
- 1/2 tsp vanilla extract
- 1/2 tsp salt, or to taste

What to do
Cake

1. Heat up oven to 350f. Spray a 9-inch springform pan with floured cooking spray or grease & flour the pan; put to the side.
2. To a big bowl, add the eggs, pumpkin, sugars, oil, pumpkin pie spice, vanilla, cinnamon, cloves, & whisk to combine.
3. Add the carrots & mix to combine.
4. Add the flour, baking powder, baking soda, salt, & mix till only combined.

5. Optionally add the raisins and/or nuts & mix to combine. Turn batter out right into prepared pan, smoothing the top lightly with a spatula.
6. Bake for about 45 min. Or till middle is set & a toothpick inserted in the middle comes out clean or with a few moist crumbs, no batter.
7. In the last 10 min., loosely drape a sheet of foil over the top of the springform pan to prevent the top from becoming overly browned.
8. Allow cake to cool completely in pan on a wire rack before frosting it so the frosting.

Frosting

1. To a big bowl add the cream cheese, butter, & beat with an electric mixer on high-speedy till fluffy, about 2 min..
2. Add the confectioners' sugar, vanilla, salt, & beat till smooth & incorporated, about 2 min..
3. Turn frosting out onto cake & spread right into a smooth, even, flat layer utilizing a spatula or knife. Unlatch springform pan, slice, & serve.

Crepe cheesecake

What you need

Crepes

- 1 c. All-purpose flour
- Tbsp sugar
- 1 tsp salt
- Cups whole milk
- Large eggs
- Tbsp unsalted butter, melted
- 1 tsp vanilla extract or 1 vanilla bean, halved & seeds take awayd
- Butter - to cover the pan

Ricotta crepe filling

- Cup ricotta cheese
- Tbsp sugar
- 1 egg
- 1 tbsp flour
- 1 c. Chocolate chips

Cheesecake filling

- (8 ounce) packages cream cheese
- Cup white sugar
- ½ or 1 c. Whole milk
- Eggs
- 1 c. Sour cream
- 1 c. All purpose flour
- 1 tsp vanilla extract or 1 vanilla bean, halved & seeds take awayd

Garnish

- Baking spray
- Ounces dark chocolate, chopped
- 1 lb. Fresh raspberries
- Powdered sugar

What to do

Crepes

1. Place eggs, milk & melted butter in a blender & mix on low - medium speed.
2. Add sugar, salt, vanilla bean seeds & flour - one c. At a time & mix in the blender/or whisk till well combined. Let the batter sit at room temperature for 15-20 min..
3. Place a 12-inch non-stick pan ver low-medium heat & when hot add a little butter to cover it.
4. Pour 1 c. Of crepe batter right into the middle of the pan & swirl to spread evenly. Cook for roughly 1 minute or till the edges of the crepe appear to loosen from the pan.
5. Using a rubber spatula, loosed the crepe edges from the pan, now utilizing your fingertips, quickly flip the crepe & cook for an additional 1 minute, till slightly golden brown.
6. Take away crepe & stack on a plate. Continue with the remaining batter & stack crepes on the plate. Cover the pan with butter as needed.
7. When done cooking, & the crepes have cooled to room temperature, cover them with a kitchen towel to avoid the edges from drying out.

Ricotta crepe filling

1. In a medium bowl, mix ricotta cheese with the egg & sugar, when combined mix in the flour, next fully incorporated add the chocolate chips. Put to the side.

Cheesecake filling

1. In the bowl of an electric mixer, fitted with the wire attachment, mix cream cheese with sugar till smooth. Add the milk, & next which mix in the eggs one at a time, mixing only enough to incorporate. Stop & scrape the bowl sides & the bottom of the bowl, utilizing a rubber spatula. Mix in sour cream, vanilla bean seeds & flour till smooth.

Bake

1. Heat up oven to 350f.
2. Spray a 8 in. Springform pan with baking spray.
3. Place 2 crepes on the bottom of the bowl & 3 on the sides, to create a crepe crust.
4. Pour half of the new york cheesecake filling right into prepared crepe crust.
5. Place a crepe on a working table, put 1 of the ricotta chocolate chip mixture a few in. From the side that is facing you, & spread it over half of the crepe. Roll it lightly right into

a tube & put it prudently right into the pan on top of the cheesecake filling. Repeat with the remaining 3 crepes.
6. Top the crepes with the remaining new york cheesecake filling.
7. Bake in the heat uped oven for 1 hour. Turn the oven off, & let cake cool in oven with the door closed for 4-5 hours, this prevents cracking. If the cake cracks, don't worry since we are covering it in chocolate so it won't be visible.
8. Once you take away the cake from the oven, the crepe edges that are over the pan will be slightly burned, trim them, & bring the crepe crust to the same level as the cake.
9. Keep the cake in the pan.

Garnish

1. Bring a medium saucepan half filled with water to a boil. Put the chocolate in a medium bowl set over the saucepan of simmering water, let it melt, mix only a few times. Take away from heat & put to the side. Pour the chocolate on top of the cheesecake, level the mixture with a spatula or spoon.
2. Top with fresh raspberries & refrigerate for at least 4 - 5 hours or better overnight.
3. Before serving, sift powdered sugar on top of the cake & take away from the springform pan.

Meyer lemon cheesecake

What you need

Blueberry sauce

- Cups fresh blueberries
- 1 c. Water
- 1 c. Sugar
- Tbsp cornstarch, mixed with 2 tbsp cold water
- 1 tbsp vanilla extract

Crust

- Cups graham cracker crumbs
- Tbsp unsalted butter, melted
- Tbsp granulated sugar

Cheesecake filling

- Packages (8 oz.) Cream cheese, softened
- 1 c. Sour cream
- Tbsp cornstarch
- Eggs
- 1 ½ c. Sugar
- 1 c. Graham cracker crumbs
- Juice of one meyer lemon
- Zest from one meyer lemon

What to do

Blueberry sauce

1. In a big saucepan over medium heat, mix blueberries, water & sugar. Mix frequently, but careful not to crush the berries, bring to a low boil.
2. In a small bowl, mix the cornstarch with cold water till combined.
3. Slowly mix the cornstarch right into the blueberries. Simmer till the homemade blueberry sauce is thick enough to cover the back of a metal spoon, about 10 min..
4. Take away from heat & lightly mix in vanilla.

5. Let the sauce cool at room temperature. Measure 1 c. For your recipe, store the remaining in jars in the fridge.

Crust

1. In a big bowl, mix the crumbs with melted butter & granulated sugar with a rubber spatula till combined.
2. Press the mixture right into the bottom of a 9inch spring form cake pan & slightly up the sides. Ensure it is tight & compact.
3. Chill the crust for 15 min..

Cheesecake filling

1. Heat up oven to 325f.
2. In the bowl of an electric mixer fitted with the whisk attachment beat cream cheese on medium speed till fluffy. Add the sugar, cornstarch, lemon juice, lemon zest & beat till combined.
3. Add eggs, one at a time, beating till only combined next each addition. On low speed beat in sour cream only till combined.
4. Take away crust from the fridge & pour the batter right into the crust.
5. In circles pour the blueberry sauce over the cheesecake & with the edge of a spatula create swirls & mix the blueberry sauce right into the cheesecake filling. Prudently not to over mix.
6. Bake for about 11 hours or till middle is just about set. Cool on a wire rack for 15 min.. Dash graham crackers on top & loosen sides of pan & continue cooling on wire rack till the cheesecake is at room temperature.
7. Transfer to the fridge. Refrigerate overnight or at least 6 hours before serving.
8. The cheesecake can be served with warm blueberry sauce.
9. Store in fridge.

Pumpkin spice cake

What you need

Cake

- Large eggs
- 1 c. Granulated sugar
- 1 c. Pumpkin puree
- 1/2 c. Canola or vegetable oil
- Tsp pumpkin pie spice
- 1 tsp vanilla extract
- 1 c. All-purpose flour
- 1 tsp baking powder
- 1/2 tsp baking soda
- 1/2 tsp salt, or to taste

Frosting

- Ounces cream cheese, softened
- 1/4 c. Unsalted butter, softened
- 1 1/2 c. Confectioners' sugar
- 1/2 tsp vanilla extract
- 1/2 tsp salt, or to taste

What to do

Cake

1. Heat up oven to 350f. Line an 8x8-inch pan with aluminum foil & spray with cooking spray; put to the side.
2. To a big bowl, add the eggs, sugar, pumpkin, oil, pumpkin pie spice, vanilla, & whisk to combine.
3. Add the flour, baking powder, baking soda, salt, & mix till only combined.
4. Turn batter out right into prepared pan, smoothing the top lightly with a spatula. Bake for about 35 to 40 minute or till middle is set & a toothpick inserted in the middle comes out clean or with a few moist crumbs, no batter. Set cake aside on a cooling rack to cool completely before .

Frosting

1. To a big bowl add the cream cheese, butter, confectioners' sugar, vanilla, salt, & whisk till smooth & fluffy or beat with an electric mixer.
2. Turn frosting out onto cake & spread right into a smooth, even, flat layer utilizing a spatula or knife. Slice & serve

Strawberry upside down cake

What you need

- 1 c. Sugar
- Tbsp corn starch
- Cups fresh quartered strawberries
- 1 tsp vanilla extract
- For the cake batter
- Cups all-purpose flour
- 1 tbsp baking powder
- 1 tsp salt
- Large eggs, at room temperature
- Cups sugar
- 1 c. Melted butter
- 1 c. Vegetable oil
- 1 c. Whole milk, at room temperature

What to do

Grease & flour a 10 in. Round cake pan very well & heat up oven to 350 degrees f. A big 9 or 10 in. Tube pan or an 9x9 square baking pan can also be used.

Cut the strawberries in half.

Mix the corn starch & 1 c. Sugar together & dash over the strawberries along with the 1 tsp vanilla extract. Toss together well & spread evenly right into the bottom of the prepared pan.

Cake batter

1. Sift together the flour baking powder & salt. Put to the side.
2. In the bowl of an electric mixer, beat together the eggs, sugar at high speed till very foamy.
3. Mix together the butter & vegetable oil in a measuring c. With a spout.
4. Slowly add this butter & oil mixture to the egg & sugar mixture as it continues to beat.
5. Fold in the dry ingredients alternately with the milk. When alternating wet & dry ingredients, always start & end with the dry mixture. =
6. Pour the batter over the strawberries in the baking pan.
7. Bake for 50-60 min. Or till a toothpick inserted in the middle comes out clean.
8. Cool in the pan for about 10 min. Before inverting onto a heatproof serving plate.

9   Serve with whipped cream or vanilla ice cream.

Apple cider bundt cake

What you need

Cake

- 1 1/2 c. Spiced apple cider
- 1 big apple, peeled, cored, & roughly chopped
- 1/2 c. Milk
- 1 tsp vanilla extract
- 1/2 c. All purpose flour
- 1 1/2 tsp baking powder
- 1/2 tsp baking soda
- 1 tsp salt
- 1/4 tsp nutmeg
- 1 tsp cinnamon
- Pinch of ground cloves
- 1/2 c. Unsalted butter, at room temperature
- 3/4 c. Sugar
- 1/2 c. Light brown sugar, packed
- Large eggs, at room temperature
- 1/4 c. Vegetable oil

Topping

- Tbsp granulated sugar
- 1 1/2 tsp cinnamon
- 1 tbsp unsalted butter, melted

What to do

1. Add the cider & chopped apple to a medium saucepan set over medium-high heat & bring the cider to a boil.
2. Reduce the heat to medium & simmer till half of the cider has been absorbed & the apples can be smashed easily with a fork, about 15 min..
3. Take away the saucepan from the heat, & permit to cool for 5 min.. Pour the mixture right into a food processor or blender & blend till pureed & smooth.
4. Measure out 1 c. Of the cider mixture & add to a big measuring cup, along with the milk & vanilla extract. Mix with a fork to combine.

5. Heat up the oven to 350 degrees f & position a rack in the middle of the oven. Grease a 10-cup bundt pan with non-stick spray & dust all over with flour, tapping out the excess.
6. In a medium bowl, whisk together the flour, baking powder, baking soda, salt, nutmeg, cinnamon, & cloves.
7. In the bowl of standard electric mixer fitted with the paddle attachment, beat the butter, granulated sugar, & brown sugar on medium speed till light & fluffy, about 3-4 min.. Add the eggs, one at a time, beating well next each addition. Scrape down the sides of the bowl with a rubber spatula as needed. Add in the oil, & beat to combine, about 1 minute.
8. Lower the mixer speed to low, & add the flour mixture in three batches, alternating with the cider-milk mixture, beginning & ending with the dry ingredients. Mix only till incorporated & scrape down the sides of the bowl with a rubber spatula as needed. Next the last addition, increase the speed to medium & beat for about 20 sec. To fully combine.
9. Scrape the batter right into the prepared pan. Bake the cake till the top is golden brown & a tester inserted right into the middle comes out clean, about 45 min.. Transfer the cake to cooling rack set over a baking sheet & let it cool in the pan for 10 min., next which invert directly onto the cooling rack.
10. Whereas the cake is still warm, mix the granulated sugar & cinnamon to make the topping. Brush the warm cake with melted butter & dash with the cinnamon sugar, utilizing your fingers to rub it onto the sides.
11. Let the cake cool completely.

Chocolate brownie cake with mascarpone

What you need

Brownie layers

- 1 c. Unsalted butter, melted
- Cup granulated sugar
- Large eggs
- 1 c. All-purpose flour
- 1 c. Unsweetened cocoa powder
- 1 tsp salt
- 1 tsp baking soda

Coconut filling

- 1 c. Walnuts, measure next which grind
- 1 c. Coconut flakes
- 1 c. Heavy cream
- 1 c. Sugar
- 1 egg yolk
- Tbsp. Butter, room temperature

Mascarpone

- Sticks of butter, softened
- Oz mascarpone cheese, chilled
- 21 c. Powdered sugar
- 1 vanilla bean
- Pinch of salt

Chocolate ganache

- Ounces semisweet chocolate, chopped
- Tbsp. Light corn syrup
- Tbsp unsalted butter
- 1 c. Heavy cream

What to do

1. Heat up oven to 350°f.
2. Grease bottom of 3 8inch round pans with melted butter or cooking spray.
3. In the bowl of an electric mixer, whisk together melted butter & sugar till smooth. Add in each egg one at a time on low speed & whisk till well combined.
4. Using a big rubber spatula, lightly mix in flour, cocoa, baking soda & salt.
5. Spread batter right into the pans & bake for 25-30 min. Till set.
6. Take away & let cool completely before assembling the cake.

Coconut filling

1. Place the butter, walnuts & coconut in a big bowl & put to the side.
2. In a medium sauce pan, on low/medium heat, mix together the heavy cream, sugar & egg yolk till the mixture starts to thicken & coats the back of a spoon (180 degrees f.).
3. Pour the hot custard straight away onto the walnut-coconut mixture & mix till the butter is melted. Cool completely to room temperature before topping the brownie layers.

Mascarpone

1. Place softened butter & mascarpone right into the bowl of an electric stand mixer that has been fitted with the whisk attachment.
2. Turn the mixer on a medium setting & cream till it smooth & combined, 2 - 3 min..
3. Add sugar, 1 a c. At a time. Add vanilla beans & a pinch of salt & whisk till well-incorporated.

Chocolate ganache

1. Place the chocolate, corn syrup & butter in a medium bowl.
2. Heat the cream in a small saucepan over medium heat till it only starts to boil.
3. Take away from heat & pour over the chocolate. Let stand one minute, next which mix till smooth. Cool to room temperature.

Assemble

1. Take away the cooled brownie layers from the pans. Set the first cake layer on a cake plate.
2. Top with a half of the coconut walnut filling, spread it evenly. Top the coconut wittier with frosting, also spread evenly.

3   Repeat the process with the second brownie cake layer. Third layer, is covered in frosting only, no coconut mixture.
    Pour the chocolate ganache on top of the cake, distribute evenly & also ice the sides of the cake whereas the ganache is dripping down.
4   Chill the cake for at least 2 hours before serving.

Chestnut chocolate cake

What you need

Chestnut layer

- 1 small egg white
- A pinch of cream of tartar
- 1 table spoon powder sugar
- 1 big egg
- 40 grams (1,4 oz) sugar
- 40 grams (1,4 oz) butter, at room temperature
- 80 grams (2,8 oz) chestnut meal boiled & peeled chestnuts
- 25 grams (0,9 oz) rice flour
- A pinch of salt

Chocolate mousse

- 100 grams (3,5 oz) dark eating chocolate
- 60ml. + 80ml. Sweetened heavy whipping cream
- 1 egg yolk
- 20 grams (0,7 oz) sugar
- 1/2 tea spoon vanilla extract
- Grams of gelatine
- Ml. Water

Chocolate ganache

- 50 (1,8 oz) grams dark eating chocolate
- 15 grams (0,5 oz) butter
- 15 ml. Heavy whipping cream

Caramelized nuts

- 40 grams (1,4 oz) sugar
- 50 grams (1,8 oz) raw nuts

What to do
Chestnut layer

1. Heat up your oven to 180c, fan-forced (350f, fan-forced). Line a baking sheet with parchment paper
2. Beat the egg white with the cream of tartar in a medium bowl till soft peaks form. Add the powder sugar & continue to beat till meringue turns glossy & light & stiff peaks form. Put to the side.
3. In an additional bowl beat the eggs with muscovado sugar till the mixture becomes fluffy & thickens a bit. Beat in the butter till all is combined.
4. Gently fold in the chestnut meal, rice flour & a pinch of salt. Mix till all ingredients combine.
5. Gently fold in the egg white.
6. Pour the batter onto the baking sheet & even the top with a spatula.
7. Bake about 7-10 min. Or till the layer turns golden brown.
8. Take away from oven.
9. Cut the chestnut layer whereas it is still hot.
10. Grease 3 rings with coconut butter or other unflavored oil/butter.
11. Using the rings, cut out of the almond layer 3 circles.
12. Place all rings on a big serving plate with parchment paper. Fit in one cake circle in every ring, press to reach the bottom & stick to the paper. Put to the side.

Chocolate mousse

1. In a small bowl mix the chocolate & 60 ml. Of heavy whipping cream.
2. Heat t in the microwave oven till cream is so hot that the chocolate will start to melt. Mix with a small spoon till the chocolate melts & the mixture is glossy & smooth. Put to the side.
3. In a medium saucepan whisk the egg yolk & sugar till pale.
4. Add vanilla extract & start cooking on medium / medium-low heat. Whisk just about continously till sugar dissolves & the egg yolk mixture is hot to the touch. Cook egg yolks on medium low heat till you temper them, continue cooking till the mixture thickens. Whisk often to avoid curdling the eggs.
5. Once the sugar dissolves & the mixture is thickened, take away from the heat & add the chocolate-cream mixture. Mix till all combines & the mixture is smooth. Put to the side.
6. In a medium-size bowl whip 80 ml. Of heavy whipping cream till soft peaks form. Don't over-beat the cream, you need it with soft peaks in order to get a smooth & light as an air mousse. Put to the side.

7. Place 5 grams (1/2 sachet) of gelatine in a small heatproof bowl with 10 ml. Water & let it sit for a few min.. Put the bowl with the gelatine over a small saucepan with simmering water. Let the gelatine heats till liquid smooth, crystal clear like water, only little yellowish. Put to the side to cool off for a bit. Add it to the chocolate-egg mixture & mix to mix completely. Fold in the heavy whipping cream & lightly mix with a rubber spatula.
8. Fill in the cooking rings with the mousse just about to the edge, leave enough room for a layer of chocolate ganache.
9. Put in the fridge to firm up for about two hours.

Chocolate ganache

1. Combine all ingredients in a small bowl & heat in a microwave oven till the chocolate starts to melt. Mix till the mixture is glossy & smooth.
2. Take away mousse cakes from the fridge & pour a little bit of the chocolate ganache over each mousse cake. Put back in the fridge for 30 min..

Caramelized nuts

1. Add sugar to a small saucepan. Set it over medium heat.
2. Cook till it melts completely & turns golden brown. Pour in the nuts & mix to cover all nuts. Take away from heat & straight away transfer the mixture to a big plate lined with parchment paper. Let the nuts cool off completely next which crush with a glass/rolling pan or in the food processor.
3. Once cakes are firm enough & the chocolate ganache is set, lightly take away each cake from the rings, put on a dessert plate & dash some of the nuts over.

Chocolate cake

What you need

- Egg whites at room temperature
- Cups extra fine granulated imperial sugar
- Tbsp unsweetened cocoa powder
- Tsp corn starch
- 1 tbsp lemon juice
- 1 tbsp vanilla extract
- Cups cold heavy whipping cream
- 1 c. Powdered imperial sugar
- 10-12 strawberries, cored & quartered
- Chocolate shavings

What to do

1. Heat up your oven to 250 degrees f. Line a baking sheet with parchment paper.
2. In the bowl of a stand mixer with the whisk attachment, beat the egg whites & granulated sugar on high, till stiff peaks form.
3. Add the cocoa powder, corn starch, lemon juice & vanilla extract & mix till well blended.
4. Transfer to your lined sheet. Use a spatula to make 6 round rings. Ensure there is an indent in the middle of each circle - the centers will rise during baking.
5. Bake for 1 hour & 30 min.. Turn off the oven & permit the meringues to cool in the oven with the door closed for at least 1 hour. When you take away them from the oven, ensure they are completely cool before assembling your pavlova cake.
6. Beat the whipping cream on high for 3-4 min.. Slowly add the powdered sugar till the whipped cream is thick & fluffy.

Assemble

1. Place one meringue on a plate. Top that with whipped cream & repeat till you have used 3 of your meringues.
2. Place several strawberry chunks right into the whipped cream & on top of the cake.
3. Dash chocolate shavings on top.

Oreo cake

What you need

- 1 box chocolate cake mix
- 1 pack of oreo cookies
- 1 big box oreo instant pudding
- Cups milk
- Ounces cool whip

What to do

1. Heat up oven to 350 f. Roughly chop oreo cookies.
2. Grease a 9x13 in. Dish. Prepare chocolate cake according to box directions.
3. Pour cake batter right into the prepared pan. Bake for 30-32 min. Or till a tooth pick inserted in the middle comes out clean.
4. Whereas the cake is cooling whisk milk & pudding together till smooth.
5. Use a wooden spoon to poke holes in the top of the cake. Evenly pour pudding over the top of the cake.
6. Dash with half of the chopped oreos. Cool cake completely.
7. Frost with cool whip. Dash with remaining oreos. Store in the fridge.

Chocolate layered cake

What you need

Layers

- 1 & 3/4 c. (220g) all-purpose flour
- 1 & 3/4 c. (350g) granulated sugar
- 3/4 c. (65g) unsweetened cocoa powder
- 1 tsp baking powder
- Tsp baking soda
- 1 tsp salt
- 1 c. (240ml) buttermilk1
- 1/2 c. (120ml) vegetable oil
- Large eggs, at room temperature2
- 1 tsp pure vanilla extract
- 1 c. (240ml) freshly brewed strong hot coffee

Chocolate frosting

- Cups (2.5 sticks or 290g) unsalted butter, softened to room temperature
- 3-4 c. (360-480g) confectioners' sugar
- 3/4 c. (65g) unsweetened cocoa powder
- 3-5 tbsp (45-75ml) heavy cream
- 1 tsp pure vanilla extract
- 1/2 - 3/4 tsp salt
- 15 oz (1.5 bags) chocolate chips

What to do

Cake

1. Heat up oven to 350f degrees. Butter & flour two 9 in. Round cake pans4, or use non-stick spray.
2. Sift together the flour, sugar, cocoa powder, baking powder, baking soda, & salt in a medium sized bowl. Put to the side.
3. Using a handheld or stand mixer on high speed, mix the buttermilk, oil, room temperature eggs, & vanilla in a big bowl till combined. Slowly add the dry ingredients to the wet ingredients with the mixer on low. Add the coffee. The batter will be very thin. This is ok.

4. Pour the batter right into prepared baking pans & bake for 23-27 min. Or till a toothpick inserted in the middle comes out clean. My cakes took exactly 24 min.. Permit to cool before frosting.

Frosting

1. Using a handheld or stand mixer fitted with a paddle attachment, beat the butter on high speed till smooth & creamy - about 2 full min..
2. Turn speed to low & slowly add 3.5 c. Of confectioners' sugar & the cocoa powder. Beat till sugar/cocoa are absorbed right into the butter, about 2 min.. Turn mixer to medium speed & add the vanilla & cream. When added, turn the mixer to high speed & beat for 1 minute.
3. Taste, & add salt to taste.

Assembly

1. Place 1 layer, flat side up, on a plate or cake stand. With a knife or offset spatula, spread the top with frosting.
2. Place the second layer on top, rounded side up, & spread the frosting evenly on the top & sides of the cake. Decorate with chocolate chips.

cinnamon sugar cake

What you need

- Cups all-purpose flour
- 1 tsp baking powder
- 1 tsp baking soda
- 1 tsp salt
- 21 tsp ground cinnamon
- Large eggs
- 1 c. Granulated sugar
- 1 c. (1 stick) unsalted butter, softened
- Tsp vanilla extract
- 1 c. Sour cream

Buttercream frosting

- 1 (2 sticks) c. Unsalted butter, softened
- Cups confectioners' sugar
- Tbsp 2% milk
- 1 tsp ground cinnamon
- 1 tsp vanilla extract
- 1 tbsp cinnamon-sugar, dash on top of cake

What to do

1. Heat up oven to 350f degrees. Spray two 9-on. Round baking pans with non-stick cooking spray. Put to the side.
2. In a medium bowl, mix flour, baking powder, baking soda, salt & ground cinnamon. Put to the side.
3. In a big bowl, utilizing an electric or stand mixer on medium speed, beat eggs & sugar for about 2 min., or till light & creamy.
4. Add the butter & vanilla extract & beat on low speed for about 1 minute, or till well blended. Beat in the dry ingredients on low speed till blended. Add the sour cream & beat till smooth.
5. Divide batter evenly right into prepared baking pans. Bake 18 to 20 min. Or till toothpick inserted in middle comes out clean. Permit cake to cool before frosting.

Frosting

1. Mix softened butter on medium speed with an electric or stand mixer. Beat for 30 sec. Till smooth & creamy.
2. Add powdered sugar, milk, ground cinnamon & vanilla extract. Increase to high speed & beat for 3 min. Or till smooth.
3. Spread the frosting between layers & over top & sides of cake. Dash with cinnamon-sugar.

Dark chocolate & yogurt cake

What you need

- Tbsp butter
- 1/2 c. Brown sugar
- 1 egg
- 1 tsp vanilla extract
- 1 1/2 c. Flour
- 1 tsp baking powder
- 1/4 tsp salt
- Tbsp dark cocoa powder
- 3/4 c. Plain greek yogurt
- 1/4 c. Milk

Dark cocoa syrup

- 1 c. Powdered sugar
- 1 tbsp dark cocoa powder
- 1 tsp vanilla extract
- 1 tsp water

Instuctions

1. Heat up oven to 350 degrees. Butter & flour an 8×8 cake pan.
2. Cream butter & sugar together till fluffy. Beat in egg & vanilla. Add cocoa, flour, baking powder & salt & mix till combined. Add yogurt & mix till batter is smooth. Add in milk & mix till batter comes together. Pour right into pan.
3. Bake for 18-20 min., or till cake is set. Cake will be thin, & appear a bit spongey. Serve with fresh whipped cream & cocoa syrup.

Dark cocoa syrup

1. Mix all ingredients till a smooth glaze forms.

strawberries cake

What you need
Strawberry cake

- 1 c. Unsalted butter, at room temperature
- Cups white sugar
- Large eggs
- Tsp freshly squeezed lemon juice
- Cups plus 3 tbsp flour
- Tbsp cornstarch
- Tbsp strawberry jell-o mix, dry
- 1/2 tsp baking soda
- 1/4 tsp salt
- 1 c. Buttermilk
- 2/3 c. Chopped fresh strawberries

Frosting

- 1/2 c. Unsalted butter, softened
- 1 (8 ounces) package of full-fat cream cheese at room temperature
- Tsp vanilla extract
- 4- 4 & 1/2 c. Powdered sugar

Topping

- 1 & 1/2 c. Sliced strawberries
- 1 & 1/2 tbsp white sugar

What to do
Cake

1. Heat up the oven to 350 degrees f. Grease & flour a 9 x 13 pan & put to the side.
2. Beat the room temperature butter with hand mixers till light & creamy.
3. Slowly add in the sugar till the mixture is light & fluffy,
4. In an additional bowl, lightly beat the eggs & next which add the mixture & mix along with the freshly squeezed lemon juice. Beat in the buttermilk.

5. In a separate bowl, sift together the flour & cornstarch 2-3 times & next which add in the jell-o mix, baking soda, & salt.
6. Add the dry ingredients to the wet & beat at low speed till only combined.
7. Take away the stems from the strawberries & finely chop. Add in the finely chopped strawberries to the cake.
8. Pour the batter evenly in the prepared 9 x 13 pan.
9. Bake for 30-40 min. Or till a toothpick comes out clean when inserted right into the center.
10. Cool the cake for at least one hour & next which chill in the fridge for an additional hour.

Frosting

1. Beat the softened butter & room temperature cream cheese till completely creamy.
2. Beat in the vanilla. Slowly beat in the powdered sugar till smooth & your desired consistency.
3. Spread the frosting over the cake

Sugared strawberry topping

1. Stir together the sliced strawberries & sugar in a medium bowl.
2. Let them stand at room temperature for about 20-30 min.. Add them to the cake when serving & not beforehand.

Carrot cake

What you need
For the cake

- 2 c. Shredded carrots
- 8 oz crushed pineapple, drained
- ¾ c. Sweetened, shredded coconut
- ½ c. Raisins
- 1½ c. Sugar
- 1 c. Vegetable oil
- 4 big eggs, room temperature
- 2 tsp vanilla extract
- 2 c. All purpose flour
- 1½ tsp baking powder
- 2 tsp baking soda
- 2 tsp cinnamon
- 1 tsp salt

For the frosting

- ½ c. Unsalted butter, room temperature
- 5 oz cream cheese, softened
- 1 tsp vanilla extract
- ½ tsp salt
- 3 c. Powdered sugar

What to do

1. Heat up oven to 350°f. Grease & flour three 8 in. Cake pans & put to the side.
2. In a big bowl, mix the carrots, pineapple, coconut, raisins, sugar, vegetable oil, eggs, & vanilla extract. In a separate bowl, mix the flour, baking powder, baking soda, cinnamon, & salt. Incorporate the dry ingredients right into the wet, stirring till well combined.
3. Evenly pour the batter right into the prepared pans. Bake for 25 min., next which permit to cool completely before frosting.

For the frosting

1. Whip the butter & cream cheese till light & fluffy, about 4 min..
2. Add in the vanilla extract, salt, & powdered sugar & whip to combine, about 2 min. More.
3. Place the first cake on a plate, next which top with ⅓ of the frosting. Layer the second & third layers, frosting in between each. Be freeform with it, utilizing a flat knife to even the top of each layer. If you'd like, decorate the top with edible flowers! Next which ensure you have friends with you when you eat it, or else you'll go nuts.

Mocha cake

What you need

- 1 stick + 1 tbsp (125g) butter
- 1 c. (50g) cocoa
- Tsp instant espresso powder
- Cup (300g) sugar
- 1 c. (150g) plain flour
- Eggs

What to do

1. Heat up the oven to 180c, & grease & line a 7 in. (18cm) cake tin.
2. Melt the butter in a medium saucepan over a low heat, & next which mix in the remaining ingredients.
3. Scrape the batter right into the pan, & bake for 20-40 min., or till the edges are set, but the middle is still gooey. Mine took 30 min., but start checking at 20.
4. Leave to cool for at least 30 min., before removing from the pan & serving with raspberries, & a dollop of creme fraiche.

Chocolate zucchini cake

What you need

- 2-1/4c all-purpose flour
- 1/2c cocoa powder
- 1t baking soda
- 1t salt
- 1-3/4c sugar
- 1/2c butter, softened
- 1/2c canola oil
- 2 eggs
- 1t vanilla extract
- 1/2c buttermilk
- 2c zucchini, grated
- 3/4c semi-sweet chocolate chips

What to do

1. Heat up oven to 325. Grease & flour a 9x13 in. Baking pan.
2. Sift the flour, cocoa powder, baking soda & salt right into a medium bowl.
3. In an additional bowl, beat the sugar, butter & oil in a big bowl till well blended. Add the eggs 1 at a time, beating well next each addition. Add the vanilla extract.
4. Mix in the dry ingredients alternating with the buttermilk in 3 additions. Mix in grated zucchini.
5. Spread right into prepared pan . Dash with chocolate chips. Bake 50 min. Or till toothpick inserted right into the middle comes out clean. Permit to cool about 15 min., slice, & serve warm.

Zesty citrus cheesecake

Yield 8

What you need
1 egg yolk
1 tbsp lemon juice
1 tsp lemon zest, grated
1/4 tsp vanilla extract
1 1/4 c. All-purpose flour
1/3 c. White sugar
1/2 c. Butter
1 egg white
24oz cream cheese
1 2/3 c. White sugar
2 tbsp cornstarch
1 tbsp lemon juice
1 tbsp orange zest, grated
2 tsp lime zest, grated
1 1/2 tsp lemon zest, grated
1/2 tsp vanilla extract
3 eggs
1 c. Sour cream
2/3 c. Orange marmalade
2 tsp fresh lemon juice

What to do
Crust:
1. Heat up oven to 450 °f.
2. Beat egg yolk, 1 tbsp lemon juice, 1 tsp lemon peel & 1/4 tsp vanilla.
3. Mix flour & 1/3 c. Sugar with a food processor. Pour in butter & continue blending. Beat yolk mixture & blend till clumps form.
4. Press crust to the bottom of a lightly greased 9 in. Pan. Cool down for 10 min..
5. Brush crust lightly with egg white. Bake for 15 min..
6. Permit to cool on rack whereas preparing filling.

Filling:
1. Reduce oven temperature to 350 °f.

2. Mix cream cheese & 1 2/3 c. Sugar. Add cornstarch, 1 tbsp lemon juice, orange zest, lime zest, 1 1/2 tsp lemon zest & 1/2 tsp vanilla. Pour in eggs one at a time, next which mix in sour cream.

3. Pour mixture right into crust.

4. Bake for an hour. Turn off the oven, open the door & leave the cheesecake inside to cool next which refrigerate overnight.

5. Boil marmalade & 2 tsp lemon juice till slightly reduced for a couple of min. In saucepan.

6. Spread glaze on cheesecake. Permit to cool for a few min..

Herry jell-o cheesecake

Yield 8

What you need
2 1/2 c. Graham cracker crumbs
1/2 c. Butter, melted
6oz lemon flavored jell-o
1 c. Boiling water
8oz cream cheese
1 c. White sugar
1 tsp vanilla extract
3 tbsp lemon juice
12oz evaporated milk
21oz cherry pie filling

What to do
1. Blend together graham cracker crumbs & melted butter. Press 2 c. Of the mixture right into the bottom of a 9 in. Pan. Put to the side the remaining for garnish.

2. Dissolve lemon jell-o in boiling water. Put to the side.

3. Mix cream cheese, sugar & vanilla. Add jell-o mixture & lemon juice.

4. Whip evaporated milk in a separate bowl. Pour milk right into the cream cheese mixture & pour right into pan.

5. Permit to cool for a few hours. Add cherry pie filling & garnish with remaining crumb mixture.

Classic cheesecake

Yield 8

What you need
1 prepared graham cracker crust
16oz cream cheese
2 eggs
3/4 c. White sugar
2 tsp vanilla extract
1/2 tsp lemon zest, grated

What to do
1. Heat up oven to 350 °f.
2. Beat softened cream cheese slightly. Add eggs, sugar, vanilla, & lemon zest.
3. Bake for 30 min. & permit to cool afterwards before refrigerating for 8 hours.

Classic new york cheesecake

Yield 12

What you need
15 graham crackers, crushed
2 tbsp butter, melted
32oz cream cheese
1 1/2 c. White sugar
3/4 c. Milk
4 eggs
1 c. Sour cream
1 tbsp vanilla extract
1/4 c. All-purpose flour

What to do

1. Heat up oven to 350 °f .
2. Mix together graham crackers crumbs & butter. Press to the bottom of a lightly greased 9 in. Pan.
3. Blend cream cheese with sugar till you achieve a smooth texture. Add milk & mix it with eggs one at a time.
4. Pour in sour cream, vanilla & flour right into the mixture & blend till smooth. Pour filling right into mixture & bake for 1 hour.
5. Turn off the oven, open the door & leave the cheesecake inside to cool for 3-4 hours to prevent it from cracking. Let it cool in the fridge afterwards before serving.

Chocolate cheesecake

Yield 12

What you need
6oz cream cheese, softened
14oz condensed milk
1 egg
1 tsp vanilla extract
1 c. Chocolate chips
1 tsp flour
1 chocolate cookie pie crust

What to do
1. Heat up oven to 350 °f .
2. Mix cream cheese, condensed milk, egg & vanilla extract till smooth.
3. Cover chocolate chips with flour & pour right into the mixture.
4. Pour filling right into pie crust & bake for 35 min..
5. Refrigerate before serving.

No-bake chocolate cheesecake

Yield 10

What you need
8oz semi-sweet chocolate baking squares, melted & cooled
16oz cream cheese, softened
3/4 c. Brown sugar
1/4 c. Granulated sugar
2 tbsp milk
1 tsp vanilla extract
6oz chocolate crumb crusts
Sweetened whipped cream

What to do
1. Mix cream cheese, brown sugar, granulated sugar, milk & vanilla.
2. Pour in melted chocolate & continue beating.
3. Scoop right into crust & cool down inside fridge.
4. Garnish with whipped cream.

Gluten-free diet cheesecake

Yield 12

What you need
16oz low-fat cream cheese
3 eggs
1 c. Splenda
1 tsp vanilla
2 c. Sour cream
1/4 c. Splenda
1 tsp vanilla

What to do
1. Heat up oven to 350 °f .
2. Mix low-fat cream cheese, eggs, 1 c. Splenda & vanilla. Pour mixture right into a lightly greased 9 in. Pan.
3. Bake for 35 min..

4. Take away from oven & permit to cool.

5. Mix low-fat sour cream, 1/4 c. Splenda & vanilla. Pour over cheesecake & bake for 10 more min..

6. Refrigerate.

Layered blackberry cheesecake

Yield 8

What you need
3 tbsp butter, softened
1 c. Sour cream
1 c. Graham cracker crumbs
1/4 c. All-purpose flour
32oz cream cheese
1 tbsp vanilla extract
1 1/2 c. Sugar
1 1/2 pints blackberries
3/4 c. Milk
Zest & juice of 1 lemon
4 eggs

What to do
1. Heat up oven to 350 °f.
2. Mix graham cracker crumbs with 2 tbsp butter.
3. Press mixture to the bottom of a greased 9 in. Pan.
4. Whisk to mix cream cheese & sugar till smooth.
5. Blend in the milk & add eggs one at a time whereas mixing.
6. Add sour cream, flour & vanilla till smooth & divide the mixture evenly right into two bowls.
7. Purée blackberries, lemon zest & juice & pour right into one bowl of the mixture along with a half pint of blackberries & mix well.
8. Pour blackberry filling right into crust & bake for 10 min..
9. Take away pan from the oven & pour the remaining of the filling over the top.
10. Return the pan to bake for an hour till topping is set & cool down in the fridge till ready to serve.

White chocolate raspberry cheesecake

Yield 12

What you need
1 c. Chocolate cookie crumbs
3 tbsp white sugar
1/4 c. Butter, melted
10oz raspberries, frozen
2 tbsp white sugar
2 tsp cornstarch
1/2 c. Water
2 c. White chocolate chips
1/2 c. Half-and-half cream
24oz cream cheese, softened
1/2 c. White sugar
3 eggs
1 tsp vanilla extract

What to do
1. Heat up oven at 325 °f.
2. Blend cookie crumbs, 3 tbsp sugar & melted butter. Press to the bottom of a 9 in. Pan.
3. Mix raspberries, 2 tbsp sugar, cornstarch & water. Boil them in a saucepan & use a strainer to take away seeds afterwards.
4. Melt white chocolate in a pan of simmering water.
5. Blend cream cheese with half c. Sugar. Beat the eggs & pour them in one at a time. Pour in vanilla & melted white chocolate.
6. Pour half of the filling over the crust & add 3 tbsp of raspberry sauce on it. Pour the second half & do the raspberry sauce again on top.
7. Bake for an hour. Open the door & leave the cheesecake inside to cool & cool down in the fridge for 8 hours before serving.

Walnut crust cheesecake

Yield 12

What you need
Crust:
1 c. Graham cracker crumbs
1/4 c. Walnuts, finely chopped
3 tbsp brown sugar
1 tbsp ground cinnamon
1/2 tsp ground nutmeg
5 tbsp butter, melted

Filling:
24oz cream cheese
1 c. White sugar
1 c. Sour cream
1 c. Heavy cream
3 tbsp all-purpose flour
1 tbsp vanilla extract
3 eggs

What to do
Crust:
1. Heat up oven to 350 °f .
2. Mix graham cracker crumbs, walnuts, brown sugar, cinnamon, nutmeg & melted butter. Press to the bottom of a lightly greased 9 in. Pan.
3. Bake for 10 min. & permit to cool.

Filling:
1. Beat cream cheese & sugar till smooth.
2. Add sour cream, heavy cream & whereas still stirring.
3. Add flour & vanilla.
4. Add eggs one at a time.
5. Bake for an hour & cool down in the fridge overnight before serving.

Savoiardi cheesecake

Yield 12

What you need
9oz ladyfingers
19oz cream cheese, softened
1 tsp vanilla extract
1 c. White sugar
1 pint heavy whipping cream
21oz cherry pie filling

What to do
1. Arrange ladyfingers on the bottom of a 9 in. Pan.
2. Whip cream till smooth.
3. Mix together cream cheese, sugar & vanilla till smooth. Pour in the whipped cream.
4. Scoop 1/2 of cream cheese mixture right into pan.
5. Layer with ladyfingers & pour remaining cream cheese mixture over the top.
5. Finish with ladyfingers, topped off with the fruit pie filling. Refrigerate.

Layered creamy orange cheesecake

Yield 10

What you need
16oz cheese, softened
1/2 c. White sugar
2 eggs
3/4 c. Sour cream
1 tsp vanilla extract
1 tsp orange extract
2 drops yellow food coloring
1 drop red food coloring
Graham cracker crust

What to do
1. Heat up oven to 350 °f .
2. Mix cream cheese & sugar together till light & fluffy. Beat in eggs & mix well. Add sour cream & vanilla extract right into cream cheese mixture till smooth.

3. Pour a c. Of cream cheese mixture right into a small bowl & mix in orange extract, yellow food coloring, & red food coloring.

4. Pour plain colored mixture right into graham cracker crust. Drop orange batter over the top of the plain batter.

5. Bake for 30 to 35 min..

6. Turn off the oven, open the door & leave the cheesecake inside to cool & refrigerate.

Moist pecan cheesecake

Yield 8

What you need
1 1/2 c. Graham cracker crumbs
1/2 c. Pecans, chopped
1/3 c. White sugar
6 tbsp butter, softened
Cream cheese, softened
2 c. White sugar
4 eggs, beaten
1 tbsp lemon juice
16oz sour cream
1/2 c. White sugar
1 tsp vanilla extract

What to do
1. Heat up oven to 325 °f .

2. Mix graham cracker crumbs, pecans, & 1/3 c. Of sugar in a bowl, & mix the softened butter right into the crumbs till mixed well.

3. Press to the bottom of a lightly greased 10-inch pan. Beat the cream cheese, 2 c. Of sugar, eggs, & lemon juice together. Spoon the batter on top of the crumbs.

3. Bake for 1 hour & 10 min.. Take away from oven & put to the side to cool.

4. Blend the sour cream, 1/2 c. Of sugar, & vanilla extract together. Pour sour cream mixture over cheesecake evenly.

5. Return to oven, & bake for 10 more min.. Refrigerate.

Tropical pineapple cheesecake

Yield 12

What you need
16oz cream cheese, softened
1 can sweetened condensed milk
1 c. Sugar
1 c. Coconut, finely flaked
1/4 c. Milk
1/4 c. Pecans, crushed
2 eggs
2 tsp vanilla extract
1 pinch salt
1 prepared graham cracker crust
8oz frozen whipped topping, thawed
15oz pineapple, crushed
3 tbsp coconut, finely flaked
1 tbsp pecans, crushed

What to do
1. Heat up oven to 350 °f.
2. Mix cream cheese, sweetened condensed milk, sweetener, 1 c. Coconut, milk, 1/4 c. Pecans, eggs, vanilla extract, & salt till smooth. Pour filling right into crust.
3. Bake for 35 to 40 min..
4. Cool down cheesecake in the fridge for 8 hours or more
5. Pour crushed pineapple evenly over cheesecake & top with whipped topping.
6. Garnish with 3 tbsp flaked coconut & 1 tbsp pecans.

Pumpkin cheesecake

Yield 10

What you need
16oz cream cheese
1/2 c. White sugar
1/2 tsp vanilla extract
2 eggs
1 prepared graham cracker crust
1/2 c. Pumpkin puree
1/2 tsp ground cinnamon
1 pinch ground cloves
1 pinch ground nutmeg
1/2 c. Frozen whipped topping, thawed

What to do
1. Heat up oven to 325 °f.
2. Mix cream cheese, sugar & vanilla. Mix till smooth. Add eggs one at a time. Take out 1 c. Of mixture & spread right into bottom of crust. Put to the side.
3. Pour pumpkin, cinnamon, cloves & nutmeg to the remaining mixture & mix lightly till well incorporated. Lightly pour the batter right into the crust.
4. Bake for 35 to 40 min..
5. Refrigerate for 3 hours or more.
6. Garnish with whipped topping.

Pineapple cheesecake

Yield 8

What you need
8oz cream cheese, softened
1/2 c. White sugar
30oz crushed pineapple, drained
1 3/4 c. Frozen whipped topping, thawed
1 prepared graham cracker crust

What to do

1. Beat together cream cheese & sugar. Add 1 can of pineapple & whipped topping & beat till smooth.
2. Pour mixture right into crust & top with remaining pineapple.
3. Refrigerate.

Peanut butter oreo cheesecake

Yield 12

What you need
4 1/2 c. Oreo cookies, crushed
1 c. Roasted peanuts, chopped
1/2 c. Butter, melted
32oz cream cheese, softened
5 eggs
1 1/2 c. Brown sugar
1 c. Peanut butter
1/2 c. Whipping cream
1 tsp vanilla extract
12 reese's peanut butter cups, broken right into small pieces

Topping:
3oz sour cream
1/2 c. Sugar

What to do
1. Heat up oven to 275 °f.
2. Blend crushed oreo cookies, peanuts & melted butter. Press to the bottom of a lightly greased 10 in. Pan.
3. Beat cream cheese. Add eggs one at a time. Add sugar, peanut butter & cream. Mix till well incorporated.
4. Add in vanilla next which add the peanut butter c. Pieces.
5. Pour batter over the crust. Put the 10 in. Pan right into a larger pan with 1 in. Water up the sides.
6. Bake for an hour & a half. Blend sour cream & sugar & spread evenly on the cheesecake.
7. Return to oven for 5 min.. Take away & permit to cool for an hour.

8. Cool down in the fridge before serving.

Lemon raspberry cheesecake bars

What you need
Crust:
30 vanilla wafer cookies
1/4 c. Butter, melted

Cheesecake:
1/3 c. Heavy cream
1/2 c. White chocolate
16oz cream cheese, softened
3/4 c. Granulated sugar
1 1/2 tsp cornstarch
1/2 c. Sour cream
1 tsp vanilla extract
2 eggs

Topping:
10oz lemon curd
48 raspberries

What to do
Crust:
1. Heat up oven to 350 °f.
2. Blend cookies in the food processor till it turns to fine crumbs.
3. Pour in melted butter & blend till mixed well.
4. Press to the bottom of a lightly greased baking dish.
5. Bake for 8 min. & permit to cool.

Filling:
1. Heat up oven to 300 °f.
2. Heat heavy cream in saucepan over low heat & mix in white chocolate. Mix continuously till melted. Put to the side.
3. Beat cream cheese, sugar & cornstarch till fluffy.

4. Add in sour cream, eggs & vanilla extract whereas slowly beating the whole mixture.
5. Pour filling right into crust & bake for 35 min..
6. Turn off the oven, open the door & leave the cheesecake inside to cool for 20 min..
7. Take away from oven & spread lemon curd on the cheesecake. Refrigerate for 3 hours.
8. Cut right into bars & finish with fresh raspberries.

Zesty cheesecake brownies

Yield 12

What you need
Brownies:
4oz unsalted butter, cut right into pieces
4oz unsweetened chocolate, chopped
1 1/2 c. Sugar
2 tsp vanilla extract
1/2 tsp baking powder
1/4 tsp salt
2 eggs
2/3 c. All-purpose flour

Cheesecake:
8oz cream cheese,
1/4 c. Sugar
1 egg
1 tsp grated orange zest
1 tbsp all-purpose flour

What to do
Brownies:
1. Heat up oven to 325 ºf .
2. Mix butter & chocolate in a bowl & set over a pan of simmering water. Mix often till smooth. Take away bowl & permit to cool.
3. Mix sugar, vanilla, baking powder & salt right into the mixture. Add eggs one at a time. Lastly, add flour.

Cheesecake:

Combine cream cheese & sugar till smooth in a separate bowl for the cheesecake mixture. Add in egg, zest & flour.

Assemble:
1. Pour 1/2 c. Of brownie batter right into prepared pan.
2. Pour cream cheese mixture over brownie batter in pan.
3. Pour the remaining brownie batter in a swirl motion to create a marbling effect.
4. Bake for 45 min. & permit to cool afterwards.
5. Refrigerate. Cut right into squares.

Caramel brownie cheesecake

Yield 10

What you need
Brownies:
8oz butter, melted
1 c. Unsweetened cocoa powder
2 c. Granulated sugar
4 eggs
1 tsp vanilla extract
1 1/2 c. Flour
12oz hot fudge sauce

Cheesecake:
8oz cream cheese
1/2 can sweetened condensed milk
1 tsp vanilla

Topping:
4 full sized caramel biscuit bars
Caramel sauce

What to do
Brownies:
1. Heat up oven to 350 °f.

2. Mix cocoa & melted butter. Mix in sugar & add eggs one at a time. Add vanilla & keep stirring.
3. Add flour & hot fudge sauce.
4. Pour filling right into a lightly greased 9-inch pan & bake for 35 min.. Permit to cool & refrigerate.

Cheesecake:
1. For the cheesecake layer, mix cream cheese, sweetened condensed, milk & vanilla till smooth.
2. Spread mixture over brownies & top with twix bars. Refrigerate before serving.
3. Garnish with caramel sauce.

Cheesecake-stuffed strawberries

Yield 24

What you need
24 strawberries
12oz cream cheese
1 tsp vanilla
3 tbsp confectioners' sugar
1/2 c. Almonds, chopped fine in the blender

What to do
1. Pour cream cheese in a bowl & microwave for 30 min..
2. Blend cream cheese, vanilla & sugar till smooth.
3. Make a hole in the middle of each strawberry, but do not go all the way through the strawberry.
4. Scoop filling right into each strawberries.
5. Garnish with almonds.
6. Cool down strawberries in the fridge before serving.

Cheesecake tarts

Yield 14

What you need
16oz cream cheese, softened
3/4 c. Sugar
2 tbsp all-purpose flour
2 eggs
1/2 tsp vanilla extract
1/4 tsp almond extract
Vegetable cooking spray
2/3 c. Gingersnap crumbs
3 c. Assorted fresh fruit

What to do
1. Heat up oven to 350 °f .
2. Beat cream cheese till smooth. Add sugar & flour, mix well. Add eggs, one at a time whereas stirring.
3. Dash gingersnap crumbs evenly between tart pans.
4. Pour cheesecake batter evenly between tart pans.
5. Bake for 20 min.. Permit to cool & take away from tart pans.
6. Spread fruit evenly over each cheesecake tart.

Cheesecake lollipops

Yield 8

What you need
24oz cream cheese, softened
3/4 c. Sugar
1/3 c. Sour cream
3 tbsp all-purpose flour
1 tsp vanilla
1/4 tsp salt
3 eggs

24 lollipop sticks
10oz white chocolate
Chocolate chips
Toasted coconut

What to do
1. Heat up oven to 350 °f .
2. Mix cream cheese & sugar till smooth. Pour in sour cream & mix well.
3. Mix flour, vanilla & salt in the mixture. Beat eggs one at a time.
4. Pour filling right into a lightly greased 9-inch pan.
5. Bake for 50 min..
6. Turn off the oven, open the door & leave the cheesecake inside to cool. Refrigerate.
7. Take small scoops out of cheesecake. Form right into 1 1/2-inch balls & put on a lined baking sheet.
8. Attach lollipop sticks to each cheesecake ball. Put the tray in the freezer till firm.
9. Heat white chocolate till melted. Dip each cheesecake lollipop right into the chocolate.
10. Garnish lollipops with chocolate chips or toasted coconut if you wish.
11. Permit covering to set. Cool down in the fridge before serving.

Toffee cheesecake bars

What you need
16oz cream cheese
1/2 c. Brown sugar
1 tsp vanilla extract
1 tsp ground cinnamon
1/4 tsp ground nutmeg
1/4 tsp ground cloves
3/4 c. Chopped toffee bars

What to do
1. Beat cream cheese till smooth.
2. Add sugar, vanilla, cinnamon, nutmeg & cloves & blend till well incorporated.
3. Dip toffee bars in mixture & refrigerate.
4. Serve with fruits, graham crackers or pretzels.

Bittersweet apple cheesecake roll
yield 10

What you need
6 tortillas
2 tbsp butter, melted
1 tbsp granulated sugar
1 tsp cinnamon
Salted caramel sauce

Apple filling:
1 tbsp butter, melted
3 c. Apple, peeled, chopped
2 tbsp granulated sugar
1 tsp cinnamon, ground
1/4 tsp nutmeg, ground
1/4 tsp allspice, ground

Cheesecake filling:
8oz cream cheese
1/3 c. Granulated sugar
2 tbsp all-purpose flour
1/2 tsp vanilla extract

What to do
1. Heat up oven to 350 °f .
2. Melt butter over medium heat. Add chopped apples, sugar & spices. Mix well. Cook for 10 min..
3. Mix cream cheese, sugar, flour & vanilla till well incorporated.
4. Arrange tortillas at the bottom of a 9 in. Pan & spread filling over them.
5. Spread apple mixture evenly over the filling.
6. Mix together 1 tbsp granulated sugar & 1 tsp of cinnamon. Dash half of it over butter.
7. Roll tortillas & put seam down. Brush it with butter.
8. Garnish with remaining cinnamon sugar. Bake for 25 min..
9. Pour over salted caramel sauce & serve.

Cranberry cheese squares

Yield 16

What you need
Crust:
1 1/2 c. Granola
1/4 c. Butter, melted

Cheesecake:
12 ounces   cream cheese
1/2 c. Greek yoghurt
1/3 c. Sugar
2 tbsp all-purpose flour
1 tsp almond extract
2 eggs

Cranberry mixture:
3/4 c. Canned jellied cranberry sauce

Garnish:
1/3 c. Sliced almonds

What to do
1. Heat up oven to 350 °f .
2. Finely grind granola & mix with 3 tbsp sugar & the melted butter till well incorporated. Press to the bottom of an ungreased 9 in. Pan.
3. Bake for 8 min..
4. In a separate bowl, mix cream cheese, yogurt, sugar, flour, almond extract & eggs till smooth.
5. Pour cheesecake batter over the baked crust. Layer with spoonfuls of cranberry on top. Top off with almonds.
6. Bake for 40 min. & permit to cool afterwards.
7. Cool down in the fridge before cutting right into squares.

Banana cheesecake

Yield 10

What you need
20 vanilla cream-filled sandwich style cookies, finely chopped
1/4 c. Butter, melted
24oz cream cheese, softened
2/3 c. Granulated sugar
2 tbsp cornstarch
3 eggs
3/4 c. Mashed banana
1/2 c. Whipping cream
2 tsp vanilla extract
Coconut, for topping

What to do
1. Heat up oven to 350 °f.
2. Blend cookies & margarine. Mix well. Press to the bottom of a lightly greased 10 in. Pan.
3. Mix cream cheese, sugar & cornstarch. Add eggs one at a time.
4. Add bananas, whipping cream & vanilla. Pour filling right into crust.
5. Bake for 15 min.. Reduce temperature to 200 °f & bake for 75 min.. Permit to cool.
6. Refrigerate.

Chocolate truffle cheesecake

Yield 10

What you need
1 1/2 c. Chocolate- cookies, crushed
2 tbsp butter, melted
8oz semisweet chocolate bars, chopped
1 c. Whipping cream
32oz packages cream cheese, softened
14oz sweetened condensed milk

2 tsp vanilla extract
4 eggs
Fresh raspberries

What to do
1. Heat up oven to 300 °f .
2. Mix crushed cookies & butter. Press mixture to the bottom of a 9-inch springform pan.
3. Microwave chocolate & cream till melted, stirring at 30-second intervals.
4. Beat cream cheese till smooth.
5. Add sweetened condensed milk & vanilla & mix well. Add eggs one at a time. Pour in chocolate mixture. Mix well.
6. Pour mixture right into crust.
7. Bake 1 hour & 5 min.. Turn off the oven, open the door & leave the cheesecake inside to cool for 30 min.
8. Refrigerate overnight.
9. Top with fresh raspberries.

Chocomint cheesecake

Yield 10

What you need
8oz cream cheese, softened
3 tbsp granulated sugar
1/2 tsp vanilla extract
1/8 tsp peppermint extract
8oz frozen whipped topping, thawed
12 mint chocolate cookies, finely chopped

What to do
1. Mix cream cheese & sugar till smooth & creamy. Add extracts & mix well.
2. Fold whipped topping right into cream cheese mixture. Add mint chocolate cookies.
3. Pour filling right into pastry bag. Cut the end of the bag & pipe batter right into serving glasses.
4. Alternate layers of the cookies & cream cheese mixture with chopped cookies.
5. Top with additional whipped topping & chopped cookies.

Green tea mousse cheesecake

Yield 12

What you need
4.8oz graham crackers, crushed
2 tbsp white sugar
3 tbsp butter, melted
2 tbsp green tea powder
1/2 c. Warm water
2 tbsp gelatin
1/2 c. Cold water
2 c. Whipping cream
16oz cream cheese
1/2 c. White sugar
1 tsp vanilla extract
1/4 c. Honey
2 eggs

What to do
1. Mix graham cracker crumbs, 2 tbsp sugar & butter.
2. Press to the bottom of a lightly greased 9 in. Pan.
3. Mix matcha powder right into warm water. Put to the side.
4. Dash gelatin over cold water. Put to the side.
5. Beat the cream to stiff peaks; put to the side.
6. Mix together cream cheese, 1/2 c. Sugar, vanilla, & honey in a bowl.
7. Add in the eggs one at a time.
8. Cook the gelatin mixture in the microwave till melted.
9. Pour gelatin & tea right into cream cheese mixture, next which add in whipped cream till smooth.
10. Pour batter over pan.
11. Refrigerate overnight.

Frozen blueberry & lime cheesecake

Yield 12

What you need
3 limes
2oz caster sugar
8.8oz blueberries

Cheesecake:
3 egg whites
5oz confectioners' sugar
8.8oz mascarpone
1/2 tsp vanilla extract
10oz double cream

Crust:
8.8oz amaretti biscuits
2oz butter

What to do
1. Grate the lime zest. Put to the side.
2. Squeeze the juice from the limes right into a pan. Add sugar & blueberries & heat till sugar dissolves. Simmer for 1-2 min..
3. Take away blueberries & put to the side. Reduce juice till slightly thickened. Pour over the blueberries & put to the side.
4. Beat egg whites till stiff, add confectioners' sugar till it forms soft peaks.
5. Mix mascarpone, lime zest & vanilla. Whip the cream & fold right into the mascarpone. Fold in egg white mixture.
6. Crush the amaretti biscuits right into crumbs & mix with melted butter. Press to the bottom of a lightly greased pan.
7. Spread the blueberries & juice over the base. Spread the cheesecake mixture over the blueberries. Dash the amaretti crumbs over the top.
8. Freeze.

Salted caramel ginger snap cheesecake

Yield 12

What you need

Cheesecake:
3 1/2 c. Ginger snaps, finely ground
1/2 c. Almonds, ground
2/3 c. Butter, melted
1 1/2 c. Ricotta cheese
16oz cream cheese
1 c. Brown sugar
4 eggs
2 tbsp golden syrup
1/4 tsp salt
1 tsp vanilla extract

Sauce:
1 c. Whipping cream
1/4 c. Butter, cubed
1 c. Brown sugar

Topping:
1 c. Whipping cream
1 c. Sour cream
1 tsp vanilla
1 tbsp confectioners' sugar, sifted
Sea salt

What to do
Cheesecake:
1. Heat up oven to 325 °f.
2. Mix ginger snaps, almonds & butter. Mix till well incorporated.
Press to the bottom of a lightly greased 8 in. Pan.
3. Refrigerate.
4. Beat ricotta & cream cheese in a bowl till smooth. Mix in sugar & mix well.
5. Add the eggs one at a time. Add syrup, salt & vanilla. Scoop mixture over the crust.
6. Bake for an hour & a half. Refrigerate.
7. Garnish cheesecake with the cream, drizzle with the caramel sauce & dash with sea salt flakes.

Sauce:
1. Mix cream, butter & sugar in a saucepan over low heat & mix till sugar is dissolved.
2. Increase & bring to boil & cook for till thickened & becomes the color of caramel. Permit to cool.

Topping:
Beat together cream, sour cream, confectioners' sugar & vanilla in a bowl.

Coffee cheesecake

Yield 12

What you need
8 whole graham crackers, crushed
5 tbsp butter, melted
1 1/2 c. Sugar
1/2 c. Whipping cream
4 tsp instant coffee powder
1 1/2 tsp vanilla extract
8oz cream cheese
2 tbsp all-purpose flour
1 c. Semi-sweet chocolate chips
Chocolate, shaved right into curls

What to do
1. Heat up oven to 350 °f .
2. Mix graham crackers, butter & 1/4 c. Sugar. Press to the bottom of a lightly greased 9 in. Pan.
3. Bake for 10 min.. Permit to cool.
4. Blend cream cheese, coffee & vanilla.
5. Beat cream cheese, 1 1/4 c. Sugar & add eggs one at a time. Mix in flour.
6. Mix espresso mixture & pour right into cream cheese mixture. Add chocolate chips.
7. Pour mixture over crust. Bake for an hour.
8. Permit to cool. Refrigerate overnight.
9. Garnish with chocolate curls.

Chocolate melt cheesecake

Yield 10

What you need
1 1/2 c. Vanilla wafer crumbs, crushed
1/2 c. Powdered sugar
1/3 c. Cocoa
1/3 c. Butter, melted
24oz cream cheese, softened
14oz sweetened condensed milk
2 c. Semi-sweet chocolate chips, melted
4 eggs
2 tsp vanilla extract
Whipped cream
More chocolate chips

What to do
1. Heat up oven to 300 °f .
2. Blend vanilla wafer crumbs, powdered sugar, cocoa & butter.
2. Press mixture to the bottom of a lightly greased 9 in. Pan. Put to the side.
3. Beat cream cheese till fluffy. Slowly add milk whereas beating.
4. Pour melted chocolate chips, egg & vanilla. Pour mixture right into crust.
5. Put cheesecake pan in a larger baking pan with warm water midway up the sides & bake for an hour.
6. Take away & permit to cool. Serve.

Mint cheesecake

Yield 12

What you need
12oz oreos, crushed
3 tbsp butter
24oz cream cheese
3/4 c. Sugar
1/3 c. Sour cream
4 eggs
2 tbsp all-purpose flour

1 tsp vanilla extract
1/2 tsp peppermint extract
1/2 tsp salt
1/3 c. Candy cane, crushed

What to do
1. Heat up oven to 300 °f.
2. Blend together oreo crumbs & butter. Press to the bottom of a lightly greased 9 in. Pan.
3. Bake crust for 10 min..
4. Beat cream cheese till smooth. Add sour cream. Add eggs in one at a time. Add flour, vanilla, peppermint extract & salt & beat till smooth.
5. Pour filling over baked crust.
6. Bake for an hour. Permit to cool afterwards & refrigerate.
7. Garnish with candy cane.

Toffee truffle cheesecake

Yield 8

What you need
Crust:
1 1/2 c. Graham cracker crumbs
1/2 c. Toasted almond, finely chopped
1/2 c. Toffee pieces
2 tbsp dark brown sugar
1/4 tsp salt
6 tbsp butter, melted

Filling:
32oz cream cheese
1 c. Packed dark brown sugar
4 eggs
1 tbsp vanilla extract
1/4 tsp almond extract
8oz chocolate-covered toffee bars, chopped

Topping:
16oz sour cream
1/2 c. Sugar
1 tsp vanilla extract
Extra crushed chocolate-covered toffee bar, for sprinkling

What to do
1. Heat up oven to 350 °f .
2. Mix graham cracker crumbs, toasted almonds, toffee pieces, dark brown sugar, salt & butter.
3. Press to the bottom of a lightly greased 10 in. Pan
4. Bake for 5 min.. Take away from oven & reduce temperature to 325 °f .
5. Mix cream cheese & sugar. Add eggs one at a time.
6. Pour half of the batter right into the baked crust. Dash with toffee pieces.
7. Pour the other half of the mixture over the toffee pieces.
8. Bake for an hour.
9. Mix topping ingredients till smooth. Pour over cheesecake.
10. Permit to cool & refrigerate. Garnish with crushed toffee.

Lime cheesecake

Yield 8

What you need
1 1/4 c. Graham cracker crumbs
1/4 c. Sugar
3 tbsp butter, melted
24oz cream cheese
1 1/4 c. Sugar
4 eggs
1 1/2 tbsp lime juice
1 pinch salt

What to do
1. Heat up oven to 350 °f .
2. Mix graham cracker crumbs, sugar & melted butter in a bowl. Press to the bottom of a lightly greased 9 in. Pan.

3. Bake for 10 min.. Take away from oven & permit to cool.

4. Mix together cream cheese, sugar & eggs till well incorporated. Add in lime juice & pinch of salt.

5. Pour mixture over baked crust.

6. Bake for an hour & permit to cool. Refrigerate before serving.

Chocolate snickers cheesecake

Yield 12

What you need
3 tbsp butter, melted
1 1/4 c. Sweet biscuit crumbs
1 tbsp white sugar
26oz cream cheese
3 eggs
3/4 c. White sugar
2 tsp vanilla essence
2 snickers bars, chopped

What to do
1. Heat up oven to 355 °f.

2. Mix together melted butter, biscuit crumbs & 1 tbsp sugar. Press to the bottom of a 9 in. Pan. Bake for 10 min..

3. Cream sugar & cream cheese till smooth. Add eggs one at a time, followed by vanilla. Add in chopped snickers bars.

4. Pour mixture right into crust.

5. Bake for an hour. Permit to cool.

Double layer creamy pumpkin cheesecake

Yield 12

What you need

16oz cream cheese, softened
1/2 c. White sugar
1/2 tsp vanilla extract
2 eggs
1 prepared graham cracker crust
1/2 c. Pumpkin puree
1/2 tsp ground cinnamon
1 pinch ground cloves
1 pinch ground nutmeg
1/2 c. Frozen whipped topping, thawed

What to do
1. Heat up oven to 350 °f
2. Mix cream cheese, sugar & vanilla. Pour in eggs one at a time. Pour a c. Of the mixture & spread over bottom of the prepared crust. Put to the side.
3. Add pumpkin, cinnamon, cloves & nutmeg to the remaining mixture & mix lightly till smooth. Pour over the first layer of mixture in the crust.
4. Bake for 40 min.. Let it cool.
5. Refrigerate overnight. Garnish with whipped topping before serving.

Caramel macchiato cheesecake

Yield 12

What you need
2 c. Graham cracker crumbs
1/2 c. Butter, melted
2 tbsp white sugar
24oz cream cheese, softened
1 c. White sugar
3 eggs
8oz sour cream
1/4 c. Brewed espresso or strong coffee
2 tsp vanilla extract

Whipped cream
Caramel ice cream topping

What to do
1. Heat up oven to 350 °f.
2. Mix graham cracker crumbs, melted butter, & 2 tbsp of sugar. Press to the bottom of a lightly greased pan.
3. Bake for 8 min.. Permit to cool.
4. Reduce oven temperature to 350 °f.
5. Beat cream cheese in a bowl till fluffy. Slowly add in 1 c. Of sugar whereas still beating.
6. Beat in eggs one at a time & slowly add sour cream, espresso & vanilla. Pour batter right into the crust.
7. Bake for an hour. Permit to cool.
8. Refrigerate before serving. Garnish with whipped cream & top with caramel ice cream.

Vanilla mousse cheesecake

Yield 16

What you need
40 wafers, crushed
3 tbsp butter, melted
32oz cream cheese, softened
1 c. Sugar
4 tsp vanilla
3 eggs
8oz frozen whipped topping, thawed

What to do
1. Heat up oven to 350 °f
2. Mix wafer crumbs & butter. Press to the bottom of a lightly greased 9 in. Pan.
3. Beat cream cheese, 3/4 c. Sugar & 1 tbsp vanilla with mixer till well blended. Add eggs one at a time. Spread over crust.
4. Bake for an hour. Permit to cool.

5. Mix remaining cream cheese, sugar & vanilla till well incorporated.
6. Beat in whipped topping. Spread over cheesecake.
7. Refrigerate.

Red velvet cheesecake cups

Yield 12

What you need
Crust:
10 chocolate sandwich cookies, crushed
2 tbsp butter

Cheesecake:
12oz cream cheese, softened
1 tbsp sour cream
1/2 c. Sugar
3 tbsp unsweetened cocoa powder
1 tsp vanilla extract
4 tsp red food color
1 egg

Whipped cream:
1/2 c. Heavy cream
2 tbsp powdered sugar
1/2 tsp vanilla extract

What to do
1. Heat up oven to 350 °f.
2. Mix crushed cookies & butter.
3. Press a spoonful of cookie mixture to the bottom 12 cupcake liners
4. Bake for 10 min.. Take away from oven & put to the side to cool.
5. Reduce oven temperature to 325 °f.

6. Mix cream cheese, sour cream & sugar till smooth. Add cocoa powder. Add vanilla & red food color, followed by the egg.

7. Pour mixture right into each liner.

8. Bake for 15-18 min..

9. Permit to cool. Refrigerate.

10. Beating whipped cream ingredients together till soft peaks form. Use to garnish cheesecake cups.

Blueberry cheesecake cups

Yield 24

What you need
8oz cream cheese
3/4 c. Sugar
2 tsp lemon zest, finely grated
1 tsp vanilla extract
2 c. Blueberries
24 vanilla wafer cookies

What to do
1. Mix cream cheese, sugar, zest & vanilla in a food processor. Add blueberries to the mixture.

2. Spread blueberry mixture evenly among 24 cupcake liners.

3. Put a vanilla wafer on top of each cup.

4. Cool down in the fridge overnight.

Honey cheese cups

Yield 8

What you need
9oz ricotta cheese
1/3 c. Caster sugar
1/3 c. Honey
4 eggs
1 tsp ground cinnamon
1 lemon zest, finely grated

What to do
1. Heat up oven to 355 ºf.
2. Mix ricotta cheese, sugar & honey till well incorporated.
3. Add eggs one at a time. Add cinnamon & lemon rind.
4. Pour mixture to 8 lightly greased muffin pans.
5. Bake for 25 min.. Permit to cool afterwards.
6. Garnish with extra honey.

Berry cheesecake cups

Yield 12

What you need
16oz strawberries, halved
1/2 c. Plus 2 tbsp sugar
1 tbsp lemon juice
20oz cream cheese
3/4 c. Sugar
1/2 tsp vanilla extract
1/4 c. Sour cream
2 eggs
3 tbsp all-purpose flour

What to do
1. Heat up oven to 350 °f.
2. Mash together half of the strawberries with sugar. Heat the pan & cook for 3 min..

3. Take away pan from heat & pour in the remaining strawberries together with lemon juice. Permit to cool.

4. Beat cream cheese & add sugar. Add in vanilla & sour cream till well incorporated. Add eggs one at a time & mix with flour.

5. Line a muffin tin with muffin cups. Fill each about 3/4 & bake for 15 min.. Permit to cool.

6. Cool down in the fridge till set & garnish each cheese c. With 1 tbsp of strawberry topping.

Mini berry cheese cups

Yield 10

What you need
1 1/2 c. Graham cracker crumbs
1/4 c. Sugar
1/4 c. Butter, melted
24oz cream cheese
14oz condensed milk
3 eggs
2 tsp vanilla
Raspberries

What to do
1. Heat up oven to 300 °f .
2. Line cupcake tin with cupcake papers .
3. Mix crumbs, sugar & butter. Press mixture right into pan lined with 24 cupcake liners.
4. Mix cheese cream cheese till smooth. Slowly add condensed milk, eggs & vanilla. Mix well.
5. Spread mixture evenly between the cupcake liners.
6. Bake for 20 min. & permit to cool. Refrigerate.
7. Garnish with berries.

Blackberry cheese cups

Yield 10

What you need
1 c. Graham cracker crumbs
1/2 c. Sugar
3 egg whites
16oz reduced-fat cream cheese
2 tbsp all-purpose flour
1 tsp lemon zest, grated
1/2 c. Low-fat plain greek yoghurt
1 tbsp vanilla extract
1 egg
2 c. Blackberries
1/2 c. Seedless raspberry preserves

What to do
1. Heat up oven to 325 °f.
2. Mix graham cracker crumbs, 2 tbsp sugar & 1 egg white in a bowl till combined.
3. Press to the bottom of each liner & bake for 5 - 8 min..
4. Blend cream cheese in a bowl till smooth. Add remaining sugar, flour & lemon zest. Pour in yogurt, vanilla, whole egg & remaining 2 egg whites, one at a time.
5. Spread cream cheese mixture evenly among the muffin cups. Bake for 30 min..
6. Permit to cool. Refrigerate.
7. Garnish each cheesecake with blackberries.
8. Mix remaining blackberries, pre yield & 2 tbsp water right into pan. Bring to a boil over medium heat.
9. Mix well till sauce has thickened.
10. Glaze over cheesecakes.

Chocolate cheesecake cups

Yield 15

What you need

1 1/2 c. Chocolate graham cracker crumbs
2 tbsp sugar
6 tbsp butter, melted
16oz cream cheese, softened
1 c. Hot chocolate mix
2 eggs
2 tbsp sour cream
2 tsp vanilla
2 tbsp flour
1 c. Cool whip
1/2 c. Kraft mini marshmallow bits
1/4 c. Colored sprinkles

What to do
1. Heat up oven at 350 °f .
2. Mix together graham cracker crumbs, sugar & butter.
3. Line baking pan with cupcake liners & put to the side.
4. Blend cream cheese & hot chocolate till creamy.
5. Pour in eggs, sour cream, vanilla & flour & blend again till fully combined.
6. Scoop mixture right into the cupcake liners & bake for 22 min..
7. Turn off the oven, open the door & leave the cheesecake inside to cool for a few min. Before refrigerating.
8. Garnish with cool whip, marshmallows & colored sprinkles.

Miniature cherry cheesecakes

Yield 12

What you need
12 vanilla wafers
16 ounces cream cheese, softened
2 eggs
2 tbsp lemon juice
2/3 c. White sugar
21oz cherry pie filling

What to do

1. Heat up oven to 350 °f .
2. Prep muffin tins with 12 paper baking c. Placing a vanilla wafer in each one.
3. Beat cream cheese till fluffy. Add eggs, lemon juice, & sugar & mix till smooth.
4. Spoon 2/3 cream cheese mixture right into each baking cup.
5. Bake for 15 to 17 min. & permit to cool.
6. Garnish with fruit pie filling or whipped cream before serving.

Sundried tomato cheesecake

Yield 24

What you need
Crust:
5 slices whole wheat bread
1/2 c. Fresh parsley, chopped
1/2 tsp salt
1/2 tsp lemon rind, grated
1/2 tsp black pepper
1 tbsp butter
1 tsp extra virgin olive oil
1 garlic clove, minced

Cheesecake:
1 1/4 c. Sun-dried tomatoes, without oil
1 1/4 c. Cottage cheese
1 tbsp lemon juice
1 tbsp all-purpose flour
1/4 tsp salt
32oz cream cheese
2 egg whites

1/4 c. Fresh basil, chopped
1/2 c. Drained canned artichoke hearts, chopped
13oz melba toast rounds

What to do
1. Heat up oven to 350 °f .
2. Prep bottom of a 9-inch pan with parchment.
3. Mix breadcrumbs, parsley, 1/2 tsp salt, rind, & pepper in a medium bowl.
4. Heat butter in a skillet. Add oil & garlic cook for a min. Whereas stirring continuously.
5. Mix butter mixture with breadcrumbs. Stir.
6. Press breadcrumb mixture to the bottom of the pan. Put to the side.
7. Cover sun-dried tomatoes with boiling water for 30 min.. Drain & finely chop.
8. Beat cottage cheese till smooth. Add lemon juice, flour, salt, cream cheese & egg whites. Mix till smooth.
9. Add tomatoes, basil, & artichoke.
10. Pour filling right into pan.
11. Bake for 30 min.. Let cool.
12. Serve with melba toast rounds.

Roasted pepper pesto cheesecake

Yield 24

What you need

Cooking spray
2 tbsp dry breadcrumbs
15oz ricotta cheese
8oz light cream cheese, softened
1/3 c. Parmesan cheese, grated
1/8 tsp salt
Pinch ground red pepper
1 egg
1 1/4 c. Roasted pepper pesto
1 tsp all-purpose flour
8oz sour cream
French bread baguette, sliced diagonally right into 24

24 roasted red bell pepper strips

What to do

1. Heat up oven to 325 °f .
2. Prep 2 9-inch pans with cooking spray. Dash breadcrumbs over the bottoms of pans.
3. Beat ricotta & cream cheese till smooth. Add parmesan cheese, salt, pepper, & egg. Mix well.
4. Pour 3/4 c. Cheese mixture right into each prepared pan. Spread 1/2 c. Roasted pepper pesto over each layer; top each pesto layer with 3/4 c. Cheese mixture.
5. Bake for an hour.
6. Mix 1/4 c. Roasted pepper pesto, flour, & sour cream in a bowl; mix well. Spread half the mixture over each cheesecake. Bake at 325 °f for 10 min..
7. Take away cheesecakes from oven, permit to cool.
8. Cut each cheesecake right into 12 wedges; serve with baguette slices. Garnish with bell pepper strips, if desired.

Feta cheesecake

Yield 8

What you need
Crust:
3oz white breadcrumbs
1 1/2oz parmesan, finely grated
1oz butter, melted
Black pepper

Cheesecake:
8oz feta cheese
8oz curd cheese
6oz fromage frais
4 heaped tbsp fresh chives, chopped
3 spring onions, finely sliced

2 tbsp lemon juice
2 tsp gelatin
2 egg whites
Black pepper

What to do
1. Heat up oven to 400 °f .
2. Mix breadcrumbs, cheese, melted butter & pepper. Press to the bottom of a lightly greased 9 in. Pan.

3. Bake for 15 min..

4. Process feta cheese, curd cheese & fromage frais till smooth.

5. Add chives, spring onions & pepper.
6. Pour lemon juice & 2fl ounces water right into saucepan. Dash in the gelatin. Mix to dissolve.

7. In a separate bowl, beat the egg whites till soft-peaks. Heat gelatin mixture to boiling point & add to the cheese.

8. Mix quickly till well incorporated.

9. Steadily add whisked egg whites.
10. Pour the batter onto the crust.

11. Refrigerate cheesecake overnight.

Garlic mushroom cheesecake

Yield 12

What you need
2 tbsp oil
8oz mushrooms, chopped
2 cloves garlic, minced
8.8oz cream cheese, softened

1/2 c. Sour cream
1/4 tsp cayenne pepper
3 eggs
1 tbsp rosemary leaves, finely chopped

What to do
1. Heat up oven to 325 °f .
2. Heat oil in big nonstick skillet. Add mushrooms & garlic. Cook & mix 5 min. Or till softened. Drain.
3. Mix cream cheese, sour cream & cayenne pepper in a bowl till well incorporated.
4. Add eggs, one at a time; mix well. Add in mushroom mixture & rosemary.
5. Pour right into lightly greased 9 in. Pan.
6. Bake for 30 to 35 min.. Permit to cool.
7. Refrigerate overnight.

Double cheese bacon cheesecake

Yield 8

What you need
5oz crackers, crushed
3oz butter, melted
6 rashers bacon, finely chopped
1 onion, finely chopped
18oz ricotta cheese
18oz cream cheese, chopped
1 1/4 c. Parmesan cheese, grated
4 eggs

What to do
1. Heat up oven to 325 °f .
2. Mix crackers & butter. Press to the bottom of a lightly greased 9 in. Pan.
3. Refrigerate crust.
4. Fry bacon & onion in a pan. Put to the side to cool.
5. Mix ricotta, cream cheese, 1 c. Of parmesan, eggs, & salt & pepper till smooth. Add bacon mixture.
6. Pour filling over crust. Garnish with remaining parmesan.

7. Bake for 45 min.. Serve at room temperature.

Vanilla layered cheesecake

Yield 16

What you need
24oz cream cheese
4 eggs
1 1/4 c. Sugar
2 tsp pure vanilla extract
1 ginger graham cracker crust
1 c. Sour cream

What to do
1. Heat up oven to 325° f .
2. Beat cream cheese till smooth. Add eggs one at a time. Add 1 c. Of sugar, 1 tsp of vanilla & mix well.
3, pour batter right into the prebaked crust. Bake for an hour.
4. In a separate bowl, mix sour cream & remaining sugar & vanilla. Pour over crust.
5. Bake again for 5 min.. Permit to cool & cool down in the fridge before serving.

Raspberry cheesecake

Yield 10

What you need
1 c. Gingersnap cookies, crushed
1/3 c. Uncooked quick-cooking oats
2 tbsp butter, melted
Cooking spray
24oz cottage cheese
8 ounces cream cheese
1 c. Sugar

1/3 c. All-purpose flour
1 tbsp lemon rind, grated
1/4 c. Lemon juice
3 big eggs
1 egg white
1 tsp vanilla extract
2 c. Raspberries

What to do
1. Heat up oven to 350 °f .
2. Blend crushed gingersnaps, oats, & butter. Press to the bottom of a lightly greased 9 in. Pan.
3. Bake for 6 min.. Take away & permit to cool.
4. Reduce oven temperature to 325 °f .
5. Mix cottage cheese & cream cheese till smooth. Add sugar, flour, lemon rind, lemon juice, eggs, egg white & vanilla.
6. Pour batter over crust.
7. Bake for one hour & permit cheesecake to cool. Refrigerate before serving.
8. Garnish with raspberries.

Vanilla cinnamon cheesecake

Yield 12

What you need
Crust:
1 1/2 c. Graham cracker crumbs
1/4 tsp ground cinnamon
1/3 c. Butter, melted

Filling:
32 ounces   cream cheese, softened
1 1/4 c. Sugar
1/2 c. Sour cream
2 tsp vanilla extract
1 tsp
5 big eggs

Topping:
1/2 c. Sour cream
2 tsp sugar
1/4 tsp cinnamon

What to do
1. Heat up oven to 475 °f.
2. Mix crust ingredients. Press to the bottom of a lightly greased 9 in. Pan. Put to the side.
3. Beat cream cheese, sugar, sour cream, vanilla & cinnamon till smooth. Whisk eggs & add to the mixture.
4. Pour filling over crust. Bake for 12 min..
5. Reduce oven temperature to 350 °f. Bake for an hour.
6. Permit cheesecake to cool afterwards.
7. Mix topping ingredients & spread evenly over cheesecake. Refrigerate.

Double berry cheesecake

Yield 12

What you need
Crust:
2 c. Graham cracker crumbs
1/4 c. Butter, melted
2 tbsp sugar
1/2 tsp ground cinnamon
Cooking spray

Cheesecake:
24oz cream cheese
1 c. Sugar
1 c. Sour cream
2 tsp lemon rind, grated
1 tsp vanilla extract
3 eggs

Topping:

3/4 c. Blueberries
3/4 c. Strawberries, sliced
2 tbsp sugar
1 tbsp lemon rind, grated
3 tbsp lemon juice

What to do
Crust:
1. Heat up oven to 325 °f .
2. Mix crumbs, melted butter, sugar, & cinnamon in a bowl.
3. Press crust mixture to the bottom of a lightly greased 9 in. Pan.
4. Bake for 10 min.. Permit to cool.

Filling:
1. Beat cream cheese till smooth. Add sugar, sour cream, lemon rind & vanilla. Add eggs, one at a time & mix well.
2. Pour filling over crust. Put pan in a big roasting pan half filled with hot water.
3. Bake for an hour & 20 min.. Permit to cool & refrigerate overnight.

Topping:
Mix berries, sugar, lemon rind & lemon juice. Spread over cheesecake.

Double-chocomalt cheesecake

Yield 10

What you need
7oz malted milk
4oz biscuits, crushed to crumbs
4oz butter, melted
5 tbsp caster sugar
21oz cream cheese
10fl ounces   heavy cream
10oz white chocolate, melted
7oz milk chocolate, melted
2 tbsp malt powder
2oz white maltesers

What to do

1. Mix biscuits, melted butter, 2 tbsp sugar. Press to the bottom of a lightly greased 9 in. Pan & cool down.

2. Divide cream cheese & cream between two bowls, evenly. Add white chocolate to one & milk chocolate, malt & remaining 3 tbsp sugar to an additional. Mix well till smooth.

4. Scoop the milk chocolate mixture evenly right into the pan. Pour the white chocolate mixture over the surface.

5. Garnish with maltesers & cool down overnight.

Creamy lemon cheesecake

Yield 8

What you need
3oz digestive biscuits
2oz butter, melted
7oz cream cheese
18oz fromage frais
7oz confectioners' sugar
5 lemons
4 gelatine sheets

What to do

1. Mix crushed digestive biscuits with melted butter. Press to the bottom of a lightly greased 9 in. Pan. Cool down.

2. Beat cream cheese with fromage frais & confectioners' sugar. Add zest of 2 lemons.

3. Dip gelatine sheets in cold water. Add the juice of 3 lemons & heat over low heat till gelatine is melted. Add right into cheese mixture.

4. Scoop over the crust. Refrigerate before serving.

Melted marshmallow cheesecake

Yield 12

What you need
Crust:
2 1/2 c. Graham crackers crumbs
1/2 c. Granulated sugar
3/4 c. Butter, melted
2 c. Mini marshmallows
1/2 c. Warmed hot fudge ice cream topping

Cheesecake:
16oz cream cheese
1 can sweetened condensed milk
2 tsp vanilla
3 eggs, room temperature
1 c. Mini chocolate chips
2 1/2 c. Mini marshmallows

Topping:
2 chocolate bars, broken right into pieces
1/4 c. Graham cracker crumbs
1/4 c. Warmed hot fudge ice cream topping

What to do
1. Heat up oven to 325 °f .
2. Mix together graham cracker crumbs, granulated sugar & melted butter. Press to the bottom of a lightly greased 10 in. Pan.
3. Arrange 2 c. Of marshmallows over crust & pour hot fudge sauce over marshmallows. Put to the side.
4. For the cheesecake, mix cream cheese, sweetened condensed milk till smooth. Beat eggs one at a time, stirring well. Add vanilla.
5. Add chocolate chips & 2 1/2 c. Mini marshmallows. Spread over crust.
6. Bake for 45 min.. Take away & add remaining marshmallows. Put back in the oven for 5 min..
7. Permit cheesecake to cool. Refrigerate overnight.
8. Garnish with graham crumbs, crumbled chocolate bars & extra hot fudge sauce.

Caramel apple cheesecake
yield 12

What you need
2 tbsp butter
1 c. Brown sugar,
4 apples, peeled, cored, sliced
6oz caramels
1/2 c. Half & half
8oz cream cheese, softened
1/2 tsp pumpkin pie spice
1 1/2 tsp vanilla
1 egg
1/2 c. Milk chocolate chips, chopped
1 pie crust, baked
Pumpkin pie spice
Whipped cream

1. Heat up oven to 375 °f.
2. Melt butter & 1/2 c. Brown sugar in a skillet over medium heat. Mix continuously.
3. Add apples & continue stirring for 15 min. Till apple looks caramelized. Put to the side.
4. In an additional saucepan on low heat, melt caramels in halves till smooth. Keep stirring.
5. Mix cream cheese & 1/2 c. Sugar. Add 1/2 tsp pumpkin spice, vanilla & egg. Mix till well incorporated.
6. Add half of the caramel mixture to the cream cheese batter. Mix apple mixture to the remaining caramel & mix well.
7. Take out apple caramel filling & pour right into crust. Spread chocolate over the filling.
8. Layer it with the caramel cream cheese mixture.
9. Bake for 45 min.. Turn off the oven, open the door & leave the cheesecake inside to cool.
10. Cool down in the fridge till cold. Add pumpkin pie spice right into whipped topping & use to garnish the pie. Return to fridge.

Butter-nutty cheesecake
yield 8

What you need

1 c. Ground vanilla wafers
2 tbsp granulated sugar
2 tbsp butter
1/8 tsp salt
8oz cream cheese, softened
1/4 c. Peanut butter
1/2 c. Sugar
1 egg
2 tbsp heavy cream
1/8 tsp salt
4 fun size butterfinger candy bars, crushed
1 c. Semi-sweet chocolate chips
2-3 tbsp heavy cream
2 fun size butterfingers, crushed

What to do
1. Heat up oven to 350 °f.
2. Mix cookie crumbs, sugar, butter & salt. Press it to the bottom of a lightly greased pan. Bake for 10 min. Next which remove.
3. Reduce heat to 300 °f. Mix cream cheese & peanut butter till smooth.
4. Mix sugar, egg, cream & salt till well incorporated.
5. Add crushed butterfingers. Spread batter over crust.
6. Bake for 22 min.. Turn off the oven, open the door & leave the cheesecake inside to cool for 2 hours
7. Melt chocolate chips. Add cream & mix till smooth.
8. Garnish cheesecake with chocolate mixture.

Lemon berry cheesecake

Yield 8

What you need
3 tbsp butter, softened
1 c. Sour cream
1 c. Graham cracker crumbs
1/4 c. All-purpose flour
32oz cream cheese

1 tbsp vanilla extract
1 1/2 c. Sugar
3 c. Blackberries
3/4 c. Milk
Zest & juice of 1 lemon
4 eggs

What to do
1. Heat up the oven to 350 °f .
2. Mix graham cracker crumbs with butter. Press to the bottom of a lightly greased 9 in. Pan.
3. Beat cream cheese & sugar till smooth. Add milk. Add eggs one at a time till well incorporated.
4. Add sour cream, flour & vanilla. Pour mixture right into two separate bowls.
5. Purée blackberries, lemon zest & juice. Add it to the cream cheese mixture & blend thoroughly.
6. Pour blackberry filling right into the crust. Bake it for 10 min..
7. Take away from oven & add the remaining filling. Return to oven & bake for an hour.
8. Refrigerate before serving.

Chocolate oreo cheesecake

Yield 12

What you need
Cheesecake
16oz cream cheese, softened
2/3 c. Sugar
3 big eggs
1/2 tsp vanilla
1 c. Chocolate chips
1 oreo pie crust

Topping

3 tbsp sugar
8oz sour cream
1 tsp vanilla

What to do
1. Heat up oven to 350 °f .
2. Mix cream cheese, 2/3 c. Sugar, eggs, & 1/2 tsp vanilla till smooth. Pour in chocolate chips & stir. Pour batter right into oreo crust.
3. Bake for 30 min.. Take away from oven & permit to cool.
4. Mix 3 tbsp sugar, sour cream, & 1 tsp vanilla. Pour over warm cheesecake & return to oven for 5 min..
5. Permit to cool & cool down in the fridge before serving.

Nutella cheesecake

Yield 12

What you need
10oz graham crackers, digestive biscuits
5 tbsp butter
13oz nutella
3/4 c. Toasted hazelnuts, chopped
16oz cream cheese
1/2 c. Confectioners' sugar, sifted

What to do
1. Mix finely ground graham crackers butter & 1 tbsp of nutella. Add 3 tbsp of the hazelnuts & continue to blend.
2. Press mixture to the bottom of a lightly greased 9 in. Pan. Refrigerate.
3. Mix the cream cheese & confectioners' sugar till smooth. Add remaining nutella to the cream cheese mixture. Mix well.
4. Pour batter right into crust & spread remaining chopped hazelnuts on top.
5. Refrigerate overnight before serving.

Smoked salmon cheesecake

Yield 15

What you need
Crust:
1/4 c. Breadcrumbs
2/3 c. Parmesan cheese, grated
2 tbsp butter, melted

Cheesecake:
16oz cream cheese, cubed
2 eggs
2 tbsp chives, chopped
2 tbsp parsley, chopped
1 tsp lemon zest
1/4 tsp salt
Ground black pepper to taste
1/2 c. Sour cream
6oz smoked salmon, chopped fine

Garnish:
Chives
Extra breadcrumbs

What to do
Crust:
1. Heat up oven to 350 °f.
2. Mix breadcrumbs, parmesan & butter in a bowl. Press mixture right into the bottom of a 9 in. Lightly greased pan. Put to the side.
3. Beat cream cheese till light & fluffy. Add eggs one at a time; beat well.
4. Mix in chives, parsley, zest, salt & pepper. Add sour cream by hand & chopped salmon.
5. Pour mixture over crust. Put pan in a larger pan filled with 1-inch hot water.
6. Bake for 30 to 40 min.. Permit to cool.
7. Refrigerate overnight.
8. Garnish with chives & breadcrumbs.

Ricotta asparagus cheesecake with swiss almond crust

Yield 8

What you need
2 c. Ground almonds
1 c. Cheese, grated
1/4 c. Butter, melted
2 c. Asparagus, chopped
1/2 c. Arugula, chopped
2 tbsp butter
Salt to taste
4oz cream cheese, softened
2 c. Ricotta cheese
4 eggs
1/4 c. All-purpose flour
1/4 c. Parsley, finely chopped

What to do
1. Heat up oven to 275 °f
2. Mix almonds, grated cheese & butter.
3. Press 1 1/2 c. Of the mixture to the bottom of a lightly greased 10 in. Pan. Reserve the remaining for the topping.
4. Bake for 15 min.. Put to the side to cool.
5. Turn oven temperature to 400 °f .
6. Sauté asparagus & arugula in butter for 10 min.. Permit to cool.
7. Puree cream cheese, ricotta, & eggs till smooth. Add flour & mix till smooth. Add salt & freshly ground black pepper to taste. Mix well.
8. Mix cheese mixture, parsley, & asparagus mixture. Pour over crust.
9. Bake for 15 min..
10. Reduce heat to 375 °f add the remaining of the almond-mixture onto the cheesecake & bake for 35-40 min..

Triple cheese & basil cheesecake

Yield 12

What you need

Crust:
1/3 c. Parmesan cheese, grated
1/3 c. Panko breadcrumbs
1 tbsp butter, melted
pinch of salt

Cheesecake:
8oz cream cheese, softened
1/4 c. Feta cheese
1/4 c. Sour cream
2 eggs
1/2 c. Basil
1 tbsp olive oil
1/2 tsp salt

What to do

1. Heat up oven to 350 °f

2. Mix together cheese, bread crumbs, & salt. Press right into the bottom of a 7 in. Springform pan. Put to the side.

3. Put basil in boiling water till leaves are bright green.

4. Transfer to an ice water bath to halt the cooking. Drain & process with olive oil & salt till smooth.

5. Beat together cream cheese & feta cheese till smooth. Beat in eggs, one at a time. Add sour cream & basil mixture & mix well.

6. Pour mixture over crust.

7. Bake for an hour. Permit to cool.

8. Refrigerate overnight.

Creamy leek cheesecake

Yield 12

What you need
16oz cream cheese
2 eggs
1 egg yolk
3 tbsp sour cream
3 tbsp heavy cream
1/4 c. Sautéed leeks, white part only
3/4 c. Cheese, grated
Salt & pepper

What to do
1. Heat up oven to 350 °f .
2. Mix all ingredients together till smooth.
3. Pour the cheesecake batter over a 9 in. Lightly greased pan.
4. Bake for an hour. Permit to cool.
5. Refrigerate.

Pecan & olive cheesecake squares

Yield 12

What you need
1 1/4 c. Breadcrumbs
1/2 c. Pecans, finely chopped
1/3 c. Butter, melted
11oz cream cheese, softened
8oz sour cream
1 tbsp all-purpose flour
1/4 tsp salt

1/4 tsp pepper
1 egg
1 egg yolk
1/2 c. Kalamata olives, pitted, sliced
1 tbsp rosemary, chopped
Fresh rosemary sprigs
Kalamata olives

What to do
1. Heat up oven to 350 °f .
2. Mix together breadcrumbs, pecans & butter.. Press to the bottom of a lightly greased 9 in. Pan. Bake for 12 min.. Put to the side to cool.
3. Mix cream cheese, sour cream, & flour. Add egg & egg yolk, one at a time.
4. Mix in sliced olives & chopped rosemary. Pour mixture right into crust.
5. Bake for 20 min. Or till done. Permit to cool.

Blue cheese & garlic cheesecake

Yield 8

What you need
Cooking spray
16oz cream cheese, softened
1/2 c. Sour cream
4oz blue cheese, crumbled
1 tbsp all-purpose flour
1/2 tsp dried parsley flakes
1/2 tsp dried marjoram
1/4 tsp granulated garlic
2 eggs

Preparation
1. Heat up oven to 325 °f .
2. Mix together cream cheese, sour cream, blue cheese, flour, parsley, marjoram & garlic.
3. Beat in eggs, one at a time. Scoop cream cheese mixture right into 12 baking cups.
4. Bake for 40 min.. Permit to cool.
5. Refrigerate.

Mexican cheesecake

Yield 12

What you need
6 corn tortillas
3 tbsp butter, melted
12oz feta cheese
12oz cream cheese
1 1/4 c. Sour cream
2 cloves garlic, minced
2 jalapenos, finely minced
1 c. Salsa
3 tbsp tomato paste
1 1/4 tsp salt
1 tsp pepper
4 eggs
1/2 c. Cilantro, chopped
2 egg whites, beaten
Watercress
Sliced avocado

What to do
1. Bake the tortillas at 200 °f for 45 min. Or till crisp.
2. Permit to cool & grind in a food processor. Put to the side. Increase oven temperature to 350 °f.
3. Press tortilla crumbs to the bottom of a lightly greased 9 in. Pan.
4. Beat cheeses, sour cream, garlic, jalapenos, salsa, tomato paste, salt, pepper & eggs till smooth.
5. Add cilantro & beaten egg whites.
6. Pour right into prepared pan & dash remaining tortilla crumbs over the top.
7. Bake for 70 min..
8. Turn off the oven, open the door & leave the cheesecake inside to cool for 3-4 hours.
9. Garnish with watercress.
10. Top with sliced avocado. Cut right into wedges & serve with tomato salsa.

Savory vegetable cheesecake

Yield 8

What you need
1 c. Breadcrumbs
2 tbsp nuts, finely chopped
3 tbsp olive oil
16oz cream cheese
1/2 c. Parmesan cheese, grated
1/4 c. Heavy cream
1 egg
Baby spinach
1 artichoke heart
2 green onions, finely chopped
2 tsp dill
1 tsp black pepper

What to do
1. Heat up oven to 325 °f.
2. Mix breadcrumbs, nuts & olive oil till well incorporated. Press to the bottom of a lightly greased 9 in. Pan.
3. Blend together cream cheese, parmesan cheese, heavy cream & egg.
4. Mix in spinach, artichoke hearts, pepper & dill. Add green onions.
5. Pour over crust. Bake for an hour.

6. Refrigerate before serving.

Chicken cranberry-orange cheesecake

Yield 10

What you need
16oz cream cheese
8oz french onion dip
1 tbsp flour
1/2 tsp dill, dried
3 eggs
1 c. Chicken, cooked , minced
1/2 c. Cranberry-orange relish, drained
2 tbsp walnuts, chopped, toasted

What to do
1. Heat up oven to 300 °f .
2. Beat cream cheese till fluffy. Add in onion dip, flour & dill.
3. Add eggs, one at a time, till well incorporated.
4. Add chicken & spread evenly in pan.
5. Bake for an hour. Permit to cool.
6. Refrigerate overnight.
7. Spread relish onto top of cheesecake & dash with walnuts.

Polenta pepper cheesecake

Yield 10

What you need
8 tbsp instant polenta

8 tbsp water
14oz cream cheese
36oz cheese, grated
4 eggs
4.2fl ounces sour cream
8 sweet piquanté peppers
Handful coriander, chopped

What to do
1. Heat up oven to 390 °f
2. Mix water & polenta together. Press to the bottom of a 9 in. Tin.
3. Mix together remaining ingredients. Pour batter right into tin.
4. Bake for an hour.
5. Permit to cool.

Blueberry cabernet cheesecake

Yield 8

What you need
1 pint of blueberries
1/2 c. Cabernet sauvignon
1/2 c. Sugar dissolved in 1/2 c. Boiling water
1/4 c. Heavy cream
1/4 c. Cream cheese
4 tbsp of sugar
1/4 c. Graham cracker crumbs

What to do
1. Puree blueberries, wine & sugar water. Put to the side.
2. Beat cream cheese till light & fluffy. Put to the side.
3. Beat cream & sugar till soft peaks form.
4. Fold cream cheese right into cream & sugar.
5. Put 1/4 c. Of mixture right into a bowl & whisk in graham cracker crumbs.
6. Right into small bowls or popsicle molds, pour 2 tbsp of blueberry mixture. Spread a tbsp of cheesecake mixture on top of blueberry layer. Spread a tsp, of graham cracker mixture on top of cheesecake mixture. Continue layering till top of bowl or mold is reached.

7. Freeze.

Amaretto cheesecake

Yield 12

What you need
Cake:
Cooking spray
1 c. Almonds, finely ground
1/4 c. All-purpose flour
1 tbsp sugar
3 tbsp butter, melted
24oz cream cheese, softened
1 can sweetened condensed milk
2 tbsp amaretto
1 tsp vanilla extract
3 eggs

Brittle:
3/4 c. Almonds, sliced
1 c. Sugar
2 tbsp water
Dash of salt

What to do
1. Heat up oven to 350 °f.
2. Mix almonds, flour, & sugar. Add butter till mixed well.
3. Press mixture to the bottom of a lightly greased 9 in. Pan.
4. Bake for 15 min.. Permit to cool. Reduce oven heat to 300 °f.
5. Beat cream cheese in a bowl till light & fluffy. Add condensed milk, amaretto, & vanilla to mixture & beat till smooth.
6. Beat in eggs, one at a time, beating well next each addition. Pour batter over crust. Bake for an hour. Permit to cool
7. Refrigerate cheesecake.
8. To make brittle, increase oven heat to 350 °f.
9. Put almonds on a baking sheet stirring twice.

10. When cool, put almonds close together in a circle.
11. Heat a saucepan over heat; add sugar, water, & salt to pan. Mix to dissolve.
12. Increase heat & bring mixture to a boil. Boil, without stirring, till caramel is a dark amber color, next which swirl the pan to even out the color.
13. Pour caramel in a circular motion over almonds.
14. Permit brittle to cool & harden. Crush brittle with a rolling pin.
15. Press remaining praline pieces right into top of cake.

Double chocolate liqueur cheesecake

Yield 12

What you need
2oz butter
8oz chocolate
Digestive biscuits, crushed
8oz dark chocolate
14oz cream cheese
4oz caster sugar
4 eggs
9.5fl ounces heavy cream
5 tbsp kahlúa
6.7fl ounces crème fraîche
2 tbsp kahlúa
Cocoa powder, for dusting
Extra kahlúa to serve

What to do
1. Heat up oven to 320 °f.
2. Mix together melted butter & crushed biscuits. Press to the bottom of a lightly greased 9 in. Pan. Refrigerate.
3. Melt chocolate over a pan of simmering water whereas stirring. Take away bowl from pan.
4. Mix cheese & sugar till smooth. Beat in eggs one at a time. Add the melted chocolate, cream & 5 tbsp kahluà.
5. Pour mixture over crust & bake for an hour.
6. Refrigerate overnight.

7. Mix crème fraîche & remaining kahluà. Spread over the cheesecake.
8. Garnish with cocoa powder dusting. Serve.

White chocolate frangelico cheesecake

Yield 12

What you need
Crust:
One package chocolate wafers, crumbed
4oz butter, melted

Cheesecake:
24oz cream cheese
3/4 c. Sugar
8oz white chocolate, chopped & melted
1 tsp vanilla
3 tbsp frangelico
4 eggs

What to do
Heat up oven to 350 °f .
Mix together cookie crumbs & melted butter.
Press firmly right into a 9 in. Pan.
Bake 10 min..
Decrease oven temperature to 325 ºf .
Beat cream cheese on low for 1 min. Next which slowly add sugar.
Add melted chocolate, vanilla & frangelico & mix only till combined.
Mix in eggs, one at a time, till only incorporated.
Pour filling right into base.
Place pan right into a larger pan half filled with water & bake 60 min. Or till set.
Allow to cool next which refrigerate.

Cheesecake icecream

Yield 16

What you need
1 quart low-fat 1% milk
16oz reduced fat cream cheese, softened
1 1/2 c. White sugar
1/3 c. Triple sec
1 tbsp vanilla extract
1 pinch salt

What to do
Blend all ingredients together & either use your icecream maker as per manufacturer's instructions, or put in freezer, stirring vigorously every 30 min..

Pecan liqueur cheesecake

Yield 12

What you need
2 c. Graham cracker crumbs
1/2 c. White sugar
1 tsp ground cinnamon
1/2 c. Butter, melted
24oz cream cheese, softened
1 1/4 c. White sugar
3 eggs
1/2 tsp vanilla extract
1/2 c. Pecan liqueur
1 c. Sour cream

1/4 c. Confectioners' sugar
1 tsp pecan liqueur
1 c. Ground pecans
1/2 c. Graham cracker crumbs
1 1/2 tbsp white sugar
1/2 tsp ground cinnamon
3/4 c. Pecan halves

What to do
1. Heat up oven to 350 °f .
2. Mix 2 c. Graham cracker crumbs, 1/2 c. White sugar, 1 tsp cinnamon, & melted butter or margarine. Press to the bottom of a lightly greased 10 in. Pan.
3. Beat cream cheese & 1 1/4 c. White sugar. Pour the eggs, one at a time. Mix in vanilla extract & 1/2 c. Liqueur, & blend for 5 min.. Pour the mixture on the crust
4. Bake for 1 hour. Turn off the oven, open the door & leave the cheesecake inside to cool.
5. Blend the sour cream, confectioners' sugar, & 1 tsp liqueur together. Spread over the top of the cooled cheesecake.
6. Mix finely ground pecans, finely ground graham cracker crumbs, 1 1/2 tbsp white sugar, & cinnamon. Garnish cheesecake with pecan mixture.

Cointreau cheesecake

Yield 12

What you need
8oz gingernut cookies
1/2 c. Butter, melted
1/4 c. Cointreau
Pinch of saffron threads
15oz cream cheese
1/2 c. Honey
1 1/2 tbsp orange zest, finely-grated
1 3/4 c. Heavy cream

What to do
1. Blend cookies & butter in a blender till moist & crumbly.

2. Press right into a 9 in. Pan & refrigerate.
3. Heat cointreau in a saucepan till it starts to steam & add saffron threads.
4. Take away from heat & put to the side for 20 min..
5. Beat cream cheese & slowly beat in honey, orange zest & saffron mixture.
6. Continuing to beat, slowly add cream till thick.
7. Spoon the mixture over the base & cool down overnight.

Coffee jelly cheesecake

Yield 10

What you need
Cheesecake:
2 1/2 tsp gelatin, plus 1 tsp
5 tbsp water
6oz shortcake biscuits, crushed
3oz butter, melted
9oz fromage frais
9oz mascarpone
5fl ounces baileys irish cream
4.8fl ounces heavy cream, lightly whipped
2 eggs
5oz caster sugar

Coffee jelly:
1 tsp gelatin
5fl ounces strong black coffee
2 tbsp caster sugar

What to do
Cheesecake:
1. Dash gelatine in water & leave to soak for 5 min.. Put the bowl of gelatine in a pan of lightly simmering water & leave till it appears clear.
2. Mix biscuit crumbs & butter. Press to the bottom of a lightly greased 9 in. Pan.
3. Mix fromage frais, mascarpone & baileys together. Pour in the gelatine & fold in the cream.

4. Beat eggs & sugar in a bowl. Add to the cheesecake mixture & pour onto the crust. Refrigerate for 4 hours.

Coffee jelly:
1. Spoon gelatine over the coffee. Put the bowl in a pan of lightly simmering water till dissolved.
2. Refrigerate the mixture. When cold, prudently pour the coffee mixture on top of the cheesecake to make a thin layer. Refrigerate.

Banana bourbon cheesecake

Yield 10

What you need
2 c. Vanilla wafers crushed
1/2 c. Chopped pecans
4oz butter, melted
3 bananas
1 tbsp lemon juice
1/4 c. Light brown sugar
1 tbsp bourbon whiskey
32oz cream cheese, softened
1 c. Granulated sugar
4 eggs
1 tbsp bourbon whiskey
1/2 c. Vanilla wafers, crushed
1 c. Heavy whipping cream
1/4 c. Powdered sugar
1 tsp bourbon whiskey
1 banana, sliced

What to do
1. Heat up oven to 350 °f .
2. Mix crumbs & pecans in a food processor. Pour in melted butter. Press to the bottom of a lightly greased 9 in. Pan.
3. Bake for 10 min.. Let it cool.

4. Mash the bananas till smooth. Add brown sugar & lemon juice. Heat over a medium heat till the sugar has melted & the bananas cook slightly.

5. Take away from heat & add 1 tbsp bourbon. Blend & let it cool down.

6. Beat cream cheese for 2 min.. Slowly add granulated sugar. Add eggs one at a time, till well incorporated. Add 1 tbsp bourbon.

7. Blend in banana mixture & mix well. Scoop filling over crust & put in a roasting pan half-filled with water.

8. Bake for an hour.

9. In a separate big bowl beat heavy whipping cream. Add powdered sugar & bourbon. Continue whisking till the cream forms soft peaks.

10. Pipe whipped cream onto each slice. Garnish with a vanilla wafer cookie & a banana slice.

Rum-infused mousse cheesecake

Yield 8

What you need
4oz semisweet chocolate, chopped
1 1/2 tsp unflavored gelatin
4 tbsp cold water
8oz cream cheese
1 c. White sugar
2 tbsp rum
2 egg yolks
6fl ounces heavy cream, whipped
2 egg whites
1 prepared chocolate cookie crumb crust

What to do
1. Dash gelatin over water & permit to soften.
2. In the top of a double boiler, heat chocolate, stirring continously till melted.
3. Put the bowl of gelatin over double boiler & mix till gelatin dissolves.
4. Cream the cream cheese & sugar till light & fluffy. Add rum, egg yolks, dissolved gelatin & melted chocolate.
5. Fold in whipped cream.
6. Whisk egg whites till stiff. Fold right into chocolate mixture.

7. Pour filling right into pie base.
8. Cool down 4 hours or more.

White chocolate cheesecake

Yield 12

What you need
White chocolate cheesecake:
4oz white chocolate
24oz cream cheese
3/4 c. White sugar
1/4 c. All-purpose flour
3 eggs
1/2 c. Heavy cream
1/2 tsp vanilla extract

White chocolate brandy sauce:
2 c. White chocolate, finely chopped
1 c. Heavy cream
2fl ounces   brandy

What to do
White chocolate cheesecake:
1. Heat up oven to 300 °f .
2. Cream the cream cheese, sugar, & flour till light & fluffy.
3. Beat in eggs one at a time, mixing well next each addition.
4. Melt 4oz white chocolate and, with mixer on low speed, mix right into cream cheese mixture. Slowly add in the vanilla & 1/2 c. Of heavy cream. Pour filling right into a greased pan.
5. Fill a larger pan 1 to 2 in. Deep with water. Put cheesecake pan right into this pan & bake for 50 to 60 min., or till middle of the cheesecake is only firm.
6. Refrigerate.

White chocolate brandy sauce:

1. Heat 1 c. Heavy cream over a medium-high heat till it boils, next which pour over chopped white chocolate. Mix till melted.

2. Add brandy. Pour over cool down ed cheesecake.

Margarita cheesecakes snacks

Yield 75

What you need
1 can sweetened condensed milk
8oz cream cheese, softened
6oz frozen limeade concentrate
1/4 c. Tequila
2 tbsp triple sec
75 scoop-style tortilla chips
1 c. Heavy whipping cream
2 tsp lime juice
2 tbsp white sugar

What to do
1. Beat together condensed milk & cream cheese till smooth.
2. Add limeade, tequila, & triple sec; & beat till 5 to 8 min..
3. Spoon 1 tbsp cheesecake mixture right into each tortilla chip.
4. Refrigerate till set.
5. Beat cream & lime juice together smooth & thickened.
6. Steadily add sugar till soft peaks form.
7. Top each cheesecake with 1 tsp lime-flavored whipped cream.

Vodka ricotta cheesecake

Yield 8

What you need
Crust:

1 1/4 c. Chocolate chip cookie crumbs
2 tbsp unsalted butter, melted

Filling:
2 pounds ricotta cheese
1 c. Granulated sugar
1/3 c. All-purpose flour
3 big eggs
2 big egg yolks
2 tsp vanilla extract
2 tsp orange zest
1/2 tsp salt

Topping:
1/2 c. Orange marmalade
1/3 c. Vodka

What to do
Crust:
1. Heat up oven to 350 °f .
2. Mix together cookie crumbs & melted butter.
3. Press firmly right into a 9 in. Pan.
4. Bake for 10 to 15 min. Or till done.

Filling:
1. Beat ricotta till smooth.
2. Beat in sugar & flour.
3. Add the eggs & egg yolks one at a time till well incorporated.
4. Blend in vanilla, orange zest, & salt till only incorporated.
5. Pour filling evenly right into base.
6. Bake 1 hour.

Topping:
1. Bring marmalade & vodka to a boil. Reduce to a low heat & simmer till reduced by half.
2. Let stand for 5 min. & pour over cheesecake. Leave 15 min. To set.

Rum praline cheesecake

Yield 12

What you need
1/4 c. Butter
1 c. Graham cracker crumbs
3 tbsp packed brown sugar
1/3 c. Pecans, chopped
16oz cream cheese, softened
1 1/4 c. Brown sugar
3 eggs
1 tsp rum flavored extract
1 tsp vanilla extract
1/4 c. Sour cream
1/3 c. Pecans, chopped
1 1/2 c. Sour cream
1/4 c. Packed brown sugar
3/4 tsp maple flavored extract
1/2 tsp rum flavored extract

What to do
1. Heat up oven to 350 °f .
2. Mix melted butter, graham crumbs, 3 tbsp brown sugar & 1/3 c. Chopped nuts. Press to the bottom of a lightly greased 9 in. Pan.
3. Blend cream cheese & remaining c. Brown sugar till smooth. Add eggs one at a time.
4. Add in 1 tsp rum flavoring, vanilla, 1/4 c. Sour cream & 1/3 c. Chopped nuts.
5. Pour batter over the crust.
6. Bake for an hour & permit to cool.
7. Mix 1 1/2 c. Sour cream, 1/4 c. Brown sugar, maple flavoring, & 1/2 tsp rum flavoring.
8. Spread batter over cheesecake & bake it again for 10 min..
9. Refrigerate before serving.

Pina colada cheesecake

Yield 10

What you need
1 1/4 c. Vanilla wafer crumbs

1 c. Flaked coconut, toasted
1/2 c. Butter, melted
6oz pineapple juice
1 package gelatin
24oz cream cheese, softened
3/4 c. Sugar
1/4 c. Dark jamaican rum*
3/4 tsp coconut extract
2 c. Frozen whipped topping, thawed
20oz crushed pineapple
1 tbsp cornstarch
2 tbsp sugar
Toasted flaked coconut

What to do
1. Mix crumbs, coconut & butter. Press mixture on bottom 9-inch pan. Put to the side in fridge.
2. Pour juice right into saucepan. Dash gelatin over juice & leave to soften.
3. Mix over medium heat till gelatin dissolves. Put to the side.
4. Beat together cream cheese & 3/4 c. Sugar. Beat in gelatin mixture, rum & coconut extract.
5. Fold in whipped topping. Pour filling right into cheesecake base.
6. Refrigerate at least 6 hours.
7. Mix undrained pineapple, cornstarch & 2 tbsp sugar in a saucepan & mix till mixture boils & slightly thickens. Refrigerate.
8. To serve, spoon pineapple mixture over top of cheesecake.
9. Garnish with additional toasted coconut, if desired.

Tiramisu cheesecake

Yield 12

What you need
12oz ladyfingers
4 tbsp butter, melted
4 tbsp coffee liqueur
24oz cream cheese

8oz container mascarpone cheese
1 c. White sugar
2 eggs
4 tbsp all-purpose flour
1oz square semisweet chocolate

What to do
1. Heat up oven to 350 °f .
2. Mix melted butter with finely crushed ladyfingers. Pour 2 tbsp of coffee liqueur & mix well. Press right into the bottom of a 9 in. Pan.
3. Blend cream cheese, mascarpone & sugar till smooth. Pour in 2 tbsp coffee liqueur & mix well. Add eggs one at a time, alternating with flour. Mix slowly till smooth.
4. Pour mixture right into crust.
5. Bake for 45 min.. Leave cheesecake to cool afterwards inside the oven with the door open.
6. Refrigerate next 3 hours. Garnish with grated semi-sweet chocolate.

Rum & chocolate cheesecake

Yield 12

What you need
1 c. Ground almonds
1 c. Whole wheat flour
2/3 c. Vegan margarine
24oz firm tofu
1 1/2 c. Demerara sugar
7 tbsp unsweetened cocoa powder
1/4 c. Sunflower seed oil
1/2 c. Soy milk
1/4 c. Dark rum
1 1/2 tsp vanilla extract

What to do
1. Heat up oven to 325 °f .
2. Mix ground almonds & whole wheat flour. Mix in margarine till a dough is formed. Press to the bottom of a lightly greased 9 in. Pan.

3. Blend together crumbled tofu, sugar, cocoa, oil, soy milk, rum & vanilla till smooth. Spread filling over crust.
4. Bake for 75 min.. Permit to cool.
5. Refrigerate before serving.

Vegan cheesecake

Yield 6

What you need
12oz soft tofu
1/2 c. Soy milk
1/2 c. White sugar
1 tbsp vanilla extract
1/4 c. Maple syrup
1 prepared graham cracker crust

What to do
1. Heat up oven to 350 °f .
2. Mix together tofu, soy milk, sugar, vanilla extract & maple syrup. Blend till smooth. Spread over pie crust.
3. Bake for 30 min.. Let it cool.
4. Cool down in the fridge before serving.

Tofu cheesecake

Yield 12

What you need
24oz extra firm tofu, drained, cubed
1 c. White sugar

1 tsp vanilla extract
1/4 tsp salt
1/4 c. Vegetable oil
2 tbsp lemon juice
1 prepared graham cracker crust

What to do
1. Heat up oven to 350 °f.
2. Mix together tofu, sugar, vanilla, salt, vegetable oil, & lemon juice. Mix till well incorporated. Spread over pie crust.
3. Bake for 20 to 30 min.. Permit to cool.
4. Cool down in the fridge before serving.

Cashew cheesecake

Yield 12

What you need
2 c. Macadamia nuts
1 1/2 c. Cashews
1/2 c. Dates, pitted
1/4 c. Dried coconut
6 tbsp coconut oil, melted
1/4 c. Lime juice
1/4 c. Raw agave nectar
1/2 sun-dried vanilla bean
3 c. Mixed berries, such as blueberries & raspberries

What to do
1. Put macadamia nuts in a bowl with cold water.
2. Put cashews in an additional bowl with cold water. Soak nuts 4 hours, next which rinse, drain, & put to the side.
3. Crush & blend macadamia nuts & dates in food processor. Spread dried coconut to the bottom of a lightly greased 9 in. Pan. Press macadamia nut batter over the coconut to make crust.
4. Mix cashews, coconut oil, lime juice, agave nectar, & 6 tbsp water in bowl to blend. Take out seeds from vanilla bean & purée till smooth.

5. Pour batter over crust, & refrigerate for an hour.
6. Garnish with berries. Serve.

Strawberry cheesecake

Yield 12

What you need
Crust:
1 c. Almonds
2 tbsp coconut oil, liquefied
3 soft medjool dates
1 tsp pure vanilla extract

Cheesecake
2 c. Raw cashews, presoaked for at least a few hours or overnight
6 tbsp coconut oil, liquefied
Juice of 1 lemon
1 tsp pure vanilla extract
1/4 c. Liquid sweetener of your choice
1 banana
2 c. Strawberries, hulled

Garnish
Extra strawberries for decorating

What to do
1. Mix all crust ingredients. Press to the bottom of 9 in. Pan.
2. Mix all cheesecake ingredients till smooth. Pour mixture over crust & spread evenly.
3. Refrigerate cheesecake overnight.
4. Garnish with extra strawberries on top.

Cashew lime cheesecake cups

Yield 12

What you need
Crust:
2 c. Raw walnuts
3 tbsp maple syrup
1 tsp vanilla

Cheesecake:
2 c. Raw cashews
1/2 c. Coconut oil
2 tbsp maple syrup
1/2 c. Key lime juice
Zest of 4-6 key limes

What to do
1. Mix finely ground walnuts, maple syrup & vanilla.
2. Put 2 tsp of walnut mixture right into 12 cupcake liners
3. For the cheesecake, mix finely ground cashews, coconut oil, maple syrup, lime juice & lime zest.
4. Dash with remaining lime zest. Pour mixture evenly between the cupcake liners.
5. Refrigerate before serving.

Dulce de leche cheesecake bars

Yield 12

What you need
1 1/2 c. Rolled oats
1 c. Walnut pieces
1/2 c. Butter, cold chopped
24oz cream cheese, softened
1 c. Sugar
3 eggs

2 tsp vanilla extract
1 can dulce de leche
1 1/4 c. Chocolate chips
1/3 c. Heavy cream

What to do
Crust:
1. Blend oats & walnuts with a food processor till it turns to fine crumbs. Mix with butter till it starts to come together.
2. Press to the bottom of the lightly greased baking pan to form the crust & let it cool down for half an hour in the fridge.

Filling:
1. Heat up the oven at 350 °f .
2. Blend cream cheese, sugar, eggs & vanilla extract in a food processor.
3. Pour 1/2 c. Of dulce de leech right into the filling mixture & blend. Put to the side the remaining half c. Of dulce de leche.
4. Pour filling right into crust & bake for 40 min..
5. Turn off the oven, open the door & leave the cheesecake bars inside to cool for 3-4 hours.
6. Pour the remaining dulce de leche over it when the cheesecake is ready.

Chocolate layer:
1. Mix chocolate chips & heavy cream & heat in the microwave till chocolate only melted
2. Permit it to cool for a few min. Before pouring over the cheesecake.
3. Let it set for a few hours before cutting right into bars.

Lime cheesecake bars

Yield 12

What you need
Crust:
2 c. Graham cracker crumbs
4oz butter, melted

Filling:

16oz cream cheese, softened
1/2 c. Granulated sugar
2 eggs plus 1 egg white
1/2 c. Sour cream
1 tsp vanilla
2 tbsp all-purpose flour
3/4 c. Prepared lime curd
green food coloring
yellow food coloring

Lime curd:
4oz butter, softened
1 c. Sugar
2 eggs
2 egg yolks
1/3 c. Plus 4 tbsp lime juice

What to do
Crust:
1. Heat up oven to 325 °f .
2. Blend graham cracker crumbs & butter to form the crust. Press to the bottom of the lightly greased pan & bake for 5 min.. Put to the side & permit to cool.
3. Mix food coloring right into 3/4 c. Of lime curd. Put to the side.
4. Beat the cream cheese & sugar till smooth.
5. Beat in eggs slowly one at a time & add sour cream, vanilla & flour to blend again.
6. Pour the mixture over the crust but put to the side a c. Of it for later use.
7. Mix the half c. Of the lime curd with remaining mixture & pour over the top of the cheesecake mixture.
8. Bake for 35 min..
9. Turn off the oven, open the door & leave the cheesecake inside to cool before refrigerating.
10. Cut right into bars to serve.

Lime curd:
1. Cream butter & sugar. Add eggs one at a time whereas mixing.
2. Add lime juice & continue blending till it looks curdled.
3. Cook the mixture over medium-heat till smooth.
4. Lightly increase the heat whereas whisking consistently till it thickens.
5. Take away from the heat & put inside a bowl. Cover the lime curd's surface with plastic wrap.

6. Cool down in the fridge.

Coffee cheesecake bars

Yield 12

What you need
2 c. Chocolate cookie crumbs
1/2 c. Butter, melted
2 tbsp heavy whipping cream
2 tsp instant coffee granules
16oz cream cheese
1/2 c. Sugar
3 eggs
1/2 tsp vanilla
1/3 c. Heavy whipping cream
1/2 c. Semi-sweet chocolate chips

What to do
1. Heat up oven to 350 °f.
2. Mix cookie crumbs & melted butter. Press to the bottom of an ungreased 13x9 in. Pan.
3. Blend whipping cream & coffee granules.
4. Beat cream cheese & sugar till smooth. Add coffee mixture, eggs & vanilla.
5. Pour mixture over crust & bake for 25 min..
6. Pour whipping cream mixture in a saucepan to heat & boil for a min.. Take away from heat & add chocolate chips, stirring till melted.
7. Pour over cheesecake & refrigerate.

ONE MORE THING...

If you enjoyed this book or found it useful, i'd be very grateful if you'd post a short review on amazon. Your support really does make a difference & i read all the reviews personally so i can get your feedback & make this book even better.

Printed in Great Britain
by Amazon